I'VE SEEN THE ELEPHANT

An Autobiography

I'VE SEEN THE ELEPHANT

William B. Saxbe with Peter D. Franklin

The Kent State University Press, Kent, Ohio, & London

© 2000 by William B. Saxbe

All rights reserved

Library of Congress Catalog Card Number 00-035222

ISBN 0-87338-668-x

Manufactured in the United States of America

07 06 05 04 03 02 01 00   5 4 3 2 1

Library of Congress Cataloging-in-Publication Data

Saxbe, William B.

I've seen the elephant : an autobiography / by William B. Saxbe with Peter D.

Franklin.

p.   cm.

Includes bibliographical references (p.   ) and index

ISBN 0-87338-668-x (cloth : alk. paper) ∞

1. Saxbe, William B. 2. Legislators—United States—Biography. 3. United States.

Congress. Senate—Biography. 4. Attorneys general—United States—Biography.

5. Ambassadors—United States—Biography. 6. United States—Politics and

government—1969–1974. 7. United States—Politics and government—1974–1977.

8. Ohio—Politics and government—1951–   I. Franklin, Peter D. II. Title.

E840.8.S29 S29 2000

328.73'092—dc21

[B]   00-035222

British Library Cataloging-in-Publication data are available.

For Dolly, Juli, Bart, and Rocky

To see the elephant (United States slang)—to see life, the world, or the sights (as of a large city); to get experience of life, to gain knowledge by experience.

The Oxford English Dictionary, 2nd ed., 5:134.

A farmer on his way to market came across a circus caravan. Scared by the elephant, his cow took off, his chickens flew away, his can of milk spilled and his eggs broke. When the townsfolk saw what had happened, they consoled the farmer.

"Oh, I don't mind," he said. "I've seen the elephant."

—*folktale*

After experiencing combat many Civil War soldiers wrote about having "seen the elephant," or variations thereof. However, the military connotation precedes that conflict. The phase also is associated with battle in the war with Mexico (1846–1848). Writing in *Civil War Times Illustrated*, Gerald Conti suggests the origin dates to the third century B.C., when "Alexander the Great's Macedonian warriors defeated the elephant-mounted army of King Porus in the Indus valley," which is in modern Pakistan ("Seeing the Elephant," *Civil War Times Illustrated*, 23 [June 1984]: 19).

CONTENTS

{ *Contents* }

FOREWORD

Who is Bill Saxbe?

It was the mid-fifties. I was a young attorney in Cincinnati, just getting interested in Republican politics, when I was approached to become involved in Bill Saxbe's campaign for Ohio attorney general.

A quick check revealed that Saxbe had alienated many Republicans in his losing effort to Congressman George Bender in the 1954 Republican primary for the U.S. Senate. I was fascinated by his boldness. We met shortly thereafter; I liked what I saw and agreed to take a large role as a volunteer in his campaign in Hamilton County, Ohio.

Saxbe defies description, yet I will try. He is a man comfortable with himself, married to Dolly in what can only be described as the perfect partnership. Dolly is special; she is Bill's rudder, his soulmate in every sense of the word; and she was willing to follow Bill's dream wherever it took them.

If he stumbled, she was there. If he misspoke, and he often did, she was there. If he was courageous in his decisions, and he often was, she was there. Dolly and their children were everything to Bill Saxbe. They were his constant companions and provided support and love during one of the most extraordinary journeys a man can travel.

One lesson I learned early. When you walk into his office, locate Bill's position in relation to his spittoon, and never get in the line of fire. Some have, to their dismay.

Aside from the campaign speeches we gave, the rallies we organized and attended, there was the job of hanging signs. It was easy, until we had to nail the double Saxbe signs on the farmers' rail fences in the rural areas. Bill's instructions were to hang the signs quickly and get out of there because "those farmers have guns."

Our reward for that effort was to be invited to the Van Darby Club for the Pure in Heart party where, among other things, they had fried fish that were best described as "barely edible." I haven't eaten fried fish since.

Following Saxbe's election as Ohio attorney general in 1956, I worked in his office as an assistant in worker's compensation matters and tried cases in various courts in Ohio. As attorney general he permitted me the same independence he enjoyed in his own work. He was extremely loyal to his friends and to the people who worked for and with him, but he demanded honesty in all matters.

When Bill was in the United States Senate, I was in the House of Representatives. We had many common constituent problems, which we attacked and solved together. He never forgot how important each individual's predicament was, regardless of that person's station in life, and each received his personal attention.

After I left Congress and Saxbe became the U.S. envoy to India, he and Dolly invited Nancy and me to India to stay with them in New Delhi. While we were there, I spoke to various groups about the U.S. Constitution and freedom of the press. (I was publisher of the *Cincinnati Enquirer* at the time.) That was shortly after Prime Minister Indira Gandhi had declared a national "emergency," in the process abolishing freedom of the press and constitutional privileges. That didn't bother Saxbe; it just made life more interesting.

There are many stories I could relate, so many Saxbeisms I could repeat. Nevertheless, I will always remember Saxbe as a fiercely independent, funny, secure, and intelligent person with an inner strength in troubled times— a man who was loyal and faithful to his mission as he discharged his duties in the various offices he held.

Bill Saxbe has fought and is fighting the good fight. He is keeping the faith. And above all, he has certainly seen the elephant.

As you read this story you will come to know Bill Saxbe for what he was and what he continues to be, a talented, forthright man without guile, a man of impeccable integrity. What you see is what you get.

William J. Keating
Cincinnati, Ohio

ACKNOWLEDGMENTS

It would be hard to imagine a treasured Bill Saxbe story that I haven't heard, but I am sure a few more will spring to life once this book is published; so much the better for storyteller and listener alike.

Most of these engaging yarns—some became legends in their own time—were told to me by Saxbe himself during the hundreds of hours I spent with him. Anecdotes and Saxbe go together like salt and pepper. I also discovered that the man has a remarkable memory for people and events that touched his life for more than four score years. I am honored that he chose me to help him record his multifaceted career.

Many others contributed their memories of Saxbe during his years of public service, and I am most grateful to all of them. I am particularly indebted to President Gerald R. Ford, Alexander M. Haig Jr., and Saxbe's many friends and associates in Ohio, Washington, India, and elsewhere he has trod since.

I would be remiss if I did not also single out the contributions of Carolyn Conrad Nassar, secretary to Charles R. "Rocky" Saxbe, who provided invaluable help, particularly during the early stages of this project, and who met me "in the alley" so many times. Also, Mike Brown deserves recognition for his computer expertise, thus saving this work from disappearing into computer oblivion.

Inestimable help came from a flock of hard-working librarians, including those at the Ohio Historical Society, where Saxbe's Washington papers are stored. The men and women at the Columbus Metropolitan Library always seemed to relish going the extra mile, and for that I am thankful. Also helpful were librarians and archivists at the National Archives at College Park, Maryland; the Gerald R. Ford Library, Ann Arbor, Michigan; The Ohio State University Libraries, including the Veterinary Medicine Library; the Otterbein University Library, Worthington, Ohio; the libraries of *The Columbus Dispatch, Cleveland Plain Dealer*, and other newspapers; and community libraries in Dublin, Upper Arlington, Cleveland, and Mechanicsburg, Ohio.

The Saxbe family was incredibly kind and forthcoming. It goes without saying that the book lives only because of their wholehearted support. Dolly fed me well and made sure her husband didn't make any mistakes in the telling of the tales. Juli, Bart, and Rocky told me stories that even their parents had not heard—and a few made it into this book!

Finally, special recognition is due my wife, Eleanor, for her love and unflagging support. She has been there for me every step of the way.

Peter D. Franklin

INTRODUCTION

Ever since Dad wrote *Seems Like Yesterday,* his account of growing up in Mechanicsburg, Ohio, his family and friends have pestered him to continue the story. He and Mom have had a fascinating life, both as private citizens and as public figures. For ourselves—my sister, Juli; my brother, Rocky; and myself—and for our children—we wanted a written record of our parents' times at Ohio State University; the military years during the Second World War and the Korean War; Dad's public service to Ohio and the nation; their experiences in India when he was ambassador; and their so-called retirement years since.

Rocky eventually persuaded Dad that this was a good idea—an obligation, in fact—and Dad tentatively began to set down some memories. Initially, we thought this would be a book for the family only. But as Dad's story unfolded, it was obvious that his accounts of his public service in the Ohio legislature, as Ohio attorney general, as U.S. senator, as United States attorney general, and as envoy to India deserved publication for their broader historical value.

On the recommendation of Columbus business executive Donald Fanta, Rocky enlisted Peter D. Franklin to work with Dad as coauthor. A Columbus journalist with several history books to his credit, Pete has admirably fleshed out Dad's recollections with details from his associates and from the public record. The Saxbe family is very grateful to Pete for his dedication and perseverance in this challenging task.

My own hobby is American family history, and I have frequent occasion to cast a critical eye on biographies and on the work of other family historians. The sorriest books in this genre are known dismissively as "the begats," because all they contain are names and dates. Good family histories convey a sense of the times in which our forebears lived, a knowledge of their unique experiences, an insight into their motivations and characters, and ideally, first-person accounts of what they did, thought, and felt. *I've Seen the Elephant* amply fulfills all these criteria. For each of us in the Saxbe family, this book is a personal treasure, and we are immensely grateful to Dad and Pete for pulling together this winning story.

For the political historian, it also contains a candid inside view of our nation's most serious constitutional crisis of this century, the Watergate affair. Dad was both witness to, and participant in, the dramatic events surrounding the demise of the Nixon presidency. For the general reader, this is the story of an extraordinary life and career, with more than a little Horatio Alger or Dick Whittington to it.

People frequently ask me if I am related to Bill Saxbe. I'm always happy to say "yes," because I'm proud of being his son—proud because he has been so clearly his own man—speaking his mind freely and doing what he thinks is right. Strangely, none of us in the family have felt that we live in his shadow, since he has always respected us as individuals and taken our opinions seriously.

Dad's courageous position in favor of national health insurance during his 1968 campaign for the Senate, capped by his support of the Kennedy Bill when he got there, may have owed a little to what I had learned about the inequalities in our health-care system—inequalities that have only grown worse in the subsequent thirty years. That position was an unpopular one with his party, but he stuck with it because he believed it was right.

Other of Dad's talents, which made him successful in politics and as a role model, are his genuine curiosity about all kinds of people and places and his ability to make a friend of everyone he encounters. I think his early life in Mechanicsburg prepared him for this, since the town was—and is—too small to support a clique. If you don't get along with everybody there, you quickly run out of people to talk to. Dad has the ability to mingle just as affably with his cronies at Don's Barbershop as he did with his colleagues in the Senate. His sense of adventure, love of travel, and receptivity to new people and ideas—traits I am pleased to say he has passed on to his children and grandchildren—also keep him interested and interesting. He's the kind of man you don't meet every day.

Elephants may be best known for their size, their shape, and their association with the Grand Old Party, but their most noble and admirable characteristics are their prodigious memories and their devotion to their kin. Such uncommon critters are well worth seeing. Read on, and you, too, will see the elephant.

William B. "Bart" Saxbe Jr.

I'VE SEEN THE ELEPHANT

The Burg

I don't recall exactly why I wanted to be on that freight train. I was only in the sixth grade, but I suppose that even then I wanted to see the elephant.

In the 1920s a local freight left Mechanicsburg, Ohio, for nearby Springfield about 4:00 P.M. every day. One day after school, I stopped at Marsh's grocery—where we had a much-abused charge account—picked up a loaf of bread and proceeded to the railroad yards, where I climbed into an empty grain car and departed forever from the Burg. In the yards in Springfield, on another track, a freight train was made up that appeared to be headed west. I was on it when it pulled out. I was positive we were rattling west, and it wasn't long before I was sure we had traveled most of the night.

The train seemed to be approaching a large town. Surely it must be St. Louis or Chicago. It was Columbus, thirty miles east of my hometown. A hobo showed me an old day coach on a siding where half a dozen bums were sleeping. I couldn't sleep; I was thinking too much of my bed at home. I gave up after an hour, slipped out of the yards, and walked to downtown Columbus in search of a telephone. After a couple of hours I went back to the yards and the day coach. About 3:00 A.M. a railroad detective woke me up and took me to his office. My father's cousin, Joe Saxbe, was the station-master of the Union Depot in Columbus, and his people had been on the lookout for me since 10:00 P.M. when the train from Springfield arrived. I wished they had found me sooner.

When they reported to my mother that I had been found, she was great-ly relieved. My father had gone to bed and simply said, "I'll get him in the morning." He arrived about 9:00 A.M. to pick me up, joked with the men in the office, and we started for home. He said nothing about my trip or my purpose. And he never did! My escapade was treated as an everyday occur-rence, and I was forever grateful. I was genuinely ashamed of the whole business and never tried it again.

The daily train that connected Mechanicsburg with the rest of the world was known as "the jerk." We were on the Delaware Bee Line of the Big Four, as it was known before it became part of the New York Central. I believe the proper name of the road was Cincinnati, Columbus, Cleveland, and New York.

When the train arrived in Mechanicsburg, there was the usual small-town bustle on the platform. The train was always met by the town dray, pulled by a fat old gray horse and—in my time—driven by Joe McEvoy, the last of his kind. Joe later bought out Leidy's soda and candy shop, and on repeal of Prohibition turned it into a beer joint.

The biggest business in town for the first twenty years of this century was livestock shipping. Almost a thousand cars of stock went out of Mechanicsburg in one year. Most went to Cleveland, but some were shipped to Cincinnati.

My maternal grandfather, Henry Clay Carey, was a stock buyer in Sidney, Ohio, near where he owned a farm on Sulphur Heights Hill. Although Sidney was only forty miles away, all his stock went to Buffalo, New York, because that was the connection on the Baltimore & Ohio. In earlier days, my other grandfather, William Saxbe, had been a trader, but trading was done in a different manner then. A man would start out with a pocketful of money, often gold, and "gypsy" to as far as twenty or thirty miles from home. He would stop in the road in front of a farm and inquire what the farmer had that he wished to sell or trade: fat cattle, a milk cow, or a yearling heifer. He would bargain, buy, sell, or trade, then move on to the next farm.

There were still market days in some of the county seats at that time. London—just fifteen miles south of the Burg—was noted as a trading town, and every Thursday, year round, the streets were filled with livestock, just as had been the custom in the old market towns of England. Small-town fortunes were made in the market; they also were lost.

My father, Bart Rockwell Saxbe; his brother, Tom; my grandfather, Bill; and other cattle buyers dressed the part. The hat was somewhat oversized and always a little raffish. A vest over an ample stomach was also a mandatory part of the uniform, with vest pockets full of pencils, account books, checkbooks, toothpicks, and the then-new fountain pen—usually large and leaky. A watch and chain with lodge pendant was added to hold the vest together, because it was usually unbuttoned and, in the summer, worn without a coat.

Only a few wore boots. My father wore leather boots he bought in the West; for years they were the only boots in town, and they were regularly borrowed for home talent plays where a cowboy was involved.

Another necessary item for a stock buyer was a cane, usually hickory. It was often broken, not on stock but in forcing gates and plugging holes to stop runaway animals. A pocketknife and a chew of tobacco completed the outfit. A lot of whittling was done while dickering, and the dickering was part of every deal. There also was a lot of whittling, tobacco chewing, and storytelling while sitting around the yards waiting for a "live one," a buyer with money to spend.

Smoking in the stockyards was forbidden, so everybody in the livestock business chewed tobacco when I was a kid. Both my grandfather and father did. I remember when I got my first taste of tobacco. One of my early jobs was driving cattle. We would unload the animals in Woodstock, then drive them back, walking seven miles from Woodstock to a farm in Irwin, the town next to Mechanicsburg.

I was driving cattle with Claude Meacham, who had a chew going. I said, "Give me some of that" and stuffed a mass of leaves into my mouth, just like I had seen so many others do. The more I chewed, the worse I felt. When we finally made it to Irwin, I went behind a shed and threw up. That was my first experience, and I have been chewing ever since. I discovered that spitting often can accentuate things. You say something strong and then splat one down. It makes the point.

Another day I was driving cattle, and they wandered into a ditch, stomping all over a nest of bees. The cattle took off in every direction. I had on a pair of bib overalls, and the bees got down inside my overalls. I ran as fast as I could, but I couldn't shake the bees. I unhooked the overalls and just ran right out of them. Every time I go by that spot I think of that day.

My grandfather, Bill, dressed more like a farmer than a stock buyer. He was born June 22, 1839, about thirty miles from Rochester, New York, and he married Sophia Elizabeth "Lib" Bamberger of Goshen Township, Ohio, in 1862. I didn't know him until about 1920. He sported the stock buyer's wider brim hat, but he wore farmer shoes—something a cowman would never do—and he wore moleskin pants with galluses. But when he dressed up to go to a Republican picnic or GAR reunion, he was a sight to see. His Santa Claus shape and full beard, his manner and size (in his prime he weighed 275 pounds), his broadcloth suit and wide-brimmed GAR or Masonic hat gave every indication that here was a man of substance, which he was. He was the owner of three farms, a stockholder and director of the Farmers Bank, and a member of the Masons and the Modern Woodmen of America. Generally, he was regarded as one of the three or four richest men in town.

My dad always said his father wasn't a money maker; he was a money

My paternal grandmother, Sophia Elizabeth Bamberger Saxbe, and my paternal grandfather, William Saxbe.

saver. He also said that the "old gent," as he referred to his father, would "chase a rag doll to hell for the buttons." Grandfather was "close," and when he died in 1934, at the age of ninety-six, he never had lived in a house with central heat or plumbing, never had owned an automobile or tractor, and never had paid more than 5 cents for a cigar or $1.50 for a shirt. His estate totaled $130,000.

Until a week before he died, he drove a fine brown mare, Katy, hitched to a spring wagon, which he called a rig. I held the mare's halter a week after his death when "Doc" (John V.) Lange gave her a shot of strychnine in the jugular; she dropped in her tracks. The family decided she had been too close to Grandfather for too many years to sell her.

His father, Thomas, was born January 1, 1810, in Stowe, Buckinghamshire, England. He came to the United States as a teen in the early 1820s, married Lucy Bowen in New York State in 1834, and moved to the Mechanicsburg area in 1847.

My father was born on the outskirts of town on August 17, 1882, the eighth of nine children. His schooling was interrupted by rheumatic fever when he was nine years old. The disease left him weakened for several years, and the consensus of the neighborhood was that the Saxbes "would never raise that boy." A wise old doctor told his parents to get the boy a gun and a dog; that would keep him outdoors. They did that, and day after day he

My father and mother took my sister, Betty, and me on vacations to Newberry, Michigan, as here, in July 1920.

roamed the nearby woods, hunting squirrel, rabbit, and quail. When he first started, he could walk only a hundred yards, with the aid of a stick, but he gradually increased his range until he could stay out all day. The game he shot added to the family larder. By the time he was fifteen, he had thrown off all vestiges of rheumatic fever and had become an excellent hunter and shot. I always was convinced that the years he spent on his own had a profound effect on his later life. His determination to be completely self-sufficient, and his sensitive independence must have stemmed from his development as a loner during those formative years.

Grandfather Saxbe was a hard taskmaster, and the family worked from daylight till dark on the farm. My dad was the weakest of the family, and he was given no quarter after his recovery. He hated farm work and resolved never to be so engaged the rest of his life, and he never was.

When he was eighteen, he left home and never lived under the family roof again. He was a thin 140 pounds, his lungs were weak, and he suffered from chest pains. He decided to go west where the climate was better, and his first stop was Wyoming, where he got a job cooking in a sheep herders' camp. He fried meat, baked biscuits, and boiled beans twice a day for ten men. He lasted for the season, grew two inches, put on twenty pounds, and learned how to take care of himself with a gang of pretty tough characters. For the remainder of his life he was a willing and better-than-average camp cook and was unsurpassed in making "scratch" baking powder biscuits.

Next stop was California, where he harvested prunes before he wound up in Redondo Beach, just south of Los Angeles. There he met T. S. Baldwin, who owned Baldwin Brothers, "Government Aeronatical [sic] Engineers and Balloon Manufacturers." Baldwin operated tethered ascension balloons filled with hydrogen at fairs and such. He'd take people up to giddy heights, a few hundred feet or so, on the end of a cable. My dad, and later my Uncle Ray, joined Baldwin as balloon "pilots."

Baldwin, a Dr. August Greth, and a group of investors decided they could make a hydrogen-filled dirigible, and they did, naming it the "California Eagle." Again my dad and Uncle Ray often were the pilots, along with Greth, an "amateur aeronaut." The mechanic was Glenn H. Curtiss, founder of G. H. Curtiss Manufacturing Company (1902) and later the Curtiss Aeroplane and Motor Company. The dirigible had a primitive, underpowered engine in the middle to turn the propellers that jutted out each side. The group tried to sell that first powered balloon in the country to the military, which had shown some interest. They even staged a flight demonstration in San Francisco in October 1903, two months before the Wright brothers achieved the first successful powered flight in a heavier-than-air craft. Unfortunately, the flight of the dirigible failed. With Greth at the controls, powerless against a strong wind, the craft was blown into San Francisco

Bay. Greth was unhurt, but that scuttled both the airship and the project.

Baldwin continued to work the fairs and expositions with his balloon ride. He, Dad, and Ray ended up at the Louisiana Purchase Exposition in St. Louis in 1904. My grandmother, Lib Saxbe, traveled there to talk the boys into coming back to Mechanicsburg, which they did. Four years later my Uncle Ray died of scarlet fever. My father's older brother, Tom, died in 1920, also of the fever.

Dad was a strapping two hundred pounds when he got back. He went into the livestock business, first with beef cattle, and then when Nestle's Milk Products Company built a large dairy in nearby Marysville, he was a successful dealer in dairy cattle. But he always had time to go on hunting trips, coming home with all manner of game, including moose from Canada.

My mother, the former Faye Henry Carey, and father were married on the Carey homestead in Sidney on September 14, 1911. He called her Maggie. My sister, Betty (Mary Elizabeth), was born a year later, and I came along June 24, 1916.

It was the second marriage for my father. His first, to a Springfield, Ohio, woman, had ended in divorce after two years. Divorce was not a subject for polite conversation then, and I didn't know about my father's earlier marriage until I was in college. My children didn't know about it until the 1970s when my son, Bart, started looking into the family history.

With the advent of trucks and refrigeration in the twenties, local shipping to central markets gradually died out. Some of the traders bucked the tiger, trying to keep going after times had changed. Most of them went broke. Some changed with the times and went into the stock cattle business.

My dad was one of those, and by the mid-twenties, that was all he did. He bought calves—usually steers up to five hundred pounds—in the west and shipped them into Ohio for feeding. He occasionally traveled to faraway and—in those days—exotic places like Texas, New Mexico, and Montana to buy stock cattle and feeding lambs, but usually he confined his buying to the stockyards in Kansas City, Chicago, or St. Paul. He traveled by Pullman, stayed in the best hotels, and wore hundred-dollar suits and twenty-dollar Stetson hats.

For a while in the late twenties he worked as a buyer for the Fred Berry Company of St. Paul, Minnesota, and made one hundred dollars a week plus all expenses, earning more money than anyone in town. But he gave up the job shortly after mother received a call from some slightly tipsy woman from St. Paul wondering where "Barty" was. My mother had a reputation to protect as an active member of the community, including three terms on the Mechanicsburg village council.

When I was eleven, my dad took me to St. Paul. We were driven to Urbana and took the Cincinnati and Lake Erie interurban line to Lima, where we boarded a Pullman to Chicago. It was first-class travel, and I really thought I was meant for that. We changed trains for St. Paul, arrived the next day, and put up at the Nicolet Hotel. That afternoon we went to a vaudeville show, followed by dinner at a fancy restaurant. I'll never forget that dinner. My father's business associate, Mr. Berry, took us, and he had a pint of whisky in his pocket. He and my father had drinks before dinner, and I was terrified that they were going to get drunk and be arrested. Then what would I do? I pictured myself wandering the streets in the snow, homeless and lost.

The other vivid memory I have of that trip is of sliding on my belly in about two inches of manure and slop while chasing cattle down an alley in the stockyards. My blue serge, short-pants suit was a mess, and it was the only suit I had. Dad did his best to clean me up, but I was plenty aromatic the rest of the trip.

Everything was new to me. We didn't have a bathtub at home, and the bathtub in our hotel room was more than I could believe. I had seen one in my aunt's house in Sidney, but I had never been in one.

My father tipped the waitress a dime, and I thought that was really high living. I was in the sixth grade at the time, and most of my friends never had been to Columbus. So when I got back to school and filled the ears of my classmates with tall tales, I was the center of attention for some time, and I liked that.

Mechanicsburg was small, about eighteen hundred souls, and like so many other small towns, it teemed with a life of its own. I guess that I was naturally curious and made it my business to know every activity and person in town. I even knew most of the dogs by name.

Stores opened early and were open every night after supper. Saturday night, the big night of the week, with stores open until eleven o'clock, was an experience in itself. The downtown had a carnival atmosphere. After the hitching posts were removed, about 1925, parking was at a premium, and some made it a practice to drive their cars downtown in the middle of the afternoon to get a choice spot for Saturday night.

Homer Rutan parked in the same spot every Saturday night for years. His wife sat in the car and visited with farmers' wives who had completed their shopping. Homer usually lounged on a fender, from where he was free to spit his tobacco. He was a storyteller and usually had a group around him to listen to stories about hunting, frogging, seining, fishing, or fighting when he was a boy down around Chuckery, Ohio.

Most folks from the country had their favorite hangout. Each had its own clubby air, and when they saw the same people for years, they developed a camaraderie that was expressed through "in" jokes, common objects of approval or derision, and sometimes a closeness that brought whole families together.

The men who spent their evenings in the poolroom never seemed to show up in Hunter's hardware next door except on business, and the loafers from Hunter's were never the same as those in Gannon's Grocery. The fast, young crowd hung out at the drug store where the banter was lively and quite a bit cleaner than that at the poolroom. Most of them had never been to college, but they talked like they had. The retired tradesmen loafed at Davis and Byer's furniture and embalming establishment. The rich respectables didn't loaf downtown at all. Each of the community's segments had its own way of life and seemed to have its own particular set of followers.

My father knew and patronized all the shops, always having some gimmick or tool that he wanted made or repaired. He was a great loafer and storyteller himself, and I have seen a whole shop or garage operation come to a complete halt as he told stories of hunting, fishing, shooting, or cattle buying in some faraway place. He always laughed like hell at his own stories, and that provided part of the amusement, for he would wind up in a high cackle that seem completely inappropriate to his size and usual businesslike demeanor.

He was completely unselfish about good hunting and fishing spots and was such a great promoter of them that he often did himself out of a choice location. He couldn't resist telling everyone where it was, what to use for bait, and where to camp.

My dad was about as good a trapshooter as there was in Ohio. When I was a boy, every grange had an annual shoot, and the grange hall would serve the meals. Churches also would have trapshoots to raise money. The prizes were turkeys, maple syrup, and so forth. Cash or sides of beef or pork were the reward in the bigger shoots. I remember coming home from one with a whole dressed hog on the running board and the back end full of sausage. My dad always was the man to beat at those shoots. In 1938 he won the North American Class A 16-yard Championship. Our house was full of silver trophies that he'd won.

On January 27, 1954, the day he died, at age 71, he was on the firing line at the Eustis (Florida) Gun Club. He had just shot ten birds at a trap shoot

My father was among Ohio's very best trapshooters.

when his friend adjacent to him heard him say, "Hold me up." They took his loaded shotgun from his hand as he said, "Let me down." That was it. He was gone, just the way he wanted.

I had started hunting with him when I was five years old or so. I'd carry a stick and beat the brush, but when I was twelve or thirteen, I got a shotgun, an Iver Johnson .410-guage single shot. It was a Christmas present from a friend of my dad's—Uncle Harry Downey. (I was taught to call all good friends of the family "uncle" and their wives "aunt.")

In a little farming community, everybody hunted. There weren't enough men in town to put out a fire on the first day of hunting season. By high school, I became a guide, booking in hunting parties from Cincinnati and Columbus and taking them out for duck or pheasant.

Subsequently I became a Class A shooter, but unlike my dad, I never reached the national level. I broke 100 straight in a state shoot one time, but it got so you had to break 200 straight to win. I'd get 194 or 195, but I never broke 200 straight. I did qualify in an international shoot in 1960 and could have gone to the Olympic tryouts, but I didn't. I was Ohio's attorney general at the time. But over the years I did win a lot of silver trophies. I also was active in the Amateur Trapshooting Association, which, thanks to my dad, I joined as a life member at the age of ten. While Ohio attorney general, I served as vice president of the organization.

I always had a dozen or so guns that I would trade and buy and sell. It was kind of a hobby for me. When I sold off my biggest batch of guns, I might have had thirty, but the insurance got too expensive. I sold off thirty thousand dollars worth at one time to my friend Marshall Coyne, who owns the Madison Hotel in Washington and many other enterprises. Another bunch of guns was sold at auction at Stratford, Ohio, just north of Columbus.

I suppose the best shotguns I had were the Purdys I bought in India for eighteen hundred dollars and twenty-five hundred dollars. They were top-of-the-line British-made shotguns with gold chasing on the bottom. A new one today costs something like thirty thousand dollars. I had some good rifles, too, but I sold most of those. My favorite was always a hunting gun. I had some top Winchester Model 21 doubles, which I used for years.

I started a hunt club in Mechanicsburg, called the Van Darby Club, in 1952, although its origins went back to 1921. My grandfather had owned Baker's Lake, on the outskirts of Mechanicsburg, and rented it out for fishing and recreation. As a young boy I used to run trap lines there, too, for muskrat and an occasional mink. Then a group of well-to-do Springfield businessmen formed the Van Dyke Club and rented the lake and the surrounding property for the club's exclusive use. Subsequently that club moved to another lake, giving me an opportunity to form the Van Darby Club on the property.

There was no private preserve shooting in Ohio prior to 1952. When I was in the Ohio House, I got together with the Senate leadership to put through a bill allowing private hunting preserves in the state. A group of old buddies and I would have a monthly shoot and a dinner at Van Darby. We had a trap and skeet range and several fields for hunting live birds. For several years the club was used for bird dog (German shorthair) field trials.

Van Darby also was the site of the "Pure in Heart" annual barbecue that I began in 1947 for Republicans throughout the state. The Beatitudes (Matthew 5) refer to the pure in heart. Pure-in-heart Republicans were invited, although a sympathetic Democrat would pop up now and then. We would have one hundred or more people there—senators, representatives, judges, city councilmen, mayors, various public officials, and supporters. Friends saw to the food, donating a hog, a whole ham, or game somebody had shot. One year Ned Crockett of Columbus donated a quarter of a moose that we made into chili. J. D. Sawyer, a Middletown, Ohio, real estate agent and a close associate over the years, bailed us out in the spring of 1959 with elk and mule deer he shot in Wyoming. Charlie Hill, who headed up Scioto Downs, the Columbus harness track, always sent over a couple of barrels of beer.

As I look back on my early years in Mechanicsburg, I realize I was rewarded in so many ways and my life enriched. My dad was strict when it came to raising a family, but he had had such a difficult youth himself. Our home was happy, and the memories are pleasant. There were love and good times, respect, and unlimited hope. You couldn't ask for much more.

Becoming Worldly

In my junior year of high school, I worked Saturdays at the drug store for Harlan West, jerking sodas, sweeping up, and such. The previous owner, Paul Slater, had left town in the night. He had made up batches of Jamaica ginger extract, which he sold to the alcoholics during Prohibition. A bad batch (Slater always was accused of mixing it) produced "Jake-leg," an affliction that crippled about twenty men in Mechanicsburg. It killed the nerves in their extremities, and they never recovered.

The drug store was old, going way back through several owners even before Slater. West was a swinger and attracted a lively crowd of regulars: Walter Allison, Skinny Neer, Neil Gest, Ben Linville, Billy MacGruder, Bill Van Ness, and Ralph Watts, the high school teacher. One time West patched up some Chicago bootleggers who were injured in a car wreck; after that they regularly delivered five-gallon cans of alcohol, and he just put it in the soda fountain. If a guy wanted alcohol in his Coke, West would give him a squirt from the fountain pump.

It got to be a pretty fast crowd, and I thought I was part of it. When I wasn't working I hung around and neglected my studies. When I was fifteen, I paid Joe Foster twenty dollars—in installments—for a 1924 Harley-Davidson Police Special motorcycle. That gave me the freedom to take off for neighboring towns, like Springfield. Along the way, there were many spills and thrills. I never told my mother about the close calls. I rode the cycle to school until one day, in the driveway, I hit a boy. He only had a small cut on his forehead, but that was the end of the motorcycle. My dad said, no insurance—no motorcycle, and insurance was not available to a fifteen-year-old without substantial funds.

I never studied very hard. In elementary school I got expelled a couple of times for acting up, and I flunked a couple of courses in high school.

That got my mother's attention. She made me buckle down and take extra courses so I could graduate with my class.

As a senior, in 1934, I almost wrecked my opportunity to graduate because I got a job delivering new International Harvester trucks for F. W. Myers Drive-Away in Springfield. The owner, Fizz Myers, wanted me to go to work right away, before graduation, but that was ridiculous. I could work one week and then not get another trip for three weeks. You had to be there when they read off the roster of drivers, so it involved a lot of hanging around.

My first trip came in my last week of high school. I had passed all my tests except typing. You had to type twenty-five words a minute, which was not too difficult, but when I got back from the trip there was a question as to whether I was going to graduate. The school must have been glad to be rid of me because I did my twenty-five words, graduated, and went back to work on the trucks.

At seven o'clock in the morning I'd be out on the road, hitchhiking to Springfield, almost twenty miles away. Then I'd hang around Myers, hoping to catch a trip. If I had fifteen cents, I'd buy a quart of chocolate milk and two donuts. That would be breakfast and lunch.

If I got a trip, I could expect to make one dollar a day, for a ten-hour day. Most of our trips were to New York—the garage was in Long Island City, Queens—and there we'd sit until ten or fifteen of us were in the city, and then Myers would send a rattletrap of a bus to pick us up. Sometimes we would wait four or five days. We got one dollar a day for food and another dollar for one night in a hotel. As a result, I slept many a night in a truck cab.

In the 1930s you could ride New York's subway for a nickel. Some days I'd go clear out to the end of the line and just walk around. I'd go in a bar and get a beer for a dime and eat their free lunch or go to a Greek or an Italian restaurant and get a blue plate special for a quarter. I became pretty well acquainted with New York.

Some of the trips were boatload trips. You drove just the chassis because the company didn't ship completed trucks overseas. So, you'd have to make a temporary windshield of some kind, and you'd have either a tow bar or a rider. Both were used to tow a second chassis. At the end of the trip you had to lug sixty pounds of windshield and rider on the subway from the docks to Long Island City.

One of the reasons I didn't get many trips was because most went to guys with families, senior guys, but I'd get picked when they had a real tough trip, like to Great Falls, Montana. It took five days to get there because you could only drive those trucks at twenty-five miles an hour. One

My Mechanicsburg High School
graduation portrait, 1934.

time we went forty-four hours without putting up in a bed. We'd stop along the road and sleep in the cab. We were in Great Falls one night, six of us. Then we loaded up an old Ford station wagon we had towed out there and drove all the way back to Springfield without stopping, except for gas and pit stops.

So I got to see a lot of country—trips to Montana, up into New England, and out to Kansas. I did that all summer. Once in a while I got a real deal; Myers also delivered new Superior Body vehicles from Lima. They made buses, ambulances, and hearses. I delivered a hearse to Boston, and that was *real* comfort—I could sleep on the gurney in the back. In New York State one night I pulled off the road into a little grove and went to sleep. I woke to a bright light shining on me, raised up, and scared the hell out of a state trooper. He thought there was a body in the hearse.

When I drove an ambulance, I could wear nice clothes. I would take the night boat from Boston, down through the Cape Cod Canal, and to New York. The smallest stateroom cost only three dollars. They had a band on board, and I had a great time.

My trucking lasted most of that summer, almost up to when I started college. I decided to go to Ohio State because two other buddies—Harold Thomas and Charles "Bus" Ackerman—decided to go there, too. My grandfather had died that summer, and I had inherited five hundred dollars. I was rich, so I bought my first car, a 1924 Buick, for twenty dollars. It died so many times, though, that when I got to college I bought a Model A Ford coupe. I think I paid something like seventy dollars for it.

The three of us got a room at a house on Indianola, just north of the Ohio State campus. That cost us fifty dollars a month. Tuition was twenty-four dollars a quarter, so I was having a pretty big time on my five hundred dollars.

I signed up for Commerce College, which was the business school. I also got a job working at the Chittenden Hotel, downtown. Each morning I'd inventory all the bars in the hotel—they had three or four of them at the time. Then I attended classes in the afternoon.

I had to put on decent clothes to go downtown and work, and I'd found that I could find good clothes at secondhand stores. I could buy a suit for ten dollars. I had to protect my clean shirt, though; the town was so dirty in those days. Everybody burned soft coal in the furnaces, and by the time you'd get downtown your shirt would be dirty just from riding on the Summit Street streetcar. The trolley had a stove in the back, and the ride cost a nickel.

In a moment of idiocy, I went out for freshman football. Every night I went to practice and got beat up by the varsity players. I weighed 190 pounds, but guys like Alex Schoenbaum, Carl Kaplanoff, and Charlie Hamrick all weighed 250 or so. In a scrimmage I'd see the fullback Dick Heekin come through the line; God, he was hard to stop! But he and I became good friends. Finally, I saw that I just wasn't big enough for that stuff, and I quit.

My parents went to Florida for the first time in 1934, so I skipped the winter quarter and went with them to hunt and fish with my dad. I came back to school again in the spring quarter. That freshman year, 1934–35, I attended two quarters because I had the idea that I wanted just a smatter-ing of college before becoming a cattle dealer. I remember one quarter I took freehand drawing, astronomy, and meat cutting instead of taking the things I should have been taking. I had a lot of dates and enjoyed the cam-pus social life. In fact, I only completed one year in the first of two years at OSU because I was off on trips and moving around a lot, from Commerce to Agriculture to Arts College. Most of the time nobody knew where I was.

I was not very smart, but college wasn't hard for me, so I didn't work at it very much. I took all the easy courses and avoided the harder ones; I could go to class and listen to a few lectures and pass the exams. Eventually I was faced with having to take required courses—languages, mathemat-ics, and such—because I had taken all my electives. But I was having too much fun to quit.

I became an ordinary seaman for the summer of 1935, thanks to a guy from Mechanicsburg who got me a job on a ship going to South America. I worked on that ship for two trips that summer, earning twenty-eight dollars a month. From the South Street piers in Brooklyn we sailed to Jamaica, Haiti, Panama, and Colombia. One time we had a whole mess of big turtles on the top deck and my job was to take care of those turtles, hosing them down. We lost quite a few and had to push them over the side.

In the fall of 1935 I returned to OSU and in November was initiated into the Chi Phi Fraternity, 2000 Indianola Avenue. They had lots of paddling, hell week, and such. The first week I told them, "Look, I've been around, and I'm not going to put up with this crap. The hell with tradition. The first guy that lays a paddle on me, I'm leaving." I thought I was a man of the world in those days. I was wearing good clothes and talking big. I had been around; I'd seen the elephant. So they took me in anyway, and the following spring they elected me president of the fraternity for the 1936–1937 school year.

While at OSU I got a job with Phillip Morris, handing out free two-cigarette sample packs on campus. That's where I first saw Ardath Louise Kleinhans. Nobody called her Ardath (the name of a field in France that her mother read about in a book); she was known as Dolly to everyone. She also earned money distributing cigarette samples. I earned a carton of cigarettes a week and thirty dollars a month to give the samples away. I never have smoked cigarettes.

I met Dolly at the Union's College Shop, 1854 North High Street, across from campus. She worked there part time as a sales clerk. The shop had a swinger for a manager, Rosalind "Rosie" Strapp. Everybody liked to hang out in there. A drink was always available in the back room. Rosie's husband also worked for The Union, but at the main downtown department store. We had hellish parties at their house. I fell in with a pretty rough crowd, including Red Comiskey, a big Irishman from Youngstown. Together we thought we could lick anybody.

In the summer of 1938 I got the idea that I'd go in the wood business if my dad and another fellow would let me cut the timber on the land that they owned near Mechanicsburg. They agreed, so I borrowed money from the bank to get started. With a small saw rig and a few guys I picked up, we cut timber that whole summer.

I thought I could haul the wood to Columbus and sell it to people for their fireplaces. I got an old truck, which broke down immediately, and there I was with this large pile of wood. I had mostly round wood—people wanted split wood—and it was greener then green. I had elm and everything else that wouldn't burn. That fall we put an ad in the paper and started selling, going house to house in Columbus. Well, we were only getting five dollars a rick for it.[1] I sold some, but most I tossed away. I lost money on the venture. In fact, when Dolly and I got married, almost two years later, I still owed twenty-five hundred dollars or so to the bank. She didn't know about that.

In January 1939, I got a job as a lecturer for the Ohio Division of Conservation, going around the state showing conservation movies to the hunters and fishermen. John W. Bricker was elected in 1938 to the first of his three terms as Ohio governor, and John T. Brown from Mechanicsburg was his director of agriculture. He got me the job. All the movies were silent, so I provided the narrative, for which I received $130 a month and expenses. That was enough to enable me to buy a used 1936 Studebaker President, which was a hot car. That thing would go one hundred miles an hour! The experience did two things for me that proved invaluable in later years. I met and made a lot of good friends throughout the state, and I became skilled at speaking to groups of people. It also was a job that I continued right up until I entered active duty in the army.

In the meantime, I joined the Masons in Mechanicsburg; my dad had said he'd pay for all the Masonry I'd take. The next thing I knew I was a candidate. He got me in more Masonic groups than I could pay dues for, but I got every rank of Masonry there was, up to the thirty-third degree.

One day in Mechanicsburg I ran into my sister's husband, Gardner Wing. He was a graduate of Ohio State in horticulture.

"What are you going to do?" he asked. "Are you going to finish up this school?"

"No," I said. "I don't care about graduating, I've seen it all, I've had the fun, and I've taken all the college I want to."

"Think of it this way, Bill: If you don't graduate, all of your life you're going to be explaining why you didn't, and it doesn't sound very good."

I got thinking about that, and I said, "Damn it, I'll graduate."

So, I had to go back and take all those courses I had avoided. By the spring of 1937, I had finished only five quarters at Ohio State, and I needed to complete twelve quarters to graduate. I really had to buckle down over the last two years. In my senior year, I moved out of the fraternity and moved in with Wilber L. "Wibby" Harrod over Larry's Grill, 2034 North High Street.[2] Harrod was a mailer at the *Ohio State Journal* and a gambler. He was broke most of the time. The apartment had a Murphy bed, and we both slept in the same bed. But he worked at night, so it worked out.

I saw Dolly again when she and her brother, Red Kleinhans, who was a pretty good friend of mine on campus, came into Hennick's restaurant on

High Street. I was there with my girl, Jean Dirkson, having a Coke. Dolly and I both had classes to go to, so I walked her on campus and left Jean and Red in Hennick's. On our way to class I asked her, "Do you like to neck?" and she said "Yea." I'll never forget it: I kissed her right in the middle of the Oval, the big common in the center of the campus.

"I thought he was pretty fresh," Dolly recalled.

After I decided to get serious about college, I saw more and more of Dolly, although we both had "steadies." Dolly was a striking young woman. She was a homecoming queen candidate at the time, so she really was a catch. I was afraid of losing her. She graduated one quarter ahead of me (December 1939) and was back home in Maumee, on the outskirts of Toledo. I visited her one day when I was up that way on a trip for the Conservation Division. She was the cashier in a Toledo restaurant and didn't like the job one bit. She had a teaching certificate in art education, so in the spring quarter she returned to osu to begin studies on her masters degree. That's when we started dating pretty steady, even though she was still "pinned" to a former classmate.

My five hundred dollar inheritance had long been squandered, and despite the many jobs I taken on, I was almost broke. But I wanted to ask Dolly to marry me before I lost her again. Pawnbroker Saul Ruben, owner of The Gun Store, 68 East Long Street, took a Colt Woodsmen and a couple of other guns in trade for a modest diamond ring.

A couple of days later Dolly and I were sitting at the soda fountain in the Varsity Drug Company store, 1876 North High Street. "If you'd send that stupid Beta pin back with that itty-bitty diamond in it," I told her, referring to her boyfriend's fraternity pin, "I'll give you this one." Obviously thrilled, she began to slip the ring on her finger. "It's too small!" she exclaimed. She meant it was too little to fit on her finger, but I thought she meant that the diamond wasn't big enough. So I went back to Ruben's with another gun and got a bigger diamond and that's the one she wears today.

We announced our engagement the day I graduated, in June 1940. My dad wasn't in favor of my getting married. He liked Dolly and her family, but he just didn't think I was mature enough and stable enough.

My lucky day came September 14, 1940, when I married Dolly Kleinhans at St. Paul's Episcopal Church in Maumee. Russell French, my roommate in the fraternity, was the best man. We were in tails and the wedding and a very nice reception went off fine. Then Dolly and I took off for the Dearborn Inn just outside Detroit. We were so exhausted after all the activity that we never got past the Commodore Perry Hotel in Toledo, about ten miles from Maumee. I told Dolly, "Now, don't tell anybody." I was

I took Dolly and my dog, Sport, on a squirrel hunt four days after our September 1940 wedding.

embarrassed that we had to stop, really, but we were both exhausted. I went down to the lobby drug store to get Dolly a milkshake, and while I was gone she called her mother and my mother, just to find out what she was expected to do. So, everyone learned about our stop.

In Mechanicsburg I rented a ten-room house, completely furnished, for twenty dollars a month. That really was more than I could afford on what the state was paying me, but it was a place to hang our hats. When we got back from Toledo, Dolly and I were pooped. We got undressed, put on our bathrobes, and sat quietly in front of the fire. Suddenly we had a yard full of merrymakers, beating on pans and whatnot, making a heck of a racket. It was a shivaree, or "belling." By tradition we had to invite them all in for a drink and something to eat. So we had a big party. That started off our life together in Mechanicsburg.

At Christmastime we did have a belated honeymoon, to Mexico. Dolly already was pregnant, and she caught Montezuma's revenge, first in Mexico City, then in Acapulco. On our way to Acapulco, where I caught a 9-foot, 129-pound sailfish, we met a dramatic-looking couple. The woman's hair was prematurely white, and the man looked very continental. We decided they were German spies, but it turned out they were chiropractors from California, the Von Waldens. They joined us on the rest of the trip and became very good friends.

Upon our return we visited both our parents, who were in Florida. That's when the mothers found out Dolly was pregnant and in bad shape. She went home to Maumee with her mother.

I went off to fight the war.

Army Daze

At The Ohio State University I joined a National Guard cavalry troop in 1937 to get out of ROTC. You had to complete six quarters of ROTC, but my friend Phil Stoltz told me, "Hell, Bill, get in the Guard. You go out there on Sunday morning, they give you a uniform, you ride these horses, you play polo, and jump and all that." So, I said, "That's for me," and I got out of ROTC and into the Guard.

In late August and early September of 1940 I went on three weeks of maneuvers in Wisconsin. It was miserable. We had all those horses up there, and it rained all the time. By then I was a corporal; it was the first time I'd had any authority, and I liked it. I found out in the Army that I could work with people. When we came off maneuvers, Dolly and I were married, but almost right away my Troop E, 107th Cavalry Regiment, was activated. World War II had begun in Europe, and we were being called up.

At the time, the Army dangled in front of young men big pay—$140 a month for second lieutenants. They were looking for young guys, particularly college men, to take what they called a Series 10 examination to become officers. I thought, boy, this could be okay, with the boots and britches, the spurs and horses, and a little whip and gloves. All that seemed very glamorous.

I took the test in the Ohio statehouse, at Broad and High Streets in Columbus. It was the first time I'd ever been to the place where the legislature met. I didn't know a thing about military science, but I didn't have to. It was the strangest exam I'd ever seen. If you didn't know the answer to a question, you could leave the room, go downstairs, and ask a question of one of the officers there, and they'd tell you. They didn't give a hoot whether you knew anything or not. My only preparation was attending three National Guard camps, and there I was—a second lieutenant.

The glamour, the excitement a young man felt on becoming an officer was just unbelievable. I made a beeline to the military store on South High Street, in Columbus, where they gave you a whole uniform on credit—boots, britches—the whole shebang.

I still had my job with the Conservation Department, and I thought I'd be selling cattle all over the state—that's what I really had in mind. My dad was phasing out of the cattle business and going to Florida where he stayed longer and longer each time.

I went down and bought my uniform, thinking we would be called up immediately. I quit my job with the Conservation Department about January, and then we didn't get called. The camp wasn't ready for us. So Dolly and I moved in with "Wibby" Harrod and slept on one cot in the hall above Larry's Grill, opposite the Ohio State campus.

Dolly was still working at The Union as a sales clerk, earning about fifteen dollars a week. We didn't have anything but a lot of free time and a lot of fun. By the time the 107th Cavalry was activated, in March 1941, Dolly was pregnant. I shipped out with the horses on the train to Camp Forrest in Tullahoma, Tennessee. Every troop was supposed to have a complement of five officers, but we had one hundred extra because so many had passed that Series 10 exam.

Less than two weeks passed, and I was feeling mighty lonely. I called Dolly. "You've got to come down here. I can't stand it without you." Fortunately, there was a whole bunch of other wives at nearby Murfreesboro. Dolly boarded a bus, so pregnant that she couldn't zip up the skirt of her one suit. Her mother was about to die. "You're going to lose the baby," she said. "This is terrible!"

No sooner had Dolly arrived than I received orders to join the 2nd Cavalry Division at Fort Riley, Kansas. We traveled there with another couple, Marge and Lee Cavey, because they had a car, and she was a nurse. When Dolly told her mother she was on the move again, her mother was very upset. "Oh, you're going to lose the baby," she kept saying, but Marge was looking out for Dolly.

The Army didn't have quarters for us so together we rented an unfurnished house in Junction City, about ten miles away. Marge and Lee had furniture in Pittsburgh, but it never arrived. We rented a couple of beds and a stove and refrigerator, and the landlady gave us two wicker chairs and a card table. That and a couple of orange crates was it.

Assigned to the 14th Cavalry Regiment, I was a platoon leader in charge of "selectees." That's what draftees were called in those days. The idea was to put together an effective regiment, but we had five hundred men who had never seen a horse, five hundred horses that had never seen a man, and one hundred officers who had never seen either. Even though the cavalry had been outdated for fifty years, I worked at it valiantly, until they needed somebody to send to intelligence school for photo interpretation at Fort Belvoir, Virginia, outside Washington. I was selected because I was the most intelligent one they had, or so I believed at the time.

At Fort Belvoir forty of us lived together in the barracks. It was at the fort that I rode in an airplane for the first time. They took us up in an old B-18 to learn how to make aerial photos. Little did I know I would become a pilot, but that is what got me thinking about it.

I was so intelligent after those two weeks at intelligence school that upon my return to Fort Riley I was assigned to G2, the intelligence section. Later I wound up as the division public relations officer in G2, cranking out a bunch of poop to hometown newspapers. In September we went on maneuvers in Louisiana, and Dolly went home to her parents in Maumee, because our first child was on its way. Dolly's father was the superintendent at the Lucas County Children's Home in Maumee.

We disembarked in Hamburg, in southeast Arkansas, and marched cavalry style down back roads into Louisiana. We kept on back roads, only to wind up in the worst swamps I had ever seen. Obviously they were not designed for cavalry. But there we were, a whole division with twelve thousand horses. While the main force was up front on maneuvers, G2 was stuck in the rear at division headquarters, pumping out press releases. We were not up in front where Gen. Dwight D. Eisenhower and other brass visited, so that was frustrating.

G2 had a little camp in the woods and a kitchen. While sitting there at a table one day, minding my business and swatting flies, a big military Packard sedan pulled up with four stars on it. Chief of Staff Gen. George C. Marshall stepped out, and he was the nicest guy you ever would meet. "I wonder if I could get a sandwich or something," he asked me. Well, of course. Talk about snapping to. Everybody did. I sat and chatted with him while he ate his lunch, just passing the time of day. He was a delight.

Before we broke camp, division called me up to be the division's assistant G2, which ordinarily called for the rank of a major, but I was only a second lieutenant. Here was a whole new world for me, putting out all intelligence reports for the whole division and mingling with the top brass. I was working night and day on important things, attending conferences, giving weather reports, and doing every other intelligence kind of thing. I was eating at the general's mess and so on. It was high-cotton time.

When Dolly went into the hospital to have the baby, we were still on maneuvers out in the real boonies. But every night I could get away I went into town where I could use a telephone. While in a phone booth in a drug store at Monroe, Louisiana, I learned that William Bart Saxbe Jr. had arrived on September 10, 1941, beet red and with a head of jet black hair that stood straight up.

The maneuvers moved on, clear down to Lake Charles, Louisiana, but I got a few days of emergency leave to visit Dolly and my firstborn. I'd received one paycheck for one thousand dollars because I hadn't had any pay since going to division. I saw an ad in the Kansas City paper for a 1937 Cadillac Convertible Sedan for $750. I took the train from Junction City to Kansas City, bought the sedan, and drove to Toledo. Then I returned to Fort Riley. When Dolly and Bart were able to travel, they followed. I had been really lonely for them both. For a few days we lived in a hotel. Bart's bed was in the dresser drawer.

When Bart was about a year old, I thought he needed a haircut. I sat him on the toilet seat, put a bowl on his head and cut away. Dolly was so mad at me. She carried on something awful because she said Bart looked just like Moe of the Three Stooges. I suppose he did, but I had the pleasure of giving him his first haircut.

Shortly thereafter I was promoted to first lieutenant. In those days you ran charge accounts; you had a PX account, an officer's club account, a commissary account. Everything was on credit. I felt I had pretty shabby duds from the quartermaster, so I went to the best tailor and ordered britches and boots. I went the limit and all on credit.

We lived in a furnished apartment over a grocery store. I earned $140 a month, but by the time we got all the bills paid, we might have $5 spending money. Meanwhile, we were running with a pretty good crowd at Fort Riley. There was hunting on Wednesdays and on Sunday mornings, polo on Saturday. We had all those great polo players out of New York—Paul Mellon, Aidan Roark, Pete Bostwick, and the like. We would go to the polo matches and the cocktail parties that followed. Then we'd go to the hunts and the hunt balls. After the hunt on Sunday morning, we'd all go to the club for a hunt breakfast and listen to the band. We were living in the days of the empire, as the Army was in those days.

It was the good life for me, playing golf or trapshooting or hunting, but not too good for Dolly. She became perturbed by my frequent absences, so she talked to my mom about it. My mother let me have it. "You had better start paying more attention to your wife and come home on time after work," she said. So I did. I didn't have a chance, anyway. My mother always sided with Dolly.

When Bart became ill, and then Dolly, her mother came out on the train. I'd get off duty 4:00 P.M. every day and go hunting. We were living on the rabbits, dove, and quail that I shot—and hickory jacks. That's a fungus on a tree, like a mushroom, and we used to have rabbit with hickory jack gravy. Just before Dolly's mother arrived, I made a big bunch of bean soup, so much that I filled every one of the ice cube trays with soup. She went to get some ice and every tray she pulled out had beans in it.

In G2 I had a first lieutenant and about six or eight guys. We had our own panel truck and a bunch of photo equipment. We took photos like crazy. Years later I gave thousands of them to the Cavalry Museum at Fort Riley.

The Army was opening an ordnance plant in Baxter Springs, Kansas, and needed to show off the military hardware there. Baxter Springs is at the corner of Kansas and Arkansas. On the morning of December 7, 1941, I was standing in the middle of the street in Baxter Springs, directing some of our military traffic. The civilians going by were yelling something about Pearl Harbor. Finally somebody stopped long enough to tell me the Japanese had attacked our Pacific Fleet base in Hawaii. We immediately went on full alert, 24 hours a day. Who the hell thought the enemy would attack Fort Riley, Kansas, I don't know, but we were on full alert there for about a week before some sense crept in.

The tense situation was not without some humor. One of the jobs was to guard the horses. We had mounted guard, armed with .45-caliber pistols. When the guard changed, they'd take the clip out of the pistols and hand them over to the guards coming on duty. Our guys weren't all that proficient changing the clip. One day during the exchange, a pistol went off and shot a horse right between the ears.

We spent the winter of 1941 at Fort Riley, not knowing if we were going overseas. We still had the horses. I rode my own horse (army issue) almost every morning, and sometimes Dolly would ride, too. That's the way we spent that winter, socializing and wondering what was happening every place else.

We did manage a few days in Ohio at Christmas. One of the children in the home Dolly's parents ran was ten-year-old Betty Toland; she had been there since she was five. She was crazy about me for some reason. She'd go around singing, "Can you bake a cherry pie, Billy boy, Billy boy?" She helped around the home a lot. She begged us to take her with us when we returned to Fort Riley, so we did. She became part of the family, remaining with either Dolly or me throughout my army career and then through the time she completed high school in Mechanicsburg.

In July 1942, our cavalry outfit became the Ninth Armor Division. The only thing I didn't like about that is that I would have to give up my cavalry uniform—the first-class boots, the Albert Moore britches, and all that. I was in hock for most of it. Plus, I didn't think much of that armor business, riding around in a tank, tearing up the reservation, and knocking over trees. Ever since that flight up to Washington, I thought I would like to get in the Army Air Corps.

The United States needed a lot of pilots by the fall of 1942. We were losing them right and left, so they loosened up the requirements, and my request was processed. Dolly and I got a house in Manhattan, Kansas, just east of Fort Riley. The tires on the old 1936 Packard Phaeton I had acquired were all but shot, but the three of us made it to Toledo, where I dropped off Dolly and Bart. I left the car there, too, and returned to Kansas by train. I wasn't back but a few days before I received orders to report for an Army Air Corps physical in Leavenworth, Kansas, and then to San Antonio for pilot training.

I took preflight training at the San Antonio Training Center, now Kelly Field, in the spring of 1943. Instead of the twelve weeks they gave regular cadets, the student officers went through as a group in only six weeks because we didn't have to take all the military training. Dolly and Bart came down to Texas, too.

I knew nothing about flying an airplane, and it was the toughest thing for me to learn. Every night I'd come home and say "Well, Dolly, I know I washed out today because I can't fly that thing," but somehow I finally made it, earning my wings in September 1943. Goodfellow Field, at San Angelo, Texas, was the next stop. We got a motel room right behind a beer joint where music blared into our room all night.

Most of the airfields in those days had grass runways. The first time I went up with the instructor in the Vultee BT-13, known as the Vultee Vibrator because it shook so. The instructor sat in the front seat, and I was behind him. He said, "I want to see what you know," so we ascended to six thousand feet or so, and that thing was shaking from more power than I thought any airplane had. Then he said to do a stall, but I thought he said do a spin. I pulled her up and kicked her into the fastest snap roll you ever saw. It scared the hell out of him. That was my start in the BT-13.

It was hot—God, it was hot—in San Angelo, and it didn't get any better when they sent me to twin-engine school at Ellington Field, in Houston. We drove there overnight because it was cooler to travel at night. In the paper I saw a house for rent and called at 6:00 A.M. It was a beautiful brick house with a nice yard and in a nice part of town. I had made captain at Fort Riley, so with flight pay, I was getting about four hundred dollars a month. It was more money than I ever had made. Once again we were living pretty good.

Twin-engine flight was easier—flying formation, night flying, and no more acrobatics. I did okay, but before you graduated they had to see if you could handle altitude. You sat in a pressure chamber, and they would take you up to thirty-eight thousand feet, without oxygen. I got a nitrogen bubble in the brain, what they call the bends, and they brought me down in a minute or two. I was out cold and wound up in the hospital. I gradually came out of it, but that limited my high-altitude flying. Meanwhile, I had put in for P-38 training at Tinker Field at Oklahoma City. Those twin-engine P-38s were hot.

My new orders sent me to a B-26 field at Dodge City, Kansas. We were there on January 1, 1944. In B-26s I was relatively safe because they couldn't climb more than twelve thousand feet. I think the most traumatic experience I had in training was the first time I went up in a B-26. I had an instructor who was scared to death of the plane. He was all over those controls; he just couldn't keep his hands off of them. I wasn't really sure I could fly because every time we'd come in for a landing, he'd be on the controls. He finally died in a crash while training another pilot.

The only time I ever came close to getting in any kind of an accident I was on the ground. We were out on the field at 5:00 A.M. I revved the engines, and the darn plane skidded on the ice, even with the brakes on. I stopped just before I plowed into another bomber. That was the closest I ever came to getting into real trouble.

My next stop was Barksdale Field at Shreveport, Louisiana. We rented a little double house in nearby Bossier City. Dolly had to do the washing in the bathtub. Bart's bed was a trunk that followed us around, and we'd make that trunk up as a baby's bed. During a physical there, they discovered that my hearing was impaired. So they took me out of B-26 training and decided I should go to Burma with light planes. I was to be a unit commander somewhere in the jungle, I guess.

So, once again we loaded up. I took Dolly and Bart to Toledo, and I reported to Jackson, Mississippi, for assignment. I was ready to go to Burma; got all my overseas stuff, my shots—everything—when orders came for an executive officer at Fort Benning, Georgia. I was it, so I joined a composite squadron that flew missions for the infantry school. We had twenty-five different kind of airplanes—bombers, fighters, observation planes, light planes—and forty veteran pilots returning from combat overseas. I was supposed to be the executive officer of the bunch. We had an easy-going CO who hadn't been overseas, either. He was a farmer and a hell of a nice guy. I kept trying to get back to flying and finally made it while at Benning's Lawson Field. I guess I just got better at cheating on the test.

On July 11, 1944, in Toledo, Dolly gave birth to our second child, Juliet Louise Saxbe. She was a pretty baby, beautiful from the beginning.

Darned if I didn't get orders to be the deputy air inspector of the 3rd Air Corps. I headed for Barksdale Field again. That time we got a big house on the post. As coordination and compliance officer, it was my job to inspect air bases and to see that they complied with regulations. A friend, who had been in the cavalry, ran the officers club there, and he asked me to help out with his gambling night. So I got out my chuck-a-luck game. I made a hundred dollars a week on that thing.

Talk about living high. As part of that inspection duty I flew all over the country. I had a twin-engine plane at my disposal, so I'd fly to Columbus and other places where I had family and friends. I'd fly down to Florida and see my folks, for example. Along the way I would drop in on a base for an inspection.

One day I had to go to Fort Dix, New Jersey, in a B-25. I picked up as my copilot a fighter pilot recently back from overseas. He held a green instrument rating card, which verified he was qualified to fly on instruments alone. Also on board were a bunch of brass I agreed to haul to Washington. When we reached Nashville and stopped for gas, the weather ahead looked poor. The report said we had only a six thousand-foot ceiling, but as long as we could fly VFR (visual) that posed no problem. Over the Blue Ridge Mountains I was told to go up to seventy-five hundred feet, whereupon we disappeared into heavy clouds. I mean, I couldn't even see our wingtips.

"Well, you're the instrument pilot, you take over," I told my copilot.

"Hell, I can't fly instruments," he told me, "and I've never been in one of these planes before!"

"Oh, shit!"

I hadn't flown instruments for almost two years, and my rating card had lapsed. I had no idea how I was going to land in Washington where the airspace was loaded with military and civilian traffic. I approached the capital with fear and trepidation. Just by chance, I spotted a hole in the clouds, and I put that bomber in a tight spiral, corkscrewing right into that hole. Down we went—down to where I thought I should be able to see Bolling Field—but it was really socked in. By the time I got low enough to see the runway, I was too low. So I pulled up and went around again—and again. It was getting spookier all the time, and I still couldn't see the runway.

On my second go-around I noticed that the nearby Anacostia Naval Air Station runway lined up the same way as the one I wanted at Bolling. With gear and flaps down, the third time around I lined up on Anacostia's runway, dropped the B-25 down through the clouds, and emerged right on Bolling's runway. When the plane rolled to a stop, my knees were shaking.

The brass in the back just thought I did a hell of a job, but they had no idea how scary it was in the cockpit. That same day, July 28, 1945, a B-25 hit the Empire State Building. A lot of people knew that I was up there trying to get into Fort Dix in a B-25. Everyone thought for sure that it was my plane that slammed into the New York skyscraper.

After VE day, all the brass that hadn't been overseas were being directed to the Pacific. I was slated for China when the atomic bomb was dropped, first on Hiroshima, then on Nagasaki. That ended it, of course, and I got to go home. Even though I never had been overseas, I had a lot of points because I'd been in five years. I also had two children. I was discharged October 1945 with the rank of major and joined the 121st Fighter Group of the Ohio National Guard at Lockborne Field, Columbus. A couple of years later the group was disbanded.

About the same time the Ohio Army National Guard established a third infantry battalion around Springfield, Dayton, Urbana, and Xenia, and they needed a battalion commander. Col. George Sheile from Cincinnati, whom I knew from Fort Benning, talked me into becoming the battalion commander with the rank of lieutenant colonel. As a colonel I was paid twenty dollars a month more, so I took it.

I had two companies in Springfield and one each in Urbana, Xenia, and Dayton. I'd visit one of those companies each week to get in my drill time, but I was in the infantry! I'd been in the horse cavalry, the armored force, and the air corps, and now I was walking. Dolly called me Pegasus.

We conducted maneuvers at Camp Perry, in northern Ohio. Surprise! We were called out on a 1948 labor strike in Dayton. I had guys who had never seen an M1 rifle, much less shot one, walking around with loaded weapons. That inadequate training was a specter that later was to haunt me, the Ohio Guard, and the nation at Kent, Ohio.

Little did I think I would be called to active duty ever again, but the Korean "conflict" broke out in 1950, and two years later they activated the 37th Division of the Ohio National Guard. Our family now numbered five, with the arrival of Charles Rockwell Saxbe on November 2, 1946, in Urbana, Ohio. We lived in the little Mechanicsburg house I built. I didn't necessarily have to go on active duty. As a member of the legislature I had an

My military career
spanned World War II and
the Korean War.

exemption, but I had talked a lot of good officers into joining up, and I
thought, boy, I just can't say no.

I reported to Fort Benning once again. Dolly and I decided she would
stay home with the kids that time; Bart and Juli were in grade school and
Rocky had just turned five. After about three weeks in Georgia, I called
Dolly: "Come on down. Everybody. I've found a house." Dolly rounded up
the troops, and with the aid of a friend, drove to the fort.

She was seven months pregnant at the time. One night she woke me up.
"Something terrible is going on," she said. I called the ambulance, but Dolly lost the baby. She became very depressed after that, crying a great deal.
One day Juli said, "Mommy, you've got to quit crying. It might have been a
boy." Dolly quit crying after that.

I was battalion commander of the best battalion in the division. We
were ready to go to Korea in the summer of 1952, but all at once the orders
were changed, and I never went anywhere. The war was winding down. I
left active duty with the rank of lieutenant colonel and continued to command a battalion in the Ohio National Guard. Finally, after serving for a
half-dozen more years in G2 and then in Selective Service, I retired as a full
colonel in 1968 with thirty-one years of service.

Throughout my military career, there always was something going on
elsewhere. I went to law school, ran for the legislature, campaigned for
Speaker of the House in Ohio, and started a family. But those are other
stories yet to be told.

Ohio's Public Servant

After five years of active duty, I really didn't know what I wanted to do as a civilian. I was discharged in October 1945 and returned to the Burg to sort things out. I had some war bonds and perhaps one thousand dollars in savings, so Dolly and I were not entirely destitute.

Again, I thought that I might go into the cattle business, which I knew something about. On the other hand I was very active in the church, so I gave some serious thought to entering the Episcopal ministry. My father's family was Methodist, but he didn't go to church, especially after he said the "kluckers"—the Ku Klux Klan—had taken over. My mother was a Presbyterian. In Mechanicsburg we didn't have a Presbyterian church, but we made up for it with two Methodist churches—the Methodist Protestant and the Methodist Episcopal, always referred to as the M.P. and the M.E. I went to the M.P. Sunday school. My mother always went to church, and I went with her. I can remember sitting there in the pew with her. I couldn't have been more than four or five years old, but I remember that. We always had one of those hellfire and damnation Methodist preachers who scared the daylights out of the parishioners.

When I became a teen, I told my mother I wanted to go where they didn't holler so much. I began going to the Episcopal Sunday school. A very soft-spoken, fine old gentleman had taken the parish as his final one. I was confirmed there in 1930, when I was fourteen. I was active in the church as a junior warden and as a lay reader. I couldn't perform any of the sacraments, but I would read the sermon.

Dolly is Episcopalian, although her family was Lutheran. When she attended Ohio State she started going to the Episcopal church, and she never misses.

When I got to Washington in 1968, we had all those violent demonstrations and trashing of the town. The Episcopal dean at the National Cathedral there harbored long-haired hippies and radicals. That's when I quit the church. I still go from time to time with Dolly, but she doesn't lay it on me so hard. I always tell people I didn't leave the church; the church left me.

While trying to determine my future path, I worked as a garage mechanic: What better place to do that than in Mechanicsburg? I earned thirty-five dollars a week at Slim Scoby's garage. Slim was a character. I'd be working under a car and he'd say, "Now, come out here and listen to me," and he'd tell me some wild story.

I'd come home so dirty and greasy that Dolly would cry. Dolly and I were living in the house we had originally rented. Her parents had liked it, so they bought it. We lived there rent free, but I paid for the ton of coal a week it took to heat the place.

One day in December I was under a car with mud and slush and winter all around. "There's got to be an easier way," I said to myself. I didn't know what it might be, but I went to Ohio State to talk with Dean Bland L. Stradley, a good old boy who had been an advisor and friend when I was an undergraduate. At the time he was vice president of student relations, but he'd been dean of the College of Arts and Sciences.

"What do you want to do for the rest of your life?" he asked.

"Well, I was thinking about the ministry."

"Oh, the hell with that. You're too damn old to start in that."

"I've thought about maybe something in politics."

"Then get over here and go to law school."

"Well," I said, "I'll be thirty-one years old when I get out of school." I was then twenty-eight.

"Hell, you'll be thirty-one no matter what you do."

So that same day—and I hadn't even talked it over with Dolly—I signed up for law school on the GI Bill. The law school was frantic for students. I think they only had eight or ten students at the time. I came home and said, "Dolly, I'm going to go to law school."

This was in December 1945, and law school started the following month. So I quit my job with Slim and got myself a two-door, Model A Ford. I never lived in Columbus when I went to law school. When I had a car I preferred to drive the thirty miles or so between Columbus and Mechanicsburg, but the Model A was so undependable. Dolly and I called it the Blue Goose, because it had been painted blue with house paint.

When I didn't have a car, I hitchhiked. There was a truck that loaded up in Columbus every night, and I rode home on that. But sometimes it wouldn't leave until nine o'clock at night. Another guy, who worked in the Pennsylvania Railroad freight yard, left Mechanicsburg every morning at five o'clock. He was very accommodating, dropping me off so I could catch the streetcar to law school. He gave me a ride home, too, as long as I made it to Buttles and High Streets to meet him at 5:00 P.M..

Shortly after entering law school I hooked up with another veteran, Allen Sophrin of Akron, for a business venture. We advertised ourselves as handymen and immediately got jobs. Our first was digging a ditch seventy-five feet long. We painted roofs, hung a chandelier, and built a two thousand-foot wood fence. Four or five other law students helped out as needed. Finally we had to give up on the business because our law studies became more demanding.

Law school wasn't all that hard for me. It wasn't easy, but I managed to get by. A law school classmate, Thomas W. Connor of Columbus, often has told the following story about me, as he remembers it:

> Rarely was Bill well prepared for class, it seems. Knowing this, Professor [Charles C.] Callahan would call on Bill to recite a particular case. Bill would begin slowly, speed-reading the case from the text as he went along. Invariably his recitation was a flawless presentation of the case and the issues involved. Each time it was an impressive performance and one that Callahan enjoyed as much as did his [Saxbe's] classmates.

I admit I didn't brief the cases, but I listened intently and attended regularly. I earned my law degree in March 1948. After I took the bar exam, but before the results were posted, I built my own house in Mechanicsburg. At its Newark, Ohio, depot, the National Guard had tons of crates once used for trucks and jeeps that they burned to dispose of them. The truck crates alone were twenty feet long and eight feet high. The pile of crates was bigger than a house, so I paid two hundred dollars for a truckload and began construction, using the crates for walls. I also bought some scrap plumbing, secondhand windows, and a two-lane bowling alley being torn out in Marysville, Ohio. As a result, I had a beautiful, finished floor in the house. I started it in April, working from plans carefully drawn out and staked on the front lawn. The plans were lost, though, when a truck buried them under a load of gravel. Despite the slight handicap, we moved in four months later.

I hadn't been in law school a full year when I saw an opportunity to earn two thousand dollars a year representing my home district in the state legislature. I not only needed the money, but I thought I was going to reform the world. The two-term incumbent from Champaign County, Joseph C.

Neer of Urbana, had done a respectable job, but I ran on the basis that I was a veteran who needed the job. That was the hot button then. On filing day in February, that prominent citizen of Urbana, who had served two terms, didn't file. He didn't have any stomach for a campaign. So, in my very first race for public office, I ran unopposed in the May 1946 primary and had only token Democratic opposition in Harry Shank of Urbana in the general election.

Whenever I ran for office, Abraham Gertner, a Columbus attorney who ran a cram course for the Ohio Bar exam, sent letters to all his students, urging them to give me their support. He was very helpful in that regard.

While I was an undergraduate, I had formed in Mechanicsburg what was reported to be the first "Bricker for Governor" club in Ohio. That was 1936, when John W. Bricker ran unsuccessfully for Ohio's top office. That got me involved in Republican politics at an early age, even before I was old enough to vote. Later I helped breathe new life into the War Veterans Republican Club, a state organization primarily made up of World War I veterans. After World War II they were looking for new members. Most of the club was made up of successful businessmen in their fifties. They were in politics up to their ears, and in later years they were very helpful to me.

One time they were having a veterans' convention in Chicago, and they wanted the young guys—the World War II vets—to attend, too, all expenses paid. Six of us from Columbus went in an old DeSoto, and we had a ball. We were all talkers. The old guard was trying to do away with price controls, and we just raised hell about that. We didn't want to do away with price controls because we were having enough trouble making ends meet at home.

The state GOP chairman, Fred H. Johnson of Zanesville, put me on the party's payroll at Republican headquarters; that meant I got expenses and a couple of hundred dollars a month. I became parliamentarian for the party and helped organize War Veterans Republican Clubs throughout the state. Often my law school classmate, Robert W. Minor, would travel with me as we visited communities in Ohio. Minor and I would drive four or five hours, attend a meeting, drive back to Columbus the same night, and make class the next morning.

As we neared graduation, Minor and I discussed setting up practice together in Urbana, but we decided there wasn't really much of a future in it. Vance Brand, president of the Champaign National Bank and a Republican politician practicing in Urbana, convinced us that there really wasn't room for two more lawyers in that small metropolis.

Also, I was gaining some prominence in the party because I had been active for more than a decade. At the state convention in December 1946, held at the old Memorial Hall in Columbus, I was the party's token veteran. Senator Robert Taft, serving the second of his three terms as Ohio's senator, was the keynote speaker, and I had the honor to introduce him to the convention.

In my second term, beginning in 1948, the legislature went Democratic. I was secretary of the House Judiciary Committee, chaired by an old boy named William J. Hart, a Democrat from Cleveland. Bill took me under his wing, and in his absence—he really didn't care about the post—I often ran the committee. So I was getting my teeth into things there, which gave me a little head start on the other new blood coming into the legislature. It was good experience, and I discovered I could get things done out of the Judiciary Committee.

We had some real political dandies back then. Edward J. Hummel, a former saloonkeeper from Cincinnati, always wore a goofy looking toupee. Eddie often ran for secretary of state, but nobody paid any attention to him until 1943. The nominated candidate died and left Hummel as the only other Republican on the ballot, so he was elected. He didn't know any

In my third race for the legislature the family graced my campaign literature. Bart is standing behind Juli and Rocky.

more about being secretary of state than a pig did about Sunday, but he served from 1943 to 1949. One day Eddie got sick over at the Neil House and lost his toupee in the toilet. Often, when he was tipsy, his "friends" would take the hairpiece and put it on him crossways. The part would run from ear to ear.

We had a Democratic legislator from Butler County, Oscar F. Hughes. At the time home permanents were just coming in. The beauty operators were incensed. They had been cooking people's hair on these big machines and making good money at it. This mousy fellow's wife was a beauty shop operator, and he introduced a bill to outlaw home permanents. The bill charged that the chemicals in home products would do great permanent damage to the hair.

Hughes pleaded his case to the Judiciary Committee. "Boys, you got to vote this bill out of committee. I don't care whether it passes or not, but if I don't get it out of committee, my wife will kill me." So we voted it out of committee, but the bill never got on the floor.

In the winter of 1950 I was elected speaker pro tem by the Republican caucus, having won election for the third time. The ninety-ninth General Assembly convened January 1, 1951. Speaker pro tem meant I was the House

In the fall of 1956 I campaigned in Ohio for President Dwight D. Eisenhower, which made Ohio GOP chairman Ray C. Bliss, center, happy.

majority leader. Gordon Renner was elected speaker. Democratic Gov. Frank J. Lausche was beginning his third term; he was to win election again in 1952 and 1954.

In 1952 Gen. Dwight D. Eisenhower carried Ohio handsomely on his way to the presidency. It was a big moment for the GOP after having a Democrat in the White House for twenty years. I led the legislature's delegation attending the inauguration in Washington on January 18, 1953. On the train to Washington, I was accompanied by three elephants from the Mills Brothers Circus, which wintered in Greenville, Ohio. They were in the inaugural parade; I was not.

The following year my political career took a giant leap forward.

The Laudable 100th

During the Second World War, the legislature was the neglected area of Ohio politics. There was money, but no place to spend it because of the all-out war effort. As a result, sessions were short, and special interests dominated.

One wag observed that the legislature was made up of retired farmers, teachers, preachers, and half-assed lawyers, who were paid two thousand dollars a year and four cents a mile for travel to Columbus. The heavy lobbies like the AFL-CIO, railroads, truckers, manufacturers, and bankers always managed to elect enough people to provide a formidable front. Well-organized, large-city political organizations like Cleveland, Cincinnati, and Columbus used the legislature to groom entry-level candidates for future election as judges, mayors, and county officers.

The legislature was often a playpen for members who had little interest in the job but looked forward to higher office or simply a frolic in Columbus at the expense of a lobby. Fortunately, however, there were always enough members to take the job seriously and perform the intended purpose and business of running the state. The effectiveness of the legislative body was said to be similar to the powertrain of a Model T Ford; it wandered around and finally came out the line of least resistance.

Ethical control was unknown, and financial reporting on contributions of gifts, trips, meals, etc., was scant to none. I remember one member who bragged that he had never paid for a meal during the session. Another complained when he had to pay his own hotel bill.

Every county got at least one representative, and the larger counties got additional members in both the House and Senate, based upon population. Cleveland and Cuyahoga County got the most, followed by Hamilton (Cincinnati), Franklin (Columbus), Lucas (Toledo), and so forth. Fractions were handled by giving areas additional members from time to time. Each ten-year census would add or subtract the number of members for the county.

By guaranteeing each county one member of the House and each senatorial district one senator, the rural counties had an advantage and the properly named "cornstalk brigade" sometimes dominated both Houses. A pair of Cleveland Democrats, Joseph H. Avellone and Michael J. Crosser, were so frustrated by the rural domination that they introduced a bill to permit Cleveland's Cuyahoga County to secede from Ohio and become the forty-ninth state.

The lobbyists usually handled the "cornstalk brigade" by courting the county party chairmen, who often selected the candidates and exerted control passed down by patronage jobs or contributions at the county level. The unions and the banking and savings companies were especially good at working the system.

The disparity of representation was remarkable when you compared Vinton County's fifteen thousand population to Cuyahoga's one million-plus, but it worked by the clever manipulation of the lobbyists.

All this began to change in the election of 1946 when the veterans of World War II began to take an interest in how things were being run in Columbus. That first occurred in rural counties, when vets challenged the lawyers, insurance agents, bankers, and union guys who ran big-town special interests. Many decided the book wasn't worth the candle. In my case, the incumbent serving Champaign County, an insurance agent I didn't even know, dropped out of the race after I filed and started my campaign. In both the 1946 and 1948 primary elections, I ran unopposed. The latter election was noteworthy in that President Harry S Truman upset the heavily favored Thomas E. Dewey of New York.

My first two-year term, beginning in 1947, was not a good one for me. I was a full-time law student. I ran an odd jobs business staffed by law students that did wiring, dug ditches, built fences, and did proofreading of the newly proposed Revised Code that later passed when I was Speaker. The pay was $1 an hour. It helped add to the $90 I got from the G.I. Bill and the $160 a month I received as a member of the Ohio General Assembly. I also received $70 a month as an officer in the Ohio National Guard. I drove back and forth to Mechanicsburg, and in bad weather I would sometimes sleep on a cot in the gym at the Columbus Athletic Club. That first term I never rented a hotel room in Columbus because I couldn't afford one. Sometimes I would share a bed with a member who had a five-dollar room at the Neil House or Deshler-Wallick Hotel.

I got off on the wrong foot with the House leadership. C. William "Billy" O'Neill was running for speaker, and I supported my neighbor from Marysville (Union County), Clifton L. Caryl, whose wife's family lived in Mechanicsburg. He didn't have a chance. As a result, O'Neill acted like he didn't know me for the rest of his career. (He later served as attorney general, governor and chief justice.) It reached a point in 1956, when he was running for governor and I was a candidate for attorney general, that I was invited to leave some of his public meetings. I didn't. I was not permitted in his attorney general's office nor ever invited to his office when he was governor.

It was different with James A. Rhodes, who served four terms as governor. Jim and I had been friends since college days, though never all that close. He had his following, and I had mine, but relations were never strained. He helped me, and I helped him, but we operated and campaigned differently. He was a good governor and loved the job.

In my second term (1949–1950), things began to look up. There was a Democrat governor, Frank J. Lausche, and a Democrat House and Senate. I was placed on the House Judiciary Committee. I worked hard and began to get a feel of how to get things done in the legislature. For the first time, I began to think about leadership.

In 1950, the election returned the legislature to the Republicans and the vets from the 1946 elections began to feel their strength. Former GOP state party chairman Ed D. Schorr, from Cincinnati, had been the strongest of the lobbyists in organizing the legislature, and he set out to do it again in 1951. A damn clever politician, he succeeded in getting a relative by marriage, Gordon Renner, elected as Speaker. Renner, an attorney from Cincinnati and a Yale graduate, was a nice little guy who drank too much, exerted little control, but followed orders. We'd set a time for one o'clock to go into session and maybe he wouldn't show up until 2:30 or 3:00. He would be at the University Club, drinking his lunch.

Ray C. Bliss was the state Republican chairman at that time, having succeeded Fred H. Johnson of Zanesville, an ineffectual party leader. Bliss was determined to break Schorr's hold on the legislature. With his help, I made a successful run for majority leader. That made for a strange combination in the leadership. I was ambitious and hardworking with no boss. Renner was a detail man, but careless when it came to organizing and running the House. He worked for the bills that Schorr wanted, but was indifferent to the rest of the business. That indifference gave me the opportunity to organize a solid block of support. Renner had lost the confidence of members.

In the 1950 election, I had my first primary opposition in Champaign

County. It had been a practice there to limit legislators to two terms, and I had served my two. Dalton D. Dowds, a popular county agent (placed in each rural county by the federal government) had left that job and gone into the real estate business. He campaigned on the basis that two terms were enough. I campaigned on the basis that seniority was essential and that one or two terms was just a warm-up to have clout.

My law practice was going well, so I bought a new Jeepster and went to work in the Republican primary. Dolly and I campaigned throughout the county almost on a house-to-house basis. We went to dances, barbecues, school functions, weddings, funerals, and lodges. I sang in a quartet that included three African-American songsters, visited bars, churches, the grange, and the Farm Bureau. It paid off: I won by a two-to-one margin and then easily defeated Democrat Harry S. Shank by forty-one hundred votes in the general election. I also won a new suit that Dowds, my confident opponent, had bet me a week before election day.

Late in 1951, after the legislature had adjourned, I learned that the 37th Division of the Ohio National Guard was to be federalized January 15, 1952, and I would be called to active duty in the Korean War. At the time, I commanded a battalion of infantry with companies in Dayton, Xenia, Springfield, and Urbana. Dolly and I and the three kids packed up and left for Fort Benning, Georgia, where I was enrolled in the battalion commanders' course at the Infantry School. When I completed the course, we moved to Camp Polk, Louisiana, where I assumed my duties as commander of the 3rd Battalion, 148th Infantry.

We were there six months when the army decided they didn't need another division in Korea and began to release those who wanted out. During my army time, I wrote personal letters to all the House Republicans and kept in touch in other ways. I even managed to attend (in uniform) a one-day special session.

I was released September 24, 1952, just in time for the 1952 election, which went strongly Republican. With Bliss's help, I organized an all-out campaign for Speaker, the most powerful post in the House. There were many new faces in the House, and I visited every one of them. Incumbent Renner relied on the remnants of the Schorr group, and to my knowledge he never campaigned beyond Cincinnati.

I was greeted warmly in counties like Lucas, Stark, Butler, Summit, Cuyahoga, and Franklin. This was as a result of the Eisenhower landslide that buried the Taft-Schorr domination in Ohio. Those counties declared their freedom from the old political organizations, which big business had controlled with money.

Becoming Speaker wasn't all that easy, and I had little money to work with. I drove myself all over the state except when Dolly could park the kids for a few days and go with me. I had no money for entertainment or travel expenses and relied on friends to put me up on many occasions. I had to keep moving: The dean of the GOP majority in the House, George H. Kirkpatrick, R-Knox, wrote to tell me that Renner was "moving heaven and earth to defeat you."

Bliss did not discourage other veteran House members from seeking the speakership, but he felt the job had to be earned. He played his cards close to his belly. He didn't want the Schorr crowd to run the 100th House session, but he had to live with the strong Cincinnati organization, the old Taft machine with its friends and moneymen all over the state.

On the night before the House caucus, on December 8, we had a reception suite in the Neil House, a downtown hotel across from the statehouse, with drinks and food. My supporters financed it, and their wives made sandwiches. The party was wet and long and ended about 2:00 A.M. I had expected to spend the night in the suite, but a passed-out new member from Cleveland occupied the bed. I finally shared a bed with Lowell "Red" Fess, R-Yellow Springs, whose father, Simeon D. Fess, was U.S. senator from Ohio 1923–1935. Red weepily told me he couldn't vote for me the next morning because the coal lobby had been paying his hotel bill for years and they wanted Renner for speaker.

Red was a character. He'd go to the Neil House and play the piano, and the management would try to throw him out. He'd be playing, "Fight the Team," and there would come the manager who would chase Red around the ballroom.

I would like to have had his vote, because winning the Speaker's job was difficult. There were four nominees, and it took several ballots for me to finally get the required majority. The final vote was a resounding sixty-eight to thirty-three over Renner. It was the first time a Speaker who sought reelection had been defeated. Bliss said my victory gave "youth a chance" in party affairs.

In a caucus immediately following the vote, I promised cooperation with opponents and supporters alike and with the Senate. I also aimed at a shorter legislative session and at ridding the floor of the House of lobbyists. I said, "I don't feel that lobbyists and persons representing trade organizations should be on the House floor when it is in session. As a public relations matter, I think that gives the people a bad impression. Many lobbyists have valuable information for us, but we should never mistake the voice of the lobbyists for the voice of public opinion."[1]

Immediately after my remarks I called Dolly in Mechanicsburg. "Dolly, I made it," I said. She seemed suitably impressed.

I had made a deal with William Schneider, the powerful GOP chairman for Franklin County. His county could have the majority leader job, but whoever it was had to earn it. Schneider was strong with the other county chairmen, and he picked Kline L. Roberts of Columbus from his stable of young, ambitious members to be the man. Kline and I had no problems during the session.

I didn't smoke cigars often, but my successful 1953 bid for Speaker seemed to call for one.

{ I'VE SEEN THE ELEPHANT }

The Speaker had almost unlimited power to organize and run the House. Gov. Frank Lausche had little interest in or power with the legislature. The few times he tried to promote or defeat a measure, the Republican majority in both houses easily overrode his veto.

As Speaker, I chose all the committee chairmen and the members of each committee. I chose chairmen who were close to me and discussed with them the makeup of their committees so as to accomplish the things we had in mind. I offered Renner the chairmanship of the powerful House Reference Committee, a post he had held before becoming Speaker, but he declined.

C. Stanley Mecham, a shoe store merchant from Nelsonville, in Athens County, was elected president pro tem of the Senate. We worked together closely, and before the session opened, we put together a program for the state. Many areas of state responsibility had been neglected during the war, and a huge surplus of several hundred million dollars had built up. What they were saving it for was beyond me. Governors Lausche, Thomas J. Herbert, O'Neill, and Michael V. DiSalle evidently believed that frugality would make them popular.

The state was rich, but in trouble. The prisons, schools, public employees, and local governments all needed a lot of money to bring them up to standard. For example, many teachers with seniority were receiving less than one hundred dollars a month and full-time judges, eight thousand dollars a year. Most state employees who traveled used their own cars and received four cents a mile, which didn't allow them to break even.

The worst situation was the highways. They were old and hadn't been maintained for years. President Eisenhower's plans for a national system of super highways required matching funds that Ohio didn't have. Lausche was determined to sit on what he called his surplus, and he did. But the surplus was a drop in the bucket to meet the need for prisons, schools, highways, and services. His parsimony did nothing to solve the big-time problems facing the state.

Lausche was so mercurial that you couldn't depend on him for anything. One day I was playing golf with him; Alvin "Bud" Silverman, the Statehouse reporter for the *Cleveland Plain Dealer*; and William C. Rhodes, executive director of the state highway department. Silverman was telling a story about the trotting-horse people. The thoroughbred races ran rain or shine, but if the weather was bad the trotters couldn't race and the track lost a day of business. Lausche said that was very unfair and something ought to be done about it.

With his approval I volunteered to get a bill through and give the trotting-track people relief, allowing the tracks to make up lost days and thus giving them parity with the thoroughbred tracks. We got a bill through the Reference Committee and the House within a week, which was unheard of, and sent it to the Senate. It passed, but when it got to Lausche, he vetoed it. That was so typically Lausche. He wanted to be all things to all people. Everybody thought he was a great governor because he didn't do anything.

Mecham and I, with help from committee chairmen, decided to tackle each problem Ohio faced and to adopt a realistic, yet ambitious, agenda and schedule. We publicly announced what the program was, and went to work. The first problem we confronted was the new legal code to streamline the laws of the state and rid the code of archaic language. It had been under revision for more than a half-dozen years. The old code had been adopted in 1912 and tinkered with from time to time, but it still remained a horse and buggy era set of laws that ill fitted a fast-moving modern age. It had been ready for adoption for the last two legislative sessions, but heavy opposition by the big law firms had killed it; they felt it would make obsolete their vast libraries of boilerplate on bond issues and courtroom pleadings. Mecham and I and the judiciary chairman, Kenneth A. Robinson, R-Marion, decided that the best way to handle the problem was to prohibit consideration of any other bills until the issue was passed or rejected. We finished the bill and were determined to get it through. The month of January was set aside, and the House and Senate Judiciary Committees went to work five days a week. The big firms brought in all their heavy hitters and wore themselves out with their outlandish arguments of the disaster to befall Ohio if it was adopted. The committees outlasted them and passed the legislation out with insignificant changes. We immediately put it on the floor. By mid-February the Ohio Revised Code had passed both Houses with big majorities and was then signed by a reluctant governor. No disasters resulted. Our first big challenge was out of the way.

Other bills were then introduced. The four weeks spent on the code gave the leadership and chairmen time to perfect their bills, get them referred to their committees, and in shape for hearings. That was in sharp contrast to previous sessions where committees went to work on the cat-and-dog favorites of committee members and bills prepared by lobbyists and introduced by members for previous support, contributions, or other debts.

One thing we did do, much to the surprise of doubters, was to achieve my earliest pledge. We barred lobbyists and visitors from the floor of the House during sessions. It's hard to believe now that prior to the 100th General Assembly, behind the seats but on the floor, the lobbyists gathered like flies on a dead horse. Some desperate ones even walked down the aisles and confronted members who hadn't voted as they promised. Confined now to the gallery with the general public, they suffered in silence—almost. Some mounted personal attacks on me, describing me as "dangerous," but it never came to much.

An *Ohio State Journal* editorial took note of my successful efforts: "Speaker William Saxbe is about as rural as they come without being an actual dirt farmer. He practices law in alfalfa famous Mechanicsburg. The lobbyists considered him easy picking when he first came to the legislature, but he fooled them."[2]

One incident relating to lobbyists really bothered me while I served as Speaker. It concerned heatedly debated legislation called the axle-mile tax, and it involved a good friend from college. I've never mentioned this before, but I should have.

The axle-mile tax was an effort to provide funds for a bond issue to build highways. Basically, it taxed commercial trucks based on the number of axles and the number of miles traveled in Ohio. Roger Cloud (R-Logan), chairman of the House Public Affairs Committee, and I came up with the idea of taxation that would raise an estimated $43 million annually from truckers and from a penny-per-gallon increase in fuel taxes. The axle-mile tax became a huge political football that was kicked around until the legislation was passed in the closing hours of the 100th General Assembly.

Sometime before the vote in the House, that friend of mine approached me on the Broad Street side of the statehouse. At a time when I was receiving twenty-five hundred dollars a year as Speaker, he said it would be worth fifty thousand dollars if I would forget about that axle-mile tax. I had never heard of that kind of money. That's the only time anybody ever offered me a bribe. I'm sure he could have denied it, and I probably couldn't have proved that the conversation took place. Nevertheless, I'll always remember that incident.

During the 100th General Assembly, we set definite times for opening the House sessions, and, unlike in Renner's day, we kept to that hour. Each session opened within thirty seconds of the agreed upon time. I suppose it was my recent military service that prompted that, but it sure put an end to the long martini lunches and brought some business discipline to the sessions. We were there to do serious government business, and in time we enjoyed knowing that everyone would show up on time.

There also had been a practice of setting a final adjournment date and then using the childish subterfuge of literally covering the clock with paper and pretending it was the same day. Sometimes that farce would last for several days while business was done in a frantic exchange of bills between the House and Senate. Most of those bills never had a chance in reg-ular sessions but were saved until the end, to skip by exhausted members who didn't dare leave the statehouse because a bill they favored or opposed might be brought up. Those thirty-six-hour (or more) marathons seemed to make even stolid members a little simple and the drinkers and jokers wild.

Food, booze, popcorn, and firecrackers added to the confusion. Always there was at least one inebriate who staggered in, throwing rolls of toilet paper and screaming "Message from the Senate."

Well, the 100th General Assembly proceeded on schedule. The major bills were introduced, referred to committee, debated, sent to the floor, and passed. Party and district factions battled over school and highway funding issues as well as the state budget, right up to the eleventh hour. We did all that in one hundred days, and when the gavel dropped at 10:31 P.M. July 14, 1953, our promises were kept. The adjournment sine die[3] created a riot in the Senate and senators came roaring over to the House saying "You can't do this! We have important business to conduct!" My answer was, "It's already done."

Mecham, of course, was not happy, either. As leader of the Senate, he always had determined when it was time to go home. On the night I ad-journed the House, he was over in the Senate, thrashing around some bill. When he got wind of what I was doing, he told an aide, "You tell the Speak-er that we're going to do this and that."

"You're going to have to tell him yourself, because they've adjourned," he was told. "They have gone."

"What?"

"You guys goofed around long enough. They have gone to plant corn."

That was the end of it. The Senate changed its attitude after that. It was somewhat friendlier to the House and certainly more attentive.

There was some business yet to be done, and that was accomplished by having a special one-day session two weeks later to settle those matters in an orderly manner.

In one of its rare effusive moments, the Fourth Estate was virtually unan-imous in its praise of the legislature and its leadership. "An unqualified 'A' for effort," said the *Akron Beacon Journal* editorial.[4] In Toledo *The Blade* noted that the General Assembly was "singularly free from obvious instances of successful pressure from lobbyists. . . . They were active, as always— getting in their licks wherever they could. But when there was a threat of wholesale surrender at one state, the GOP leadership—especially House Speaker William Saxbe—had the courage to stand up and demand that legislators make good on party promises to the electorate."[5]

The *Cleveland Plain Dealer* editorial began:

Take a good look at it, citizens of Ohio, for it has been a long time since this state has seen a more impressive record of legislative accomplishment than the one compiled by the 100th General Assembly.

Omissions and imperfections are so vastly outweighed by constructive enactments . . . that the record of the Legislature that has just closed its working session in orderly fashion is not likely to be surpassed for a long time to come. . . . We say the 100th General Assembly is one for the people gratefully to remember.[6]

I would be remiss if I didn't mention some of the unusual and sometimes sad, but also sometimes amusing, behavior of members on and off the floor. Remember that the job of representative only paid two thousand dollars a year.

Each desk had a wastebasket and a spittoon. When feelings ran high, members would kick the basket or spittoon under the desk and bang the wooden, hinged desktop, creating a horrendous racket. On my thirty-seventh birthday, in 1953, House members presented me with a new spittoon. It worked, too.

One unruly member would not stop talking on the floor. The Speaker, after a prolonged effort to quiet him, directed the sergeant at arms to eject him from the floor. That was accomplished with some difficulty, but the member soon appeared in the public gallery and continued his harangue until he was ejected from the statehouse. We had another member who was a solid, honorable, and sober citizen in his rural county. However, when he came to Columbus he would get drunk and stay drunk the entire session, propped up on the floor from time to time when his vote was needed. When he went home he never took a drink.

Drinking was a problem in Columbus with all the free booze from the various lobbies. Several lobbies that had open suites in the nearby hotels offered free food and drink. The downtown restaurants and nightspots did a land-office business during the sessions. There were occasions when some members wound up in the gutter or some low dive where they fell into the hands of the law. The police lobby (the Fraternal Order of Police) quietly handled those affairs.

Name voting was common in large counties, especially in Cuyahoga County (Cleveland), where voters would have to select from as many as twenty names on what was known as a bed-sheet ballot. Many candidates adopted popular political names, well known to voters, such as Marshall, Day, O'Brien, Calabrese, etc. Likewise, complete unknowns were sometimes sent off to Columbus. One, I recall, spent the entire session in Columbus but showed up in the House only on payday.

An elderly Irishman born on St. Patrick's Day, Patrick J. Dunn, declared on one occasion that he voted "'No' 95 percent of the time and was right 95 percent of the time." In nineteen years of service in the House, the Democrat from rural Tuscarawas County never missed a roll call. He would come to Columbus on the bus even when there was no session and sit in the chamber and chat with the tourists who visited the statehouse. The door-keeper once reported that Dunn was in his seat with his shoes and socks off, pruning his toenails, when a large group of Democratic women visited the room. He continued with the job and kept up a lively conversation with the ladies.

Some members did not let the sessions interfere with their private affairs. One accountant announced he would attend no sessions before income tax filing day, March 15 at the time, and he didn't. A. G. Herman, a crusty farmer from Auglaize County, said he would be gone after haying season began, and he was. We had our share of womanizers, and there again the lobbyists could accommodate. One day a member was walking from the Deshler-Wallick Hotel to the statehouse and spied a likely prospect seated on a bench in the Capitol yard. He tossed her a room key, told her to go up and take a bath, and he'd be right over. She was a police decoy and even the police lobby couldn't keep that incident out of the papers.

Benjamin F. Turner was a railroad brakeman from Meigs County. He thoroughly enjoyed the legislature. He would sing and dance and perform with or without an invitation. On several occasions he did a clog dance in the well of the House, in front of the Speaker's rostrum. He never missed a vote when it involved the railroads.

Some members had favorite bills that they introduced every session. They were usually tax bills that had little chance of passing. There was always one that called for a one-cent tax on each soft drink bottle. It had no chance, but always caught the attention of the pop lobbyists, who paid the author to withdraw the bill. That scheme made everybody happy: the author, the lobbyists, and the companies.

Before one man-one vote, House membership varied between 125 to 135, as counties gained or lost population or the fractioned counties picked

Being Ohio House Speaker for the 100th General Assembly (1953–1954) was the highlight of my political career.

up additional members. Of that group, there were perhaps twenty eccentrics like the ones I've set out above. The rest came to Columbus to do the best they could; they showed remarkable dedication and efficiency as they seriously performed their duties. They made the system work. Many of the young gained by the experience and went on to higher office or to be successful lawyers, businessmen, and teachers.

The women members, without exception, gained the respect of all the members and their constituents back home. They were returned year after year, among them Clara E. Weisenborn, R-Dayton; Anna F. O'Neil, D-Akron; and Golda M. "Goldie" Edmonston, R-Columbus.

Looking back on those days, I think being Speaker was the highlight of my political career. I was able to do things in the legislature that needed to be done, and that was immensely satisfying.

Losing a Good Fight

If the Speaker's post was a high-water mark for me personally, the 1954 primary race for the U.S. Senate was a watershed politically—even in defeat.

In December 1953 the party's political lineup in Ohio was cloudy, to say the least. Sen. Robert A. Taft, known as "Mr. Republican" throughout the land, had died on July 31, giving Gov. Frank J. Lausche the opportunity to appoint a Democrat to Taft's Senate seat. His choice in October 1953 was former Cleveland mayor, Thomas A. Burke.

The GOP delayed making known its choice of Burke's opponent in a special May primary election to determine who would fill the two years remaining in Taft's unexpired term. Also, State Auditor Jim Rhodes and State Attorney General C. William O'Neill, both Republicans, were making noises like they wanted to run for governor against the incumbent Lausche. I was on the fence, waiting to see which way those guys jumped.

O'Neill, who also eyed the U.S. Senate, eventually decided he would seek to keep the job he had, but Rhodes dillydallied, waiting for some hoked-up grassroots movement to hand him the nomination. I made it known that I looked unfavorably on his "reluctant bridegroom" posturing. "I don't think we should let any grass grow under our feet in getting started" on the campaign, I told reporters.[1] The filing deadline was February 3.

What few knew at the time was that just a few weeks earlier State GOP Chairman Bliss approached me about running for governor in 1954. He wanted me to immediately begin a gubernatorial campaign around the state with the idea of exposing me to the voters and building up my name recognition. I told him I wasn't interested. Furthermore, Dolly and I were leaving on vacation in Europe the day after the 1953 fall elections. "God, you've *got* to stay here and go to work on being a candidate for governor," he told me. "You're pissing it away!" Dolly and I took off anyway, leaving the chairman mad as hell.

When we got back, things were still up in the air for the GOP. I was attending a U.S. Chamber of Commerce conference on highway financing in Washington when the newspapers picked up the story again. "Saxbe Ready to Enter Race for Governor," said *The Columbus Citizen*. In a page one, screaming headline, the *Urbana Daily Citizen* said, "Saxbe May Be Governor Candidate." I told the press, "I had not had any plans at all to run for governor until I heard O'Neill may not run."[2]

George H. Bender, who represented the twenty-third district (Cleveland) in Congress and was party chairman of Cuyahoga County, announced on December 14 that he would seek Taft's Senate seat, and Rhodes, who disliked Bender, tossed his hat in the gubernatorial race. I decided to sit that one out.

About five minutes later my conscience got the better of me. I was so disappointed that the party had endorsed Bender. He was a political hack who had served six terms as congressman-at-large and, as a result, was quite well known around the state. Bliss wasn't too sympathetic to Bender, either; he really didn't like him. Bliss told me as much when I first told him of my unhappiness with the endorsement. But Bender was the darling of big money in Cleveland because he did exactly what big money told him to do. Also, one of his biggest supporters was George Humphrey of Cleveland, who at the time was treasury secretary in President Dwight D. Eisenhower's cabinet. Humphrey was very important to the GOP and to Bliss as party chairman.

I continued to fume over Bender's candidacy. Calling around I discovered there were a lot of Republicans who felt as I did. I talked to Bliss again about it, but for him the die was cast. The party had made its choice. During this period, John J. "Jack" Chester came into my office in the statehouse. "That guy's no good," I told him. "We don't need *him* in the Senate. I'm thinking about running against him," which is what I told Bliss, too.

"I'd like to participate, to help out," Jack said, and I enthusiastically embraced his support. He was just the kind of guy I needed on my side.

Jack was running in 1954 for his second term in the House. He also had a bold, rebellious streak in him. In his first race for the Ohio House two years earlier, he had successfully bucked Franklin County's powerful GOP chairman, William Schneider, and his political machine. No other member of the Franklin County delegation would have dared do that.

Together we quietly plumbed the waters around the legislature and elsewhere. Wherever we turned, it seemed, I was urged to run. Even Dolly got on my case. On January 13, 1954, a week after Bender received the party's nod of approval, Dolly and I were sitting at the breakfast table with the kids, and I again began my diatribe against Bender. "This is ridiculous. This guy is a clown and an insult to the Republican party." Dolly said, "If you feel that way about it, why don't you run?" I heard myself say, finally, "Okay, I will." Dolly later told a reporter that if I hadn't decided to run "he would have lost me to the Democrats."[3]

When I got to my statehouse office, Bob Boyd came in and sat on the couch, sensing something was up. He was a young attorney who recently had been appointed House parliamentarian. He became invaluable to me in many ways. Boyd himself said his job with me "was to keep one corner of that couch from moving and observe and listen to everything that went on in that office." That's what he was doing that morning when I picked up the telephone and called Bliss yet again. "Ray, I'm going to run," I said with finality. There was a long silence, then Bliss pleaded: "Don't do that." He mentioned the importance of party harmony and what bucking the party would mean to my political future. He desperately wanted me to give it up. "I can't do that," I said.

Jack walked in. I told him I had made my decision to run. He said, "Where did you get the money?"

"I don't have any money. I'm just going to run—in protest." At the time, I had $761 in voluntary contributions.

That afternoon I dropped my "bomb" on the Republican caucus in the House, shaking up the state organization. I explained that I had hoped someone else, like O'Neill, would have come forward to give the voters a choice. No one had, so I felt if I had the courage of my convictions, I had an obligation to enter the race. Most of the members were surprised but supportive. They applauded my decision.

My next stop was the press conference I had called at the statehouse. The room was jammed with reporters, the word of my intentions already having leaked out. My candidacy came about, I explained, because Bender represented "the old-style, ward-heeler type of politician" that the Ohio GOP had tried to get away from. "I also feel that many people remember Bender as a psalm-singing, bell-ringing voice of doom in the national convention of 1952, an exhibition that gave us little confidence in Republican leadership."

My reference was to the GOP convention in Chicago when Eisenhower beat Taft for the nomination. Bender had been one of the floor leaders of the Ohio delegation. He rang a cow bell at the convention and then he sang. He made an ass of himself and led the Taft faction to defeat.[4]

The reporters immediately called Bliss for his reaction. He issued a statement: "In view of the endorsement of the Republican state committee and the interest of party harmony in Ohio, I strongly urged him not become a candidate. I also told him that the Republican state committee would wage a vigorous and aggressive campaign to nominate its endorsees, and that included George Bender for United States senator."[5]

Many party stalwarts privately congratulated me but publicly described my candidacy as "political suicide." One unidentified Republican leader said, "Saxbe is a big shot now, but he soon will feel like the lonesomest man alive."[6] I knew, of course, that the odds would be against my winning, but at least my conscience would be clear.

I chose Martin A. Coyle, a friend and Republican chairman from Butler County, as my campaign state chairman. We set up campaign headquarters in space Chester provided at 8 East Broad Street. We knew we had an uphill battle ahead.

"Except for the enthusiasm and the youth and the inexperience of 90 percent of the people who were involved in it, it would not have been much fun," said Boyd. "I didn't have anything to lose. I was closer to the top than I'd ever been before, so what the hell; I didn't care. Anyway, we were young and eternally optimistic."

We put together a campaign staff, made up mostly of young folks in Columbus, but some from Cleveland, Cincinnati, and other parts of the state. I had Boyd, Huntington Carlile, Henry Pierce, and so many others, but Chester was the heart of it. They were all very energetic.

Shortly after my hat went in the ring, I met with the crowd that was financing Bliss's whole state operation. Among them were Charles White, president of Republic Steel and a member of the Republican national finance committee; R. L. Ireland and Arthur J. Genthols of the Pittsburgh Consolidation Company; and Ed D. Schorr, former GOP state chairman. At first they promised me the world if I would step down.

"If you step aside and let George have this, your future is assured. If you want to be governor, you want to be president, you want to be anything at all, we'll help you."

"No. I am in this race to stay," I told them.

Then they began with the threats. "You're not going to be able to run for dogcatcher!" They made it clear that that could be the end of my political career, that people in politics have long memories. "This might well be the end of any ambitions you have in this state," they warned.

I came away grimly more determined to pursue my course. They had said the wrong thing to the wrong guy. They made their position clear: No longer was I a Republican in good standing in their eyes. I looked at them as disappointed friends rather than dedicated enemies.

As my campaign progressed, I did gather substantial support from the business community. Among those who made contributions were Fred E. Jones, Columbus, a good friend and president of Ohio State Life Insurance, as well as other companies; Preston Levis, Toledo, president of Owens-Illinois; L. A. McQueen, Akron, vice president of General Tire and Rubber Company; and Wayne Brown, Columbus, president of the Big Bear supermarket chain; and so forth.

Around the state I also gained considerable overt and covert support because a lot of county chairmen didn't like Bender, either. In some places the county chairman would say, "I'd love to help you, but I can't openly," so he would refer me to someone else who could serve the campaign. Then they would add the caveat, "But you can't tell anybody that I sent you there." It was a touchy situation for many in the party, but chairmen in Logan, Clark, Champaign, Union, Greene, Clinton, Madison, and Warren Counties all publicly endorsed my candidacy.

On the whole, Ohio's daily newspapers were very supportive. I received endorsements from the *Toledo Blade,* the *Cleveland Press,* the *Dayton Journal-Herald,* and numerous others. They gave me some excellent exposure. I recall that Bender had little newspaper support because everybody thought he was a jerk.

Bender tried to ride the coattails of the deceased Senator Taft, but the Taft organization would have nothing to do with him. Robert A. Taft Jr., in fact, said he would vote for me. Bender relentlessly attacked me, as one would expect in a campaign, but to me it felt like being beaten over the head with a big bag of wind.

I enjoyed a lot of family support during the campaign, some of which I only learned about in detail later. My son, Bart, for instance, formed the "Junior Saxbe for Senator Club" among a dozen or so of his high school buddies in Mechanicsburg. The reason the club had an equal number of boys and girls became clear later: the club was a front for kissing games—spin the bottle, post office, and so forth. After forty-five seconds of business on behalf of my candidacy, the club got down to the real purpose of the meeting.

Being the oldest of the children—Dolly often said Bart was "a man from the day he was born"—Bart became more involved than the others in my early political career. Many times he would accompany me to the legislature and wander through the statehouse on his own. I recall a floor debate in the House to raise the price of dog license fees, and for some reason, when they called the roll, I was out of the chamber.

Bart, all of eleven, was sitting in my House seat, soaking up the proceedings. When it came time my turn to answer the roll call vote, he voted against the measure. "I've got a dog," Bart explained afterwards. "I thought that was a terrible idea to increase the cost of dog tags." Of course, everyone in the House thought that was pretty funny, but what they didn't know was that Bart also was prepared to vote "no" for Robert R. Shaw, R-Columbus, who was absent from his desk next to mine. Bart didn't get the chance to register the second vote because there was so much laughter. His vote was ruled out of order, and I reversed my son with a "yes" vote.

When he got older, Bart occasionally would hit the campaign trail for me, too. He thought campaigning was a lot of fun. As a handsome twenty year old, he spent a whole summer on the stump in 1962 when I was running for attorney general. In my absence he'd make short speeches—less than two minutes—and the voters loved it.

"My greatest triumph" on the campaign trail, Bart recalled, "was at a picnic in Lancaster where I got up after the meal and asked if the lady who baked the fresh peach pie had any eligible daughters. They loved that."

Although Bliss was bound by the Republican party, tacitly he was helping me, at least up to the time I pissed him off again. The campaign was going well up until then. In an offhand remark at a press conference in Washington on April 14, three days before Easter Sunday, I referred to Bliss as the "Judas goat leading the Republicans to the slaughter pens in November."[7] In the Bible and in the cattle industry—both of which were familiar to me—a Judas goat is an animal that leads others to slaughter. Also, of course, Judas betrayed Christ for thirty pieces of silver. By endorsing Bender, I felt Bliss was leading the Republicans to defeat in the election.

When told of my comments, "Bliss just sat back and laughed,"[8] but others weren't laughing. Although I immediately tried to explain what I had meant, the damage was done. Roy E. Browne, Summit County (Akron) party chairman, was the first to break away. "Saxbe's unwarranted and intemperate statements against Mr. Bliss clearly demonstrate that Saxbe lacks the stability and sound judgment so necessary in the U.S. Senate during these crucial times," he said in a statement.[9]

Said Chester: "The campaign was over. And we could feel it. The whole campaign died overnight, like somebody let the air out of the tires. You could feel it every place you went. It was something that you sensed. The campaign that was vigorous and thriving and moving shut down."

The word was out that Bliss really went to work then for Bender to beat me, and spent considerable money doing it. We lost virtually all the support

When Dolly and I voted in the GOP primary May 4, 1954, we were all smiles. Later that evening I learned that I had lost my first race for the United States Senate. Reprinted with permission of the *Columbus Dispatch*.

we had worked so hard to gain. It just stopped, right then and there. Volunteers, many who were Bliss people, quit dead in their tracks. They just didn't like what they perceived to be an attack on him.

On election night, when the votes were coming in, we were in Mechanicsburg with Meg and Dick McDermott, our friends who campaigned for me in Akron. I ran strong but behind all night. I carried twenty-two of eighty-eight counties, including Bliss's home Summit County. I didn't win, but I ran well with 44 percent of the vote. The vote total was 254,013 to 188,649. Where they knew me best, I swamped Bender, who won only 337 votes in Champaign County where I received 2,650 votes.

"All evening long everybody kept saying, 'Just wait until the farm vote comes in,'" Dolly recalled. "It came in, and Bill had lost."

It was the first election seven-year-old Rocky remembered. "I listened to the returns on the radio and went to bed knowing that dad had lost. I didn't understand how my dad could lose an election. Who could not like him?"

Tackling Ohio Law

Losing to Bender was no fun, but looking back on it, I'd never have been elected Ohio's attorney general if I hadn't run for the Senate. Up until then, I had no statewide political base, but during the Senate race I put together committees and made contacts all over the state. That was invaluable. On the other hand, I became known as the black sheep of the party for having bucked it.

I returned to Mechanicsburg to practice law. Dolly and I paid five thousand dollars for eleven and one-half acres on the edge of town and a disaster of a house, parts of which dated back to 1820. It had four bedrooms, water came from a hand-pumped well, and there was an outhouse. The house was in deplorable condition. Once restored, the farm became known as Jubarock, an acronym derived from the names of our children. Dolly and I live there today.

I was in the middle of restoring that home when Bob Boyd and Malcolm M. "Mack" Prine came visiting. They suggested we form a law partnership, so we established Saxbe, Boyd, and Prine. Our main office was on the third floor of the Guaranty, Title, and Trust Company on East Gay Street in downtown Columbus, but I also maintained an office in Mechanicsburg. We lawyered together for two years. It was not the most successful or busiest law firm in town, but I was getting by. Prine, who had been cochair, with Charles Chastang, of my Franklin County campaign, wound up being president of Ryan Homes and president of the Pittsburgh Pirates, but at that time we were all struggling lawyers.

In the spring of 1955, Chester, Carlile, and Boyd took me to lunch. "You've got to run for attorney general in 1956," they said. But that was the furthest thing from my mind. I was making a little money. My first substantial fee was five thousand dollars, which I spent on a Cadillac and a mink jacket for Dolly. I even joined the Columbus Club. I sure didn't want to piss away that money on necessities.

Anyway, the more the three friends talked, the more I thought, what the hell. I agreed to run. (Carlile was to become my first assistant and Boyd a special counsel. He also held a number of other important jobs through the years, including first assistant.)

Initially my biggest obstacle was in Columbus, in the person of Chalmers Wylie. He wanted to run for attorney general, too. So, on behalf of the GOP, John W. Bricker, now back in private practice after two terms in the U.S. Senate, got into the act, suggesting the flip of a coin to see who was going to be the GOP candidate. "No, I'm not interested," I told him. "I can beat Chalmers, and I will."

Wylie's prime support came from the insurance and banking interests and the C. William O'Neill camp, which always was antagonistic towards me. O'Neill was running for governor in 1956. In any event, Wylie's coffers totaled some fifty thousand dollars for his campaign, while I ran with less than ten thousand dollars.

Another tough opponent in the primary was Harry T. Marshall. He was a Jewish lawyer from Cleveland who had changed his name because Marshall was a great name in Cleveland. The whole Cleveland organization was for Marshall. He had a bunch of hangers-on working for him who were comical. They would show up at county rallies, looking like fugitives. That was the old Bender gang. J. Eugene Roberts, the fourth candidate, was from Youngstown. He ran for attorney general every two years, hitting the campaign trail by public bus.

On primary election night, Chester, Boyd, and Lewis H. Hausman, who was to become supervisor of public information and of claims investigations in the attorney general's office, stayed up all night, sitting in Secretary of State Ted W. Brown's office at the statehouse. The Cleveland people got tired of counting votes, so they got up and walked out, leaving ballots uncounted and unguarded. You could have walked in, grabbed all the Cuyahoga County votes and burned them. Eventually Brown got the city police to put a guard on the door until they could round up the counters and get them back to counting.

I narrowly defeated Marshall by less than 3,000 votes out of 513,000 cast. Wylie ran a distant third. I thought he was going to be a red-eyed candidate, but he never really campaigned statewide.

During the primary campaign, and subsequently, Louis B. Seltzer, publisher of the Cleveland Press, made it clear he really didn't like me for some reason, so I took a hell of a beating in that paper. Strangely enough, the paper endorsed my candidacy in 1954 when I ran against Bender. After that, though, Seltzer just pounded me mercilessly and shamelessly.

In the 1956 primary, the *Press* supported Wylie. Seltzer thought Wylie *looked* like Abe Lincoln and *was* Abe Lincoln. But in the middle of the primary campaign, the *Press* went on strike and Seltzer lost his voice; the paper didn't come back until December. At my press conference after my victory, I was asked, "What are you going to do now, after winning such a close election?" I said I was heading for Cleveland right away so I could get back on the picket line at the *Press*. Seltzer hated that.

Another of the comical things that came out of that 1956 primary campaign occurred at a big picnic at the fairgrounds in Lucasville. Through the War Veterans Republican Club I had a lot of old drinking buddies throughout the state, and they were pretty rough and tough. The county GOP put on a picnic and political stump. Wylie had a supporter named Lee Fitch, a prominent young lawyer in southern Scioto County. Fitch was telling that crowd of locals what a no-good I was. A local committeeman named Apple, who lived at the head of the "holler," had been drinking pretty heavily. He listened to Fitch and kept creeping up on him. Next thing he let loose and hit him on the jaw. He just didn't like what Fitch had been saying about me. There's a saying in southern Ohio that they wouldn't know they had had an election unless there was blood and hair on every stump.

In the general election of 1956 I was up against Clevelander Stephen M. Young, a perennial candidate for everything. He was a congressman-at-large from Ohio who eventually ended up being a U.S. senator. He and Bender took turns running for congressman-at-large. He ran a vigorous campaign.

O'Neill was one of the very best at campaigning and had a good organization. Consequently, we often followed him around the state, riding his shirttails. He had tent shows, inviting every Republican within miles, taking everybody's picture, shaking everybody's hand, giving them a little bite to eat and drink, and whatever else made them happy. It cost a fortune. It was a marvelously oiled machine, and we just thrived on it.

O'Neill got so many people to turn out, all coming to shake his hand and have their picture taken, that some would have to wait in line for an hour or more. My campaign staff—Gerald A. Donahue, Dick Sims, Boyd, and several others—worked the line, passing out my campaign literature.

Of course, when O'Neill's guys caught on, they were fuming. They had their backs up. "Get out of here!" they growled. Everett H. Krueger Jr., one of O'Neill's assistant attorneys general, told my guys they had to leave the grounds. "This is an O'Neill function. We paid for it, and you're not allowed in here."

Donahue looked at Krueger and said, "You go get [Alvin I.] 'Buddy'

Krenzler (architect of the O'Neill campaign and later a federal judge in Cleveland).[1] He isn't going to like this, because he told me to do it. Now you go back and tell Krenzler that first of all, he's going to have to get a cop to get us out of here, and second, I see a whole bunch of reporters over there. If you kick us out, the first place I'm going is over there to those reporters."

"Damn it," Krueger said, knowing when he held a losing hand. "We're asking you to leave. We're not going to force you to do anything." So my crew just kept on working the line. We showed up at other rallies after that, too, and they left us alone.

In the general election that year I captured better than 52 percent of the vote, defeating Young by nearly one hundred sixty thousand votes. O'Neill also won his only term as governor.

O'Neill and I never got along. He was a damn poor attorney general and a poor governor, but later a good supreme court judge. During his one term as governor, I was attorney general, of course, but he still thought he was both governor and attorney general. It was a rough first two years for me.

A group of young attorneys worked for me; the attorney general's office was a stepping-stone to private practice for many of them. Some would get

Former Ohio attorney general C. C. Crabbe joined Dolly and me in my 1956 campaign for that office.

Governor Rhodes, seated right, witnessed my oath for Ohio attorney general, January 15, 1957.

off on the wrong foot, though, drinking their lunch at Paoletti's Restaurant and Bar on South Third Street. One bad day in particular, I assembled the lot of them and read the riot act. "Damn it! I hope you're drinking gin, because I want the people to know you're drunk and not stupid." They got the message.

I had a driver named Carris F. Marmie. He was a former deputy in the county courts, and he liked to eat at truck stops. Donahue was running our program schedule at the time. Marmie often drove Dolly to various functions, invariably stopping to eat at one of these greasy spoons. Each time he would tell her, "Now don't tell Jerry," but when Donahue found out he'd raise hell.

The legislature dumped on me the Ohio Un-American Activities Commission when I was in my first term as attorney general. During the McCarthy era, everyone was looking under rugs for communists, in Ohio as elsewhere. Columbus attorney, Rep. Sam Devine, a former FBI agent, headed the joint House-Senate commission, established in 1951 during the ninety-ninth General Assembly. He had a bunch of sleuths running files on people.

I was never a Joseph McCarthy supporter. I thought the guy was nuts. In any event, after McCarthy's string ran out in the Senate in Washington, and Governor Lausche vetoed key legislation to give the commission even broader powers in Ohio, the legislature turned the commission's work over to the attorney general's office.

That's how I inherited Marmie and couple of gumshoes. Donahue nicknamed one of them Deputy Dog—that was Jim Worster—and the other, Jack Preble, was called Quick-Draw McGraw. Those guys were filling filing cabinets full of suspects. I never paid much attention to it. When the commission's work dried up, we put Deputy Dog and Quick-Draw McGraw on the bunko squad for statewide scams. George Mingle, former superintendent of the state highway patrol, headed up the attorney general's fraud investigations.

Fred Jones was a good friend who had a farm in the Mechanicsburg area. He also was a wealthy insurance executive in Columbus. As chairman of my campaign finance committee, he had a habit of donating his own money when it didn't come in from other sources. When we were desperate for money, which was often in the early campaigns, Boyd would go out to Fred's office and pick up a check. That's how we had money for the campaigns in 1956 and again in 1958.

Jones headed a group of insurance companies, and at the time, Ohio had a law that insurance companies couldn't write more than one line of insurance. He had different, separate companies—Buckeye Union Insurance and Ohio State Life among them—while many of the big nationals were combined into one company. So Jones was very interested in keeping the Ohio law that said you couldn't be a conglomerate company, because he had a big advantage.

When Jones and his associates in Ohio State Life acquired control of Columbus Mutual Life Insurance Company for $6 million in 1956, it wrote only mutual policies. Jones wanted to change the charter and convert it into a stock company. He approached Arthur I. Vorys, Ohio superintendent of insurance, who asked the attorney general to determine the law. Our opinion was that you couldn't convert, or if you did, you had to do it a certain, restrictive way. That was a blow to Jones. He was used to having his own way. He was a very positive fellow and did not take well to being told no about anything. But we remained friends.

In 1954 the voters approved a constitutional amendment to change the terms for governor, attorney general, and secretary of state from two years to four years, effective January 1959. When I was elected in 1956, it was for a two-year term, but when I ran again in 1958, it was for a four-year term.

Nineteen hundred and fifty-eight was the infamous right-to-work year. Herschel C. Atkinson, executive vice president of the Ohio Chamber of

Commerce, decided that Ohio needed a right-to-work law, which would effectively put an end to union shops. He couldn't get it through the legislature, so he got O'Neill to endorse it and petition signatures to put it on the ballot. Organized labor did not take well to that, and it launched one of the most effective political drives that the Democrats have ever had in Ohio. Labor raised the money and grass-roots opposition, and the Republicans were in deep trouble.

Republican Party Chairman Ray Bliss gathered the statewide candidates every Sunday morning in a dining room on the mezzanine level at the Neil House for a weekly strategy session. Usually all the GOP candidates or their representatives were there: O'Neill, Bricker, State Treasurer Roger Tracy, Secretary of State Ted Brown, me, and others who drifted in and out.

Some of us were not all that friendly with each other, but Bliss could keep the peace. It got harder toward the end because O'Neill supported right to work and Atkinson. Bliss knew almost from the time the campaigning for the right-to-work initiative began that we were in trouble on that issue. He begged, threatened and did everything else he could with both O'Neill and Atkinson to can it. But Atkinson had allies in the Ohio Manufacturers Association, headed by Executive Director Donald W. Wiper, and some of the other traditional business groups. They really wanted it and thought they had a chance. They'd done polling and said it was going to win, but it turned out that they were wrong. Among the Republicans there were no survivors, except for Brown and Rhodes, who didn't run. It was an off year for the auditor's office.

During the campaign we rented a trailer and loaded it up with assistant attorneys general, such as James F. DeLeone, Davis J. Myers, Louis H. Orkin, and others. We took the trailer to some thirty-five county fairs that summer and fall. There we would respond to questions from the populace. It was a great showcase for me.

My opponent in the general election was Mark McElroy, a Cleveland Democrat and a nice guy. There was not a lot of political acrimony between us in that campaign. But three or four weeks before election day, it became apparent that we might lose to him. The right-to-work forces and money were just too strong. Jack Chester, who was campaign chairman for each of my attorney general races, made a special trip to Mechanicsburg to discuss the campaign. As he remembers it, "I'd made up my mind that we were going to lose. I told Bill we were going to lose, but he didn't like to hear it. We had a serious discussion of some length. It cooled our relationship for awhile."[2]

Jack was right of course. McElroy beat me but not not by much—

51.6 percent to 48.4 percent. He got 1.5 million votes, and I received 1.4 million. The party lost control of the Ohio Senate and House, the United States Senate, and every key state-contested post except secretary of state.

In the fall of 1957, Dolly and I hosted a party at Jubarock for a number of politicians. Dolly played matchmaker, inviting confirmed bachelor Jack, along with Cynthia Johnson, daughter of William M. Johnson, my finance chairman for Champaign County. Cynthia was late, arriving just as Jack was leaving. Dolly ran down the drive to stop him and bring him back inside to meet her. He did, and he married Cynthia not long after that.

Gen. Carlton S. Dargusch Sr. had been after me to join his Columbus law firm, so after my defeat in 1958 I joined Dargusch, Saxbe, and Dargusch on State Street. That was a tax and big business firm, and they offered me one thousand dollars a month to practice there. I got another one thousand dollars a month from the Ohio Trucking Association, and so I was doing all right. I got in some big lawsuits and made a lot of money. I thought I was through with politics. I just quit.

For four years I spent a lot of time in Mechanicsburg, enjoying the family and the farm. In the spring of 1962 Bart had completed three years at Amherst College, and Juli had earned her diploma at Mechanicsburg High School. She took off for the University of Kansas at Lawrence on an art scholarship but shortly after transferred to the University of Wyoming at Laramie. Rocky finished his freshman year at the Columbus Academy, a private school that Bart had graduated from in 1959.

In Mechanicsburg I was a lawyer, worked at real estate, fixed flats; I did everything. But I also had some fun with those who enjoyed hunting and fishing as much as I did.

Perhaps the "fishing" trip Dolly remembers best—but not fondly—was one I took with J. Patterson "Pat" Williams, a good friend for many years. On the way back from a day of hunting, we stopped at John Sawyer's house for a couple of drinks while Dolly continued on home with the children. Sawyer, who lived just south of Mechanicsburg, was the son of Charles Sawyer, secretary of commerce under President Harry S. Truman, and Pat Williams was Charles's son-in-law. John showed us some film of his recent fishing expedition to the Dry Tortugas. I said something like, "That looks like fun. I'd like to do that."

"Well, let's go then," Williams said.

"When?"

"Right now." So he and I jumped in the car, still in our hunting clothes, drove to Cincinnati, caught a flight to Miami, and arrived in Key West by

Rocky, Bart, and Juli hit the campaign trail with their mother and me during my 1962 race for Ohio attorney general. Reprinted with permission from the *Columbus Dispatch*.

seven the next morning. We didn't tell our wives or anybody that we were going.

We discovered that it would be three days until the next boat to the Dry Tortugas, so we flew to Havana, Cuba, where for three days we enjoyed ourselves tremendously. When I got back to Mechanicsburg, the air at home was frosty. I tried to make amends with peace offerings I picked up at a tourist trap—a faux alligator purse for Dolly and castanets for the maid. Still, it took some time for home to warm up. Pat didn't fare so well; his wife divorced him.

My first trip to Cuba came in 1958 for a conference of all of the attorneys general in North and South America. Dolly was with me that time, as was Boyd, then a special counsel to the Ohio attorney general's office, and his wife, Barbara.

The conference program put me to sleep, so Boyd and I decided to depart. We tried sneaking out a side door, set off a burglar alarm, and were immediately surrounded by President Fulgencio Batista's trigger-happy guards waving assault weapons. They made us go back into the conference.

That was less than a year before Fidel Castro seized control of the government, and everyone seemed a little on edge.

Another night we were invited to President Batista's palace for dinner, but I declined, believing it would be politically incorrect to attend. As far as I know, every other U.S. attorney general at the conference attended the lavish party, as did Dolly and the Boyds.

Cuban attorney Arturo Bengochea took Boyd and me duck hunting on twenty thousand acres of marshland he owned. We also met Roberto Madura, another wealthy businessman who owned the Sugar Kings, a Havana baseball team in the same league as the Columbus Red Birds.

In 1967 I became involved in the Valley High ski resort at Bellefontaine, with three or four other investors. After an initial investment in two hundred shares of Ohio Resorts Inc. stock at about $1.60 per share, I kept buying up more until I was the biggest stockholder, with about twenty-five thousand shares. When I sold out in the late 1970s, I had made one hundred thousand dollars or so. I also bought a 460-acre farm with Chester in Madison County. We bought it for three hundred dollars an acre and sold it three or four years later for four hundred fifty dollars to five hundred dollars an acre.

In the summer of 1962, Boyd invited me to play in a little three-day golf tournament at the Scioto Country Club, which Chester G. Hawley and I won. Boyd took the occasion to work on me to run again for attorney general. After three days of his pestering, I finally agreed to do so. That night at the awards dinner, Dolly made it clear she was upset, and she told Boyd as much while they took a spin around the dance floor together. "This is the first normal life we've ever had and you go and ruin it!" she told him, but the decision was made. The race was on.

"Saxbe Ready to Run" said the newspaper headline, but it was over a photograph of Rocky in his track uniform at the Columbus Academy. Nevertheless, I was ready, too.

Even before the primary campaign began, I had a run-in with one of my opponents, John Lloyd. He was the son of a wealthy Cincinnati insurance executive who claimed that through his family and friends he had all the money that was necessary to win. He also had been very active in party politics, such as being chairman of the Ohio Young Republicans. A debate arose within the party as to who were going to be the nominees for governor, attorney general, and so forth in 1962.

Lloyd kept telling me, "I'm going to run, and I'm going to beat you" in the primary because "I have all the resources it takes to get that done." I guess he was hoping I would lie down and roll over for him, giving him the

Dolly has always enjoyed a good party, such as this one in Dayton in 1965.

nomination unchallenged. I won with 350,000 votes (66 percent); Lloyd got 136,000 votes (25.7 percent), and Robert L. Marrs received 44,000 votes (8.3 percent).

Robert E. Sweeney, a Cleveland attorney and father of eleven, from Bay Village, was my Democratic opponent in the general election. Again I won a narrow victory, capturing 1.5 million votes from the 2.9 million cast in our race. For the GOP, it was a landslide year.

When I ran for the third time, in 1966, Donahue agreed to return to my office as first assistant state attorney general, a post he held from 1963 to 1965.[3] He first came to my attention through Boyd. While still in law school at Ohio State, Donahue worked as a salesman in a clothing store Boyd managed in Upper Arlington, a Columbus suburb. When Donahue got his law degree in 1956, he asked Boyd for an introduction to the attorney general's office. Carlile hired him as an administrative assistant, and Donahue became a key figure in my campaigns and in the attorney general's office. Donahue was a handsome, very smart young man from Toledo, who often took care of the store when I was away from the office of the attorney general. He was regarded as having one of the brightest political minds in Ohio, but he became quite a disappointment to me. He drank too much and had trouble keeping focused. He couldn't get along with everybody, either.

After I left for the Senate, Donahue became involved in a statehouse loan scandal as a partner in a Columbus firm called Crofters, Incorporated. He was indicted but not convicted of bribery charges. Subsequently,

Rocky held the Bible when Judge Kingsley A. Taft swore me in as Ohio attorney general in 1963. On the right, Dolly watches. Reprinted with permission from the *Columbus Dispatch*.

{ I'VE SEEN THE ELEPHANT }

he became a lobbyist for the Associated Industries of New York and then returned to Columbus to practice law. In any event, when I ran for the Senate in the summer of 1968, Donahue was my campaign manager, but the campaign did not appear to be well organized. I brought in J. D. Sawyer to make the thing a little more orderly. He and Donahue shared many of the campaign responsibilities after that.

Sawyer was a prominent realtor in Middletown, ninety or so miles south of Mechanicsburg, and was well positioned in the industry statewide. He helped me first by raising funds in the 1956 campaign and volunteering his services. He got some of the industries in the Middletown area to sponsor a fund-raising luncheon. We raised eleven hundred dollars, which doesn't sound like much today, but it came at a time when I desperately needed it. We spent most of it on printing campaign handouts and banners, each with the slogan, "Let Your X Be For Saxbe." Through the years, Sawyer proved to be an enormous asset as an organizer.

My most famous case as Ohio's attorney general was that of Dr. Samuel Sheppard, a Cleveland-area osteopath convicted of murdering his wife, Marilyn, in their home in July 1954. It was a murder that captured the attention of the Fourth Estate like no other. Ten years later he was released from the Ohio Penitentiary in Columbus on a writ of habeas corpus, but the U.S. Appellate Court in Cincinnati overturned federal Judge Carl A. Weinman. That put the issue in the U.S. Supreme Court. I had my first assistant, Donald M. Colasurd, with me on February 24, 1966, when I went to Washington to argue the case. David L. Kessler and William A. Greene, both attorneys in my office, were along, also. Colasurd was a former FBI agent who did a bang-up job as head of my liquor control and workman's compensation sections. He also was a great help on the campaign trail in northeast Ohio. Anyway, I argued that Sheppard belonged in the penitentiary. Trial attorney F. Lee Bailey, who was to make his name and his career defending Sheppard, argued in his brief that "there was presented at Dr. Sheppard's trial no sufficient evidence to sustain a conviction."

As the *Cleveland Press* reported, I argued in my final brief that

Sheppard told eight different stories about the murder of his wife, Marilyn, from the time it was reported through the time he testified.

Two hundred sixteen times during cross examination Sheppard replied he couldn't remember concerning "facts and circumstances that took place in his claimed presence and which were material to the issues to the case."

In some statements, Sheppard said he saw a form standing over his wife's battered body and in others he said he could not see the bedroom because it was dark.

First it was "they" who killed Marilyn, then later it was one person, and at times Sheppard was unsure whether it was a man or a woman.

His stories varied as to whether the "intruder" attacked him in the bedroom or in the hallway upstairs.

"As far as the jury was concerned there was no answer as to what was in the room where Mrs. Sheppard was killed," Saxbe said. "As many times as Sheppard's changed his story, he could have been struggling with a yellow ape—that is, if there was a struggle."[4]

I lost the case, though, because the court considered evidence that news hawk Dorothy Kilgallen had talked to the judge before the trial and that the judge had said Sheppard was guilty as hell. I argued that that was the worst kind of hearsay and shouldn't be considered because both Kilgallen and the judge were dead. Later I concluded that Sheppard won release because he had spent ten years in the penitentiary, and he was deranged. In 2000, forty-six years after the murder and long after Sheppard's death, the case was still being appealed in the courts.

One of the trickiest of times politically arose during my second term as Ohio's top attorney. It involved the reapportionment of the Ohio House as a result of a U.S. Supreme Court ruling in June 1964. While the court did not specifically rule on Ohio's apportionment system, its decision requiring one-man, one-vote representation in six other state cases clearly affected Ohio.

Since 1903 and the Hanna amendment to the state constitution, each county in Ohio, regardless of population, was entitled to at least one House representative. That put the power in the hands of rural interests and created an imbalance as the state's urban centers grew. A Clevelander, James Nolan, declared as much in his suit filed against the state in 1961, seeking equal representation under the Fourteenth Amendment to the U.S. Constitution.

The issue was a political hot potato because Democrats feared the Republicans in power would shape the new legislative districts in the party's favor. More than a few representatives on both sides of the aisle feared that they would lose their seats, and justly so. To avoid open acrimony and influence, the Ohio apportionment board, composed of Governor Rhodes, Secretary of State Ted Brown, and State Auditor Roger Cloud, agreed with me that the redistricting work would need to be done in virtual secrecy.

The task of evaluating every district and redrawing the lines for equal representation fell to a politically astute, twenty-six-year-old history graduate, Nodine Miller, today a common pleas court judge in Franklin County, Ohio. I grabbed her out of the auditor's office where she worked as an administrative assistant and stuck her in the basement of a savings and loan across the street from the statehouse. There she sat, virtually alone, for ten months, poring over every inch of the state's district lines. Few knew she was there or that she had such a monumental responsibility on her hands. That was the only way we could keep her sheltered from every concerned politician in the state.

"The only thing Bill Saxbe told me at the time was to 'do what is right . . . and I will sell it,'" she recalled.

In the end, and despite many legal challenges, the plan she prepared and I submitted was accepted by the U.S. District Court and upheld by the U.S. Supreme Court. It took effect with the 1966 elections. A constitutional amendment that established a ninety-nine-member House and a thirty-three-member Senate was adopted the following year.

Many have asked me about James A. Rhodes and what I thought of him. Rhodes and I spent thirty years in politics together, but we were never socially close. There was rivalry under the surface, I suppose. When we didn't have Democrats to fight, we jockeyed with each other. I didn't always approve of the way he went about his business. He probably saw me as being too frivolous and too liberal, or worse.

Rhodes had great control over the party throughout our careers, and he played that to the hilt. Much to the dismay of some, he gave away Ohio's GOP delegation, first to Barry Goldwater in 1964 and then again in 1968. That year he held back Ohio's fifty-five votes in the hope that his friend and fellow governor, Nelson A. Rockefeller of New York, would be able to unseat Richard M. Nixon, who won the nomination on the first ballot. Rhodes always tried to hold himself out as presidential timber, but I never regarded him as having the right stuff.

Still, in the main, I was an enthusiastic Rhodes supporter. He had a political organization that helped me in my statewide races. Many in his organization in Cincinnati were "bolivers," a term that originated there for the precinct committeemen, the ward chairmen, and other party regulars who held patronage jobs. Rhodes was head hog in the wallow there. So, when we set up a meeting in Cincinnati, Rhodes's people would ask if we wanted the bolivers to attend. Most of them were factotums, but when you rang the bell they responded. Cincinnati was about the only place bolivers operated effectively. A few existed in Toledo, perhaps, but they were getting

Governor James Rhodes, right, and I attended the 1963 inauguration with Roger W. Tracy, left, state auditor, and Lieutenant Governor John W. Brown. Reprinted with permission from the *Columbus Dispatch*.

tired. In Cleveland, George Bender's bolivers were so disreputable you just would rather most of them didn't show up.

Rhodes was the one to give Juli the final nudge on her first trip to the altar. When she got back to Columbus from college in Wyoming, Juli dated Sam Lopeman, who was my chief counsel for a time. They became engaged, and a big wedding was set for April 23, 1966, in Mechanicsburg. At the eleventh hour Juli got cold feet. Just before going to the church, she was a wreck. Rhodes knocked on the door to her room at Jubarock: "Juli, I think maybe you ought to go on up there [to the church]," and so she did. The marriage lasted seven years.

Rhodes ran for a second term as governor in 1966, and I ran for my third term as attorney general. Cleveland attorney and Democratic Congressman-at-Large Robert E. Sweeney won his party's primary against Mark McElroy and the right to oppose me again in November. With the backing of most of Ohio's major newspapers—but not the *Cleveland Press*—I won reelection rather easily in a campaign that was virtually devoid of issues. In the primary I was unopposed, and in November I beat Sweeney 1,522,038 votes to 1,233,805 votes.

Less than a year passed before I began to hear voices telling me I should make another run for the U.S. Senate.

The Last Campaign

The jump from attorney general of Ohio to the U.S. Senate was enormous, even for someone who had "seen the elephant." Getting there required not only extreme physical exertion but organization and financing—lots of financing. Television had become such a major political instrument that no statewide candidate could ignore its effectiveness. Yet, it was expensive. It was largely because of the money issue that I was lukewarm about launching another political campaign, especially on the heels of having run one in 1966. Still, almost from the moment of victory that year, I was being urged to seek the U.S. Senate. I tired of hearing about it and walked away when anyone brought up the subject.

One day Jack Chester sat down with Don Colasurd, my first assistant attorney general in 1967. "Bill Saxbe is the most logical person to run for the United States Senate against Frank Lausche," said Chester. They—and others—both coaxed and coddled and urged me to give it a try. Even if I lost, Chester argued, I couldn't get hurt very much by it, given that my term as attorney general ran until 1970.

"Damn it, Bill," Colasurd told me one day in frustration at my unresponsiveness, "We've got two years to get the campaign rolling. This guy's (Lausche) going to die; he's too old for the Senate. You have to give it a shot."

The seventy-two-year-old Lausche was Ohio's only five-term governor, and now he was completing his second six-year term as Ohio's senator. His primary opponent was former congressman John J. Gilligan of Cincinnati.

Several weeks later I walked into Colasurd's office and said, "Okay, I'm going to make you happy. I'm going to go down and talk to those guys."

"What does that mean?" Colasurd asked.

"You know, what you've been after."

"You're going to go talk to John?"

"Yep."

"Good for you. Go get him."

So I hiked over to office of John S. Andrews of Toledo, who was then chairman of the Ohio Republican Party. Bliss had moved up to chair the party's national organization. Andrews and the party told me that Robert Taft Jr. was going to be the party's first choice. They didn't tell me I couldn't run, but they made it clear that Taft was going to get the nod.

"That's bullshit," said Colasurd when I told him what happened. "I can't believe you're going to stand by and let them tell you that you can't run."

He was right, of course. I had no intention of backing down, but I sure felt down. In the end, Taft decided he didn't want to take on Lausche. Chester was convinced that I could beat Lausche. Other than in 1958, the right-to-work year, I always enjoyed good labor support: Lausche did not. Chester felt that that and age were Lausche's Achilles' heel. Most everyone else felt as I did, that my chances against Lausche were not as good as they would be against Gilligan. Lausche pulled a lot of GOP votes down state, such as in Cincinnati's Hamilton County. He also enjoyed considerable strength in Cleveland's Cuyahoga County, where perhaps I was weakest.

Everything we did in gearing up for the fall campaign was aimed at

Both Richard Nixon and I, here on the steps of the statehouse in Columbus with Governor Rhodes, were hard-charging candidates the fall of 1968.

beating Lausche. That was our focus. The GOP primary wasn't much of a contest for me. I began statewide campaigning in February 1968, but the Gilligan-Lausche race received most of the press. Nevertheless, when May 7 rolled around, I got 575,178 votes against William L. White of Mt. Vernon, who had 71,191 votes, and Albert Edward Payne of Springfield, 52,393 votes.

The big surprise was that the forty-seven-year-old Gilligan proved to be such a tough opponent for the incumbent Lausche. Gilligan won the primary, pulling in some 56 percent of the slightly more than one million votes cast.

Only after the primary did the Ohio GOP feel I had a good shot at winning. Gerald A. Donahue, Sawyer, and Bill Hoiles began to staff up. Chester became chairman of my Franklin County campaign. William Klucas, who was sent to us by the Republican National Committee, came on board to staff the advance team, on leave from Ashland College.

This also was to be the first campaign that I had with me Vincent W. Rakestraw, a young man just out of Capital University Law School. He hung around the statehouse, talking to a lot of lawyers. Most of them believed the best thing a young lawyer could do was go to work with the attorney general for a couple of years, get some litigating and administrative experience, and then go to a firm or hang out a shingle. Rakestraw got a clerk's job through Hoiles, with the promise of greater responsibility after he passed the bar, which he did before the campaign began.

I never had had any formal polling, but one of the first things we did was hire Robert Teeter of Market Opinion Research, Detroit. He was a young guy then, but he ended up in Washington, working as a pollster for presidents. An early statewide poll showed Gilligan was well known by the electorate as a result of his tough race against Lausche. I had to play catch-up to Gilligan and get myself known to voters throughout the state. We began by erecting 150 billboards around the state. "It Should Be Saxbe for United States Senate," they read. We also went heavily into television advertising, which was still relatively new for me.

I could tell this was going to be an expensive campaign, much more so than any campaign I had run before. When all was said and done, it cost about $1.25 million. My problem was that I never had been that close to big money interests in Ohio. Raising money was of major concern. Among my largest contributors were

Ohio Medical Political Action Committee	$15,000+
Ireland family, Hanna Mining, Cleveland	$11,600
Joseph E. Cole, Cleveland	$ 7,500

Kyle F. Brooks, Cincinnati	$ 7,476
Kelvin Smith, Cleveland	$ 6,000
Joseph E. Cole business associates	$ 5,500
Carl and Robert Lindner, Cincinnati publishers	$ 3,000
Louis Nippert, Cincinnati	$ 3,000
Gov. Nelson A. Rockefeller, New York	$ 3,000
Edward J. DeBartelo, Youngstown developer	$ 2,500
Sam Klein, Bally Corp.	$ 2,500
Armco Steel officers, etc.	$ 2,200
David G. Gamble, Taft Broadcasting	$ 2,000
T. Spencer Shore, Eagle-Pitcher Industries	$ 2,000
Thomas F. Patton, Republic Steel	$ 1,000+
Vernon Stouffer, Stouffer Foods	$ 1,000+
Carl D. Glickman, Shelter Resources	$ 1,000+
John O. Doerge, Columbus	$ 1,000

The 1968 campaign was a lot more fun because we had a bus, like a Greyhound. It cost us sixteen thousand dollars to purchase and another three thousand to refurbish. It had a little kitchen and a loud speaker system so we could play the campaign songs and such. We launched the bus tours July 15 and had a great time with a bunch of young, enthusiastic, advance men preparing the way. Bill "Chomp" Hunter, my good friend from Mechanicsburg, was our driver. Once he got the bus stuck underneath an underpass. We had to let air out of the tires to free it.

Gaining labor votes from my Democratic opponent was the cornerstone of my campaign, and that proved to be decisive in the general election. Gilligan received the endorsement of the Ohio AFL-CIO, but he was never very comfortable face to face with the blue-collar workers. I won the endorsement of the powerful Teamsters union as well as support from the old-time trade unions, such as the carpenters, sheet metal workers, and operating engineers. I also gained some respect from the union leadership when, while visiting the campus of the University of Dayton, I refused to cross a picket line formed by striking food service and custodial workers.

We stopped the bus at a lot of plants and talked to a lot of workers. I visited General Fireproofing and Youngstown Sheet and Tube, Youngstown; Ohio Brass, Barberton; Tyson Roller Bearing, Massillon; Transue and Williams Steel Forging, Alliance; the McNeil-Akron division of McNeil Corporation, Akron; American Shipbuilding, Lorain; Ohio Screw Products, Elyria; and a host of others. At each stop I'd put a plug of Mail Pouch chewing tobacco in my cheek before I left the bus, and it became my calling card with the plant workers. They seemed to love it when I directed a stream of juice into a nearby trash bin. I became one of them; they began to listen to what I had to say, and I listened to them, too. The two major issues in the Senate campaign were Vietnam and crime. The voters wanted an end to both, and I promised I would do what I could to get that accomplished in Washington.

Not everything ran as smooth as silk during in the early days of the campaign. Behind the scenes there was a lot of maneuvering by those looking to feather their nests at my expense—win, lose, or draw. I asked Sawyer to work with Donahue to bring more order and direction to the campaign. I gave him full authority to do what was necessary. He read the staff the riot act. "You're selfish as hell; you're fighting for your own turf, and I'm not going to put up with it," Sawyer said. "Bill has told me that I have full authority to speak for him and on his behalf to hire, fire, and do anything I want to do. I am telling you now, I'm going to have the ass off of the first guy that I see move that far out of line." We had few personnel problems after Sawyer took charge.

There were other problems, though, and not without some humor. For example, one day a week we put aside for the staff to prepare the week's schedule. It was a lot of work. One day we handed our only copy of the campaign schedule to Duke Portman, a bright young attorney on the advance team. He was to make copies so everyone would know their assignments. Unfortunately, that evening he wasn't tied together very well. He ran the schedule through the shredder by mistake, forcing the staff to start all over. The trouble was few could remember what they had put on the schedule. It took four or five hours to redo it. From then on Portman was known as "The Shredder."

One night, in a motel, one of our advance guys put a quarter into the bed vibrator machine, and the darn thing went all night long. The next morning he arrived at the bus with his eyeballs still bouncing in their sockets.

Dan Rather from CBS got on the bus to interview me and was so nice. When the program came out he was not very nice. All he talked about was how I chewed tobacco and what a big farmer I was.

At a campaign stop in Toledo, a confused Republican voter came up to Dolly and said, "Oh, Mrs. Nixon. Your husband will make a wonderful president." Dolly did not attempt to unravel the woman's confusion.

Nixon, who was running hard against Hubert H. Humphrey, came to Columbus August 20 and again October 22. Both times I was pictured with Nixon in newspapers across the state. I joined Nixon one more time, in Cleveland, on October 30. As Nixon stepped off his plane, he noticed Rhodes

When Nixon arrived in Cleveland for a 1968 rally, Governor James Rhodes, center, pushed me next to the GOP presidential candidate. Also greeting Nixon are United States Representative Frances Bolton and William Minshall. Reprinted with permission of AP/World Wide Photos.

standing behind a group of dignitaries. "Why are you in the second row, Jim?" Nixon asked. "Because he's not a candidate," I explained facetiously. I was first in line to greet Nixon and his wife, Pat. Actually, it was Jim who had pushed me forward to be first in line.

Other national political figures came into Ohio to give my campaign a lift. I was with Sen. John Tower of Texas on a campaign swing in Middletown on October 29 when I was given heavy security. The police had arrested a thirty-year-old mental patient who, when stored safely in a jail cell, was still thrashing around and yelling, "I am going to kill Saxbe!" I never was in any real danger, though.

Near the end of October, Lausche gave me his endorsement, saying that he felt I was "the most able and he [Gilligan] the least able, to help cure the grave sicknesses besetting our country."

Throughout the summer Gilligan pushed for a debate, but I declined at that time. In a *Columbus Dispatch* poll at the end of August, I led Gilligan by 73 percent to 27 percent, so I didn't want to give him a forum. Also, many warned me about Gilligan's skills as a debater and urged me not to take him on. When we did meet at the Cleveland City Club on November 1, I still held a lead in the polls, with just four days to go, but it had narrowed to less than ten points. Some seven hundred attended the luncheon.

I don't know who won the debate; some said I crucified him. At the very least, it was a draw.

In the last week of the campaign, our pollster, Teeter, said we had to spend seventy-five thousand dollars more on television commercials. If we didn't do it, he said, I could lose. I was asked to sign a note for that amount, but I refused. He said, "Well, you are going to get beat."

"So, I'll get beat, but I'll walk away and won't owe anybody any money."

At the time my net worth didn't total seventy-five thousand dollars, and I wasn't going to spend the next five years paying off the debt if I lost. I got stuck for three thousand dollars when I ran against George Bender, and it took me two years to pay that off. Fred Jones and John Galbreath came through, securing a seventy-thousand-dollar loan at City National Bank, but it was GOP State Chairman John S. Andrews; Rhodes; his chief aide, John M. McElroy; and Donahue who signed the note, not me.

Ralph Waldo was with me on Election Day. Dolly fixed us breakfast, and then we hunted pheasants for a couple of hours. We left there and went right to the golf course and played nine holes of golf at the Urbana Country Club. Then we took off for Bellefontaine, to an A-frame ski lodge I owned at the Valley High ski development there, and took a nap. Afterwards, we went fishing at the trout club.

Many said my 1968 debate with John Gilligan at the Cleveland City Club was critical to my winning the Senate race. Reprinted with permission of the *Cleveland Press* Collection, Cleveland State University Library.

"I don't remember bagging any birds, catching any fish, or getting any conversation out of Bill," Waldo said. "As usual, all you get is grunts when he has something on his mind."

We returned to Mechanicsburg and Dolly and I fixed dinner for Waldo; his wife, Lorna; and about four other couples. After dinner, we drove to election-night headquarters at the Neil House, where we had a big suite with an opulent spiral stairway in it. We had hoped to celebrate my victory early, but as the first returns came in, I was losing.

Shortly after midnight I addressed the party in the ballroom and thanked them for their hard work during the campaign. Then Dolly and I went to bed, thinking I had lost. About 5:00 A.M. it was announced that I had won, but I went over to Governor Rhodes's office about 7:00 A.M. to have it confirmed. Gilligan waited until 10:00 A.M. before he conceded.

When the smoke cleared, the race was much closer than I had expected it would be. I narrowly defeated Gilligan by 114,000 votes: 1,928,964 to 1,814,152. Nixon and Spiro T. Agnew won Ohio over Humphrey and Edmund S. Muskie by an even smaller margin, 1,791,014 to 1,700,586.

On Wednesday afternoon I bumped into Vince Rakestraw at the attorney general's office. "Dolly and I are going to Germany Thursday. We want you to go to Washington to be on my Senate staff," I said. He accepted as my legislative assistant.

I already had put Sawyer in charge of setting up the Washington staff. He was a detail man, and a darn good one, too. I told him on election night, "You got me into this thing, so get down there to Washington and start digging up some personnel. Take with you people from the campaign and from the attorney general's office that you think will be useful."

Ready or not, I was headed for Washington, leaving behind my last campaign.

9

Here I Come, Ready or Not

My first trip to Washington, at the height of the Depression, was every bit as meaningful as my second, thirty-three years later. In 1936, when I was in one of my drifting periods out of college, I got a job in the Department of Agriculture cafeteria, busing dishes for twenty-five cents an hour. I began at nine o'clock in the morning, got free breakfast, and worked through lunch. So, I got two meals and one dollar a day for four hours of work.

I stayed with a friend from Mechanicsburg. I paid him two dollars a week for a cot in the hall, which was about half of his room rent. I had a ball in Washington, taking trips and seeing the sights. At that time, on the weekends, a boat went down the Potomac River and into Chesapeake Bay to Old Port Comfort, Virginia, and back. I'd take a girl and have a great time.

I thought while I was in Washington that I would help run the government, but I didn't have much chance in the Department of Agriculture cafeteria. So after a month or so, I quit. Little did I know that thirty-three years later I would be back as a U.S. senator.

Shortly after my election to the Senate—within days, actually—Sawyer presented me with a Senate study he had prepared. It detailed my office structure, staff, and organization; pay scales; office space; committee assignments open to me; a list of important things to do, such as presentation of my certificate of election; and a "potpourri of gratuitous and solicited advice." Among his invaluable points:

Organize your office at once and be ready to roll on January 3. You
    will be frantically busy after then.
Pick top people. Pay to get top.
Attend all GOP Policy Committee luncheons even if they bore you.

Vice President Hubert H. Humphrey re-enacted my Senate swearing in as Senators Everett Dirksen, left, and Mike Mansfield looked on. AP/Wide World Photos.

The old senators view this as a prerequisite to a young new senator who wants to get ahead.

Hang out in the GOP Senate cloak room and the Senate dining room. You get acquainted there and impress the old-timers.

Don't pop off, but don't fail to speak up when you have something worthwhile to say.

Do *not* get pinned in Senate by "liberal" or "conservative" groups. The press is very sensitive to this, and will box you in if they can.

Be careful of letting old senators pump you as to your vote on basic issues. Destroys your leverage and bargaining power, and makes you appear vest pocket to senators or Senate groups.[1]

Sawyer also saw to my Senate office space, securing a very good office—for a freshman senator—on the first floor, directly on the left as you walked in the front door of the Senate's newer Senate Dirksen Office Building. In those days the senior senators wanted to be in the Senate's old, more elaborate Senate Russell Office Building, but I thought I was in the best location to the Senate chamber.

The office was not big enough for the whole staff, so I was assigned space on the floor upstairs. In the main office, Sawyer had the suite next to mine; then Rakestraw; William Hoiles, administrative assistant; former *Akron Beacon Journal* reporter Robert H. Feldkamp as press assistant; my secretary, Maryellen Portwine Toughill; and a receptionist. Just about everyone else was on the other floor.

The Senate had a whole law firm, the Legislative Counsel, on the sixth floor of the building. You told them what you had in mind for a bill, and they'd reach back and pull an old one off the shelf that was similar in form and content. Then they would change this and that and all of the sudden you have your own bill to introduce. My legislative assistant, Rakestraw, took charge of doing that sort of thing. By the same token, the Library of Congress wrote speeches on any subject for any senator. It was, and is, a great basic resource.

Frances Griffin was my office manager. Sawyer hired her on his first trip to Washington to set up the office. He tells a great story about that first meeting, when he was still temporarily set up in space loaned to us by Sen. George Murphy, R-California.

I was sitting in Senator Murphy's office when a knock came at the door. This woman poked her head in. "I understand you're recruiting personnel for Senator Saxbe," she said with a thick southern accent.

"That's right."

J. D. Sawyer, left, and Bill Hoiles were my invaluable aides in the Senate and at the Justice Department. Reprinted with permission of the *Cleveland Press* Collection.

"Well, I am Frances Griffin, and I just want to come in and tell you something, boy. Have you ever been on the Hill before?"

"No, I haven't."

"I'm here to tell what you don't know, boy. I'm from Culpeper, Virginia, and I've been on this damn Hill for eighteen years. I've been legislative assistant to Senator [Frank] Carlson [R-Kansas] and administrative assistant to Representative [Clifford R.] Hope [R-Kansas], and you don't know it, but every office needs a son-of-a-bitch. I know how to kick ass, and I know how to cover my own ass and whose ever ass I'm working for. You need somebody like that."

"Well, you sound. . . ."

"You ain't so smart, you know. They don't put political know-how in your head automatically there in Ohio. I know. I can help steer you away from the bad apples, and believe me, I know who they are. I know who the good ones are and who the bad ones are. And I'm here to apply for the job."

"You sound like my kind of woman," I said, and hired her on the spot.[2]

Frances did a super job for the office. She also often looked after Dolly's houseplants when we were both away. Dolly always talked to her plants and played nice music for them. One time she came home and discovered all her plants drooping. "Frances, you've got to talk to them nice. Quit swearing at my plants."

Shortly after arriving in Washington and setting up shop, a functionary from the secretary to the Senate's office came to see me. "Senator, you're still a colonel in the National Guard. It's impossible for you to hold a position as United States Senator." What he was telling me was that I would be double dipping into the federal payroll.

"Fine," I said. "Now tell me how I resign as a senator." That's the last I ever saw of that guy.

As Sawyer predicted, once we hit Washington we were busy all the time. Dolly was in the Senate gallery January 3, 1969, the day I took the oath of office. Ohio's other senator, Democrat Stephen M. Young, greeted me and escorted me down the aisle of the Senate, which I thought was a nice gesture. Vice President Hubert Humphrey swore me in. I checked out my desk and discovered a special request I had made had been fulfilled. A foot-high brass spittoon sat on the right hand corner of the desk. Sen. Herman Eugene Talmadge, D-Georgia; Harrison A. "Pete" Williams, D-New Jersey; and I were the only ones to chew tobacco in the Senate.

Congress was about the furthest I had been from reality since my army days.

My first standing committee assignments were to Labor and Public Welfare and to Aeronautical and Space Sciences, but I also was seated on the following subcommittees: Migratory Labor, Housing, Long-term Care, Consumer Interests, and Health.

While I was becoming acquainted with the quaintness of Congress, Dolly sought suitable accommodations. At first we rented a townhouse at Tiber Island. Dolly told everyone that whenever we moved, I always sent her ahead as the "designated lifter." Billie (Eileen) Smith, her friend from Columbus, and Dolly decorated the apartment with lots of fur and incense.

Being a realtor who knew a thing or two about buying a home, Sawyer also helped Dolly. Everyone thought you had to live in Georgetown, so Dolly tramped all over that area until she had bloody feet. Finally Sawyer found a newly renovated townhouse in Harbour Square. It was one of the historical eighteenth-century townhouses on what was called Wheat Row. A former sea captain originally occupied each house. We paid seventy-five thousand dollars for it. The house had an English basement under the street with a huge bedroom, a fireplace, and a bath. It was Rocky's "party pad" when he visited. The kitchen and dining room were on the first floor, the living room and a bedroom on the second floor, two more bedrooms and a bath on the third floor, and another living room and our master bedroom on the top floor. We put in a little elevator up to the fourth floor.

It was a fun place because it was within a twenty-minute walk of the Capitol. When I'd get time off, everybody would gather at our house because they could get back quickly for a roll call. We discovered that Sen.

Strom Thurmond, D-South Carolina, and his wife, Nancy, and Sen. Hubert H. Humphrey, D-Minnesota, and his wife, Miriam, lived at Harbour Square, too. Among other "regulars" at our home were Sen. Hugh Scott, R-Pennsylvania, and Marion; Sen. Mark O. Hatfield, R-Oregon, and Antoinette; Sen. James B. Allen, D-Alabama, and Maryon; Sen. Ernest "Fritz" Hollings, D-South Carolina, his first wife, Pat, and later his second wife, Rita ("Peatsy"); Gaylord Nelson, D-Wisconsin, and Carrie Lee; and Gen. Elwood R. "Pete" Quesada, former head of the Federal Aviation Administration, and Kate.

Before we left for Washington, Harriet Bricker, wife of Ohio's former senator and governor, John W. Bricker, told Dolly, "Be sure and join the Senate Ladies Red Cross when you get to Washington, because then you get to meet all the Senate wives." It didn't matter if you were a Republican or a Democrat, because in that gaggle everybody loved everybody else. That's how Dolly always knew which spouses were being dumped.

Betty Talmadge, wife of Georgia's senator, bounced into the Red Cross one day and said, "Guess what happened to me last night? I was fixing dinner in the kitchen, and Herman was in the living room, watching television. I heard over the television that Herman was divorcing me. I asked him, 'Herman, did I just hear what I think I heard?'

"'Yep.'"

That's how she learned about her divorce.

Betty was really funny. Somebody once asked her, "Mrs. Talmadge, do you talk to your husband when you're having sex?" and she said, "Only when he calls me on the phone."

Some senators were invited to the White House all the time, but Dolly and I seldom were because I voted my conscience, not the administration's line, and that rankled some of the folks back home. I had my first private session with Nixon in May 1969 and didn't meet with him again privately until May 1971.

However, we were at the White House when the Nixons entertained some of the nation's governors, including Ohio's Jim Rhodes. The governor approached Dolly on the Q.T. and told her that she had better get me straightened out, that I wasn't voting the party line.

In 1972 we attended a Nixon reception with the junior senator from Ohio, Robert Taft Jr., and his second wife, Kay. She arrived at the White House in tennis shoes under her long dress, which wasn't zipped up in the back. We got right up to the president in the receiving line and Kay whipped out a harmonica and began playing "God Save the Delta Queen."

Taft was elected in the fall of 1970, taking Young's seat. Even before he was sworn in, Nixon met with him several times. I suppose that was meant to be a signal to me that I was out of favor. A year after my election, I had been to the White House one time and probably no more than three or four times in the first two years.

Neither Dolly nor I liked "belly rubbers," the crowded, noisy cocktail parties held by lobbyists, who expected to sway votes with a free glass of bourbon—and often did. We quit going to a lot of those things after we bought the townhouse. There we had lots of parties of our own, but even some of those dragged on too long. I would have to loudly announce, "Come on, Dolly, let's go to bed so these good folks can go home." It always got a laugh—and the desired result.

I do remember bumping into Alice Roosevelt Longworth, the daughter of President Theodore Roosevelt, at a dinner party. She told me, "If you want to say something nasty about somebody, come sit next to me." She was feisty and fun. She told Dolly and me that she always carried a switch-blade knife just in case anyone attacked her chauffeur.

I came to Washington ready to slay a lot of dragons, but in less than three months I realized that was not going to happen. I had a front row seat, but I still was waiting for the show to start. Part of the problem was that I stood ninety-seventh out of one hundred in seniority, and I was a member of the minority party. That doesn't buy you a lot of effectiveness. Second, everyone had an axe to grind. I couldn't go anywhere without somebody collaring me with a point of view. In Washington everybody talks to each other, and soon they begin to believe themselves.

The Congress was about the furthest I had been from reality since my army days. I found the Senate to be "a paper tiger, full of hot air and little real substance or meaningful action."[3] I also abhorred the nitty-gritty of a senator's duties, such as being an errand boy for the constituency. As I told Robert J. Havel of the *Cleveland Plain Dealer,* "One letter tells me why Johnny should not go to Vietnam and another is from a guy who wants his teeth fixed."[4]

As I looked around I realized that the first six months in the Senate you wonder how you got there. The next six months you wonder how the rest of them got there. The Senate is supposed to be the greatest deliberative body in the world, but I discovered that it was no such thing. There was very little debate. The average visitor to the Senate could walk in at noon and find one guy reading a boilerplate speech and another half asleep. We might as well have mailed our important speeches to the *Congressional Record* rather than deliver them on the floor of the Senate.

I hadn't been in office more than a month when I found myself under attack from conservative Republicans. In the January issue of the American Conservative Union's *The Republican Battle Line*, my voting record was described as being "one of commitment to liberalism, GOP brand." What the ACU didn't like at all was my "backing GOP moderate Hugh Scott of Pennsylvania for the Senate minority whip's post and then joining Senate liberals the next day in condemning the United Nations for censuring Israel for its attack on the Beirut, Lebanon airport. . . . If his present liberal streak continues," the ACU added in its publication, "he may make Ohio voters wish they had stuck with former Sen. Frank Lausche."[5]

Because I stood beside a few liberal Republicans and a Democrat or two, *The Wall Street Journal* wrote of me, "If he isn't yet a bomb-thrower, he certainly has been tossing a few firecrackers. . . . The 53-year-old Mr. Saxbe seems quite unruffled by all the fuss—and indicates he plans to continue to follow a markedly independent course."[6]

Obviously my firecrackers didn't attract a lot of attention outside Washington and Ohio. On the February 3, 1970, television show, "Jeopardy," none of the three contestants was able to name me as an Ohio senator. I wrote to show host, Art Flemming: "As you may know, we here in the Senate have our own little show every day about the same time yours is aired. Only we play a kind of "Reverse Jeopardy." We get all the questions and are supposed to find the answers. Sometimes we, too, come up empty."[7]

Early in my term I initiated the Wednesday Group. At informal luncheons, a few moderate-to-liberal freshmen GOP senators gathered to discuss policy and political matters. Among the original members were Senators Charles McC. Mathias Jr. of Maryland, Richard S. Schweiker of Pennsylvania, and Marlow W. Cook of Kentucky. We became known as "The Fearless Four" for our willingness to oppose the president. Later the club expanded to include ten to twelve additional moderate senators. Some of the Republican senators who came later were Lowell P. Weicker Jr., Connecticut; Jacob K. Javits, New York; James B. Pierson, Kansas; Clifford P. Case, New Jersey; Charles H. Percy, Illinois; Ted Stevens, Alaska; Mark O. Hatfield, Oregon; and Charles E. Goodell, New York.[8] We were not well regarded by the White House, where we were viewed as a bunch of renegades.

Wearing a "Charlie Goodell is a good egg" button, I joined other Wednesday Group members on a campaign swing in Albany, New York, October 26, 1970. We did this for Goodell, an ultraliberal Republican ignored by Nixon and slammed verbally and publicly as a "radical liberal" by Vice President Agnew. Joining me on the campaign trail were Javits, Percy, Cook, and Hatfield.

Nixon viewed Goodell as a radical, and he told his political staff in September 1970 that "we are out to get rid of the radicals.... We are dropping Goodell over the side. Everyone knows it.... Of course, if I thought Goodell had a chance of winning, we would be for him. Since he doesn't, we drop him over the side. This is a signal for others to stick with us in the future. Let's be tough."[9]

I got "tough" in my speech at a GOP luncheon in Albany. I pointed out that the New York race Goodell eventually lost to Conservative James Buckley would "determine whether the Republican Party will accept new ideas or whether we're going to write off the young and the black and just concentrate on the middle. If we do that," I said, "we're headed for a political catastrophe."[10] That's exactly where Nixon/Agnew took us.

Agnew was not a favorite of mine, and I said so on several occasions. I found him to be divisive within the party. In fact, shortly after my campaign swing for Goodell, I told the press that I could think of "thousands" of Republicans who would make better vice presidential candidates than Agnew. In that same interview, I referred to two of Nixon's assistants, John D. Ehrlichman and H. R. Haldeman, as "Nazis," because they epitomized the strong-arm tactics the White House used to keep its "sheep" in Congress in line.[11]

I felt much the same way about Sen. Robert J. Dole, R-Kansas, when in late 1970 he ran hard for GOP national chairman. I saw him as a negative, narrow man who clearly was "a hatchet man in and out of the party.... We can't go around making enemies" if we expected to win the 1972 elections, I maintained. "We are not going to win with the image of a reactionary farm-bloc policy."[12]

One of the more visible battles I entered was the 1969 debate on the administration's proposal for the deployment of the Sentinel antiballistic missile system. It was a hot issue that consumed the Senate for twenty-nine days, at the time the sixth longest deliberation since 1945. So volatile was the issue that it often was called "Nixon's Vietnam," and it had a lot of senators running for cover. GOP freshmen senators in particular were expected to vote with the administration—in other words, to be seen but not heard.

Nixon saw ABM as a "bargaining chip" in the SALT (Strategic Arms Limitation Talks) with the Soviets and "a turning point in America's credibility. I knew that a vote on ABM would reverberate around the world as a measure of America's resolve" to stand up to the Soviets, he said.[13]

"The Fearless Four" (Schweiker, Cook, Mathias, and I) felt compelled to let the White House know of our opposition to the Sentinel ABM system.

"From the scientific and military standpoint," we said in a letter to Nixon on March 13, "there is grave doubt that the Sentinel could function effectively against increasingly complex weapon systems and amidst the chaos and confusion of a nuclear attack." Later other members of the Wednesday Group joined us, such as Goodell and Hatfield. I also hooked up with Democratic Sen. Gaylord Nelson of Wisconsin as a bipartisan cosponsor of the National Science Advisory Committee on the ABM.

The following day, March 14, Nixon announced a modified version of the system, called Safeguard. Instead of protecting cities, as the Sentinel system would have done, Safeguard would protect a dozen intercontinental missile launch sites.

The opposition activity from "The Fearless Four" and others stirred up the White House as the vote neared on ABM. Agnew did considerable arm twisting, making calls to GOP senators and warning them that a vote against ABM was a vote against the administration. For Nixon, it was "war."[14] At his press conference on April 18, Nixon was asked about the pressure being applied to Senate party members.

"I want to make it crystal clear that my decision on ABM was not made on the basis of Republican versus Democrat," he said. "It was made on the basis of what I thought was best for the country. . . . I respect others who disagree with me on this. . . . I am going to fight as hard as I can . . . but [the battle] is going to be fought on the basis of asking each Senator and Congressman to make his own decision."[15] Quite a different picture is painted in "Nixon—The Triumph of a Politician." Historian Stephen E. Ambrose details Nixon's determination: "Nixon put more effort, and more of his prestige, into ABM than any other issue in his first year in office. As the vote approached, he told political counselor Bryce Harlow, 'Make sure that all our guys are there [to vote]. Don't let anyone get sick. Don't even let anyone go to the bathroom until it is all over.'"

Harlow sent Nixon a memorandum (July 1, 1969), saying that I had a $250-thousand campaign debt.[16] The Ohio Republican Party was ready to pay it, in the process letting Saxbe know that he "was wrong in opposing the President on the ABM." The party leaders thought the message would get through "loud and clear" and felt that holding up the money until Saxbe publicly promised support for ABM would be counterproductive. On the memo, Nixon wrote, "I disagree—make the deal tougher with Saxbe—he doesn't understand anything else."[17]

On August 6, 1969, the Senate voted on three amendments to the bill, and I voted against the administration each time. Sen. Margaret Chase Smith, R-Maine, introduced the first two amendments. Her second, to restrict ABM funding, ended in a tie. Agnew's deciding vote in favor of the legislation gave Nixon a victory.

A year later I cosponsored the Cooper-Hart amendment to delete $322 million for deployment of Safeguard. I voted for it and against the administration's position once again. As I told my constituents, my vote in opposition was based on three key factors: deployment of the Safeguard ABM system would contribute to the arms race; the high cost of an ABM system was another step in the skyrocketing military expenditures at a time our domestic needs, particularly in social services, were so great; and I didn't believe the ABM system, as proposed, would work or be effective.

Nixon didn't forget my role in the ABM vote or my opposition to the Vietnam War and his Supreme Court nomination of Judge Clement F. Haynsworth Jr., two subjects I will discuss in detail later. In a "Dear Bill" letter dated December 11, 1969, he both chided and praised me:

> We have had our differences this past year—some, to my regret, aired publicly. I hope for fewer ahead—and none public.
>
> But I do want to take specific note of your blemishless record of opposition to fiscal irresponsibility, in your votes on the parade of grotesque amendments to the tax reform bill. I do not construe those votes as votes for Nixon; I do regard them as proof that we stand together for responsible management of this government.
>
> And for that, I am greatly pleased.[18]

I received a number of "Dear Bill" letters from Nixon. One, in which he thanked me for helping sustain his veto of the Political Broadcasting Bill limiting campaign spending, was rather amusing. "It was most helpful to the final effort and I want you to know that I appreciate how difficult this was for you," he wrote. Actually, I supported the bill initially. During the Senate effort to override the veto, I paired myself with the ill and absent Sen. Carl E. Mundt, R-South Dakota, and eliminated any vote I might have made to override. Nixon was grateful for that.

During my time in Washington, much was made in the press about my trips. My first two came back to back four months into my term. During the April 1969 Easter recess, I went first to the Ninth Mexico–United States Inter-Parliamentary Union Conference in Mexico for six days, then I flew directly from Mexico City to Anchorage, Alaska, to join a fact-finding tour by the Senate Labor and Public Welfare subcommittee on Indian Education. My being there at first caused eyebrows to be raised, then my not being there erupted into a furor of sorts.

"Republicans are groaning over Saxbe's disdain for the customs and etiquette of Washington political life," reported the *Cleveland Plain Dealer*.[19] The groans were heard after I elected to go to Alaska with subcommittee chairman Sen. Edward M. Kennedy, D-Massachusetts, eschewing a White House dinner honoring Ohio's Ray Bliss, retiring chairman of the GOP National Committee. Dolly and Rocky went instead. As I explained, Kennedy asked me first, but subsequent events in Alaska earned me even more press.

Upon arriving in Anchorage on April 8, I joined what was, quite literally, a circus. Not only were there forty or so in our delegation, there also was a score of newsmen, plus Kennedy's and the subcommittee's staff aides. Their interest was in Kennedy, the heir apparent to the family's political fortunes following the assassination the previous June of his brother, Sen. Robert F. Kennedy, D-New York.

The first day we flew to Bethel, in western Alaska, and visited three Eskimo villages near there. I thought it was a humiliating experience for the native Eskimo, being put on stage like that. Clearly we were invading the privacy of the Alaskan natives, rubbing their noses in their poverty. But what really turned me off was our visit to a tiny hospital in Bethel. We swarmed through the wards with muddy boots, bumping into people, going into maternity wards. The pushing and shoving by the staff people and the media was outrageous—and it went on all day.

I decided that night that I had seen enough and made arrangements to fly back to Washington. I didn't tell Kennedy I was leaving because I figured he was asleep. Republican Senators Murphy and Henry L. Bellmon of Oklahoma also pulled out of the trip, but I did not know that at the time. I acted independently.

I had no gripe with Kennedy. I wouldn't have seen anything if it hadn't been for him. Several times he pulled me through the crowd so I could talk to the people, too. But his staff was determined to let the press get photographs of him and only him, elbowing out the rest of us. I'm not good at elbowing my way to the front.

When I got back to the Washington office, I ran into Rakestraw. He asked me what happened. "Did you have a falling out with Ted Kennedy?"

"No," I replied. "I just broke a bottle of bourbon in my suitcase, and I didn't have any other clothes to wear, so I came home."

Dolly and I were off again October 24, 1969, for a fifteen-day tour of Russia, India, Pakistan, Thailand, Korea, and Japan with seventeen other senators and representatives and their wives. The Inter Parliamentary Union and the Senate Foreign Relations Committee sponsored the trip, aboard an air force plane.

In Moscow they put us up in suites in an old hotel. We talked into the lampshades the entire time because we figured everything was tapped by the Soviets. Whether it was or not, I don't know. One member of our delegation—I don't remember who it was now—had a suite that had five pianos in it, and he didn't even play.

I didn't go on every trip available to me. For instance, in July 1969, I refused to take part in a NASA-sponsored congressional junket to Cape Kennedy for the launch of Apollo 11, even though I was a member of the Senate Aeronautical and Space Sciences Committee. I saw no reason in the world why so many people (454 congressmen and their guests, plus 33 who went alone) should have an expense-paid trip to see the event, with taxpayers footing the bill.

After all the noise in Ohio and Washington that I "wasn't voting right," my first year ended on a positive note. The *Ohio Republican News* reported on January 10, 1970, that I voted in favor of Nixon proposals nearly 80 percent of the time in 1969. Among twenty-six key issues I supported were ratification of the nuclear test ban treaty; the 5 percent income tax surcharge extension; the military procurement bill; the foreign aid bill; a bill deferring closing Job Corps camps; and the confirmation of Chief Justice Warren Burger.

Those percentages came out of my office. Not everyone added up my voting record the same way. The *Congressional Quarterly* reported that of nine major issues on which Nixon took a stand, I opposed five. Americans for Democratic Action gave me a sixty-one, meaning I took a "correct liberal" stance 61 percent of the time. From the conservative Americans for Constitutional Action, I voted "conservative" only 27 percent of the time.

I never did like labels such as conservative or liberal. They meant little. So, I just continued to do my job as I saw it. I had no idea that the growing specter of Watergate soon would affect me, too.

Vietnam All Over Again

It was no secret that I opposed the nation's overcommitment in Vietnam, and I repeatedly said as much during the Senate campaign in 1968—and before even that. I believed that trying to put backbone into Vietnam was like trying to push a truck uphill with a towrope. Furthermore, I felt it was a war that could not be won and believed strongly that we should pull out.

At the time, the Johnson administration couldn't decide whether Vietnam was a political or a military war. If it was political, then I felt it was time to bring the boys home. If it had a military objective, then I urged that the military take charge and win the thing. The nation just wasn't going to stand for ten years of stalemate, and I was right in saying that.

Speaking those things as a candidate in Ohio and saying them as a freshman senator in Washington were two different things, though, as I was to quickly find out. I voted against the White House in favor of a Senate resolution that reaffirmed the Congressional role in foreign affairs; opposed the president's proposal for an antiballistic missile system and his nomination of a Supreme Court justice; and suggested publicly that the war would bring down Nixon, just as it had Lyndon Johnson. In Ohio, the GOP natives became restless.

One letter opposing my stands was typical. It came from a Cincinnati supporter, and it appeared in part in *The Wall Street Journal*.[1] I suppose he was a supporter at the time of the campaign. In any event, he wrote: "Had we wanted a left-winger to represent us, we would have voted for Jack Gilligan. At least he was honest about his liberal persuasions." During the 1968 Senate campaign, I suppose I did appear conservative up against Cincinnati City Councilman John J. Gilligan, but then almost anyone would have. When I arrived in Washington, I discovered that the Senate was ultraconservative, and in some eyes that put me a little to the left of center. Gilligan himself said of my performance in Washington: "If I had known Saxbe was going to act like this, I would have voted for him myself."

In any event, getting back to the matter of the Vietnam War, I thought it was wrong and said so. If there ever was a war fought with one hand behind our back, that was it. We learned nothing from Korea.

After he took up residence in the White House, Nixon made it a point to invite freshmen senators over for a little heart-to-heart chat in the Oval Office. It was May before he got around to my name. I don't know if the lateness of the invite had anything to do with my criticism of some administration proposals, but he was very cordial. Perhaps my endorsement of his Vietnam speech May 14 helped his demeanor towards me. It was Nixon's first speech on Vietnam as president, and I thought it was a good one. He proposed an eight-point peace plan that included an internationally supervised cease fire and the withdrawal of all foreign troops from South Vietnam a year after a peace agreement was reached.

President Nixon took his time in inviting me to the White House. White House photo.

"I commend President Nixon for his speech of May 14," began my remarks entered into the *Congressional Record* of May 20, 1969. "I thought it was a fine speech. The president demonstrated most convincingly that he realizes the war must be brought to a peaceful but honorable conclusion as rapidly as possible. I have said for many months that American troop withdrawals should begin as soon as possible, hopefully by this summer. From his statements, it is apparent that troop withdrawals are a key part of Mr. Nixon's thinking as well."

The day following Nixon's speech (May 15), the White House canceled the president's planned speech at The Ohio State University graduation, ostensibly for fear of antiwar demonstrations. To get out of the commitment, the White House scheduled a meeting in Midway Island with South Vietnamese Premier Nguyen Van Thieu. "The scheduling process was used to create a conflict which would provide a reason for not attending an event that would cause problems because of demonstrators," according to H. R. Haldeman.[2]

Sitting together on the sofa in the Oval Office, Nixon and I talked for an hour and half on a wide range of issues—from taxes and relations with the Soviet Union to, of course, Vietnam and ABM missile defenses. He wanted me to be a part of his team on the Hill on these and other issues.

When I came to Washington, I was anxious that Nixon succeed. I wanted him to be a great president. We had met first when he was vice president in the Eisenhower administration and I was Ohio attorney general. We had lunch in his private office in the Senate building, just he and I and a Duke University Law School classmate of his, Lyman Brownfield, who also was from Columbus. I was impressed: I never had met a vice president before.

I seized that occasion to introduce my sixteen-year-old son, Bart, to Nixon. "He was very gracious and asked me where I was going to college," Bart recalled. When he said he wanted to attend Harvard, Nixon said, "That's the problem. All the bright kids in America want to go to Harvard, and they ought to realize that there are lots of other good schools out there." Nixon suggested Bart should consider Whittier College, which Nixon attended. Bart wound up at Amherst College.

After he narrowly lost his bid for the presidency in the 1960 election, Nixon came to Columbus on private business. I still was Ohio attorney general, so we broke bread together once again at a private luncheon set up by Gen. Carlton S. Dargusch Sr. in a suite at the Neil House—just the three of us. Dargusch, who served as tax commissioner in Gov. George White's administration, later became a law partner of mine.

In 1968 Nixon and I spent time together on the campaign trail in Ohio. He campaigned in Ohio at least three times, maybe more. I remember introducing him at an August rally in Columbus at which he told stories about his father's days in Columbus as a motorman for the Columbus Street Car Company.[3] That year, both in Ohio and nationally, Nixon squeaked by with a narrow victory over Hubert H. Humphrey and George C. Wallace, carrying Ohio by ninety thousand votes. I wouldn't say I rode to victory on his coattails: I ran ahead of Nixon statewide. Nevertheless, I appreciated his support.

You have to remember that the Democratic candidate running against me lost his own Hamilton County by nearly eighty-seven thousand votes. I received about 63 percent of the vote there, considerably more than the 51.5 percent I received statewide. But I would rather carry my hometown than any other place in Ohio. That's where people know you, and if you can't have their support you shouldn't be in politics. I had a five thousand-vote margin over Gilligan in my own Champaign County.

When I got to Washington, I felt I owed Nixon my loyalty for the support he had given me and the whole GOP ticket during the campaign. I wanted to be a part of the "team." As we talked that May day in 1969, in the Oval Office, it was obvious to all but a stunned mullet that Nixon wanted my allegiance—to the party line; to him as president; and to the administration's agenda, including his most recent Vietnam peace initiatives. I suppose I had been somewhat of a thorn in his side on that issue. Nixon knew my position; as I said, it was no secret. I thought the Johnson administration had not come to grips with resolving the war, either politically or militarily. The president explained to me in some detail the military and political issues he faced with Vietnam and how important it was to the administration to present a united front. Finally I said, "You know, Mr. President. This is [Lyndon Baines] Johnson's war, and you've got six months to wind it up. If you don't, it's going to be your war."

That's what I remember having said. In his 1990 memoir, *In the Arena*, Nixon remembers the remark a little differently. He writes, "As one of my supporters bluntly put it, you can withdraw our troops now and put the blame for whatever happens on [John F.] Kennedy and Johnson, who sent them there. If you continue your policy, it will become Nixon's war."[4]

Nixon goes on to explain that if he had made Vietnam "Nixon's war," he would not have had the political support he needed "to give my policies of troop withdrawals and Vietnamization a chance to work. Instead, I had to make it *America's* war, something no president had yet attempted to do."[5]

At the time of our chat in the Oval Office, telling the president the blame for the war might end up in his lap apparently was the wrong thing for me to say. I was not invited back to the White House for two years.

A few months later he told a cabinet meeting that he wished "everybody would 'shut up' about the war" for just one month. Then "we would be a long way toward getting it over."[6]

My views on the war didn't change following the meeting with Nixon, but I believe I may have been somewhat more temperate and restrained in my public remarks. Sen. George D. Aiken, a moderate Republican from Vermont, listened as I suggested that the only way to get out of Vietnam was to say we won and pull the troops out. Aiken made speeches to that effect and got his name in the paper, but I was the one who set him up.

In Henry Kissinger's opinion, "Nixon was probably the only leader who could disengage from Vietnam without a conservative revolt."[7] Yet Nixon's secretary of state believed the hatred of Nixon's flaming partisanship and the "virulence of dissent" throughout the nation deflated foreign policy initiatives and "destroyed any compassion for the complexity of the task the Nixon Administration had inherited" from the administrations of John F. Kennedy and Lyndon Baines Johnson. "By the end of Nixon's first term," Kissinger wrote, "rational discourse on Vietnam had all but stopped, the issue was fought out by recrimination and vilification in the Congress and the media and by demonstrations and riots on the campuses and periodically in the streets."[8]

The war dragged on, of course, and all the while the opposition to it at home grew larger. People were becoming very uneasy, particularly the young folk. One of those who was unhappy with the lack of closure to the war was my own son, Rocky. And that led to a revelation that I did not know until I began this book. I'll let him tell it.

When I graduated from Columbus Academy, a private school, in 1965, I decided to go to Southern Methodist University in Dallas because I wanted to be out from under the shadow of my father. He was Ohio attorney general at the time. It wasn't that I wasn't proud of him; I was. I just felt I had to live my own life and have a conversation with someone without being asked, "Are you Bill Saxbe's son?"

In December of 1967, my junior year in college, I was dating this girl from Chicago. I liked her a lot, but she also had a hometown boyfriend. Finally I told her she had to make a choice: him or me. She told me, "Well, put that way, it's him."

The next day I walked into the smu Student Center, and the Marine Corps recruiter was there in the lobby. I walked up and said,

"Where do I sign up?" I suppose had it been the French Foreign Legion recruiter sitting there, I would have joined the Foreign Legion. I was feeling sorry for myself and decided that this would be a macho demonstration of what a hard guy I was.

I called Dad and told him. At first there was silence at his end, then he said, "Well, you don't have to be crazy to join the Marines, but it sure helps."

I didn't have the courage to back out at that point because I didn't know how I could explain myself to either one of my uncles (both of whom were in the Marines) or my dad. Everyone seemed fairly proud that I had chosen to do my duty, and to some extent, I felt that I was trying to please my father, and so I was stuck.

As I said, I never knew the reason Rocky joined the Marines. I always thought he joined because he was the son of a public official and believed he had an obligation to do so. If he had gotten killed because of that, I would have felt very guilty.

Rocky completed his ten-week officer candidate training at Quantico before he graduated from SMU in May 1969. Dolly and I went down for his graduation, and we had a wonderful party for him and his friends. Graduation day I swore him in as a Marine second lieutenant, and then for graduation itself he put the cap and gown on over his uniform. It was a potboiler in Dallas and the last thing I would want to do is put on more clothes. But, that is what Rocky wanted, which led to an amusing—albeit somewhat macabre—exchange between him and the mother of a fellow graduate.

"What is this uniform you have on?" the mother asked Rocky.

"I was just sworn into the Marines."

"Are you going to wear that to graduation?"

"Yes. Why?"

"Boy!" she exclaimed, thinking of how hot it was going to be for him. "You're going to die in that uniform!"

With all the young men dying in Vietnam at the time, that is the last thing Rocky wanted to hear!

I was a senator at the time of his graduation and already was doing battle in Washington. Rocky went on active duty in August 1969 and was assigned to Quantico, which put him close to his mother and me. Even before graduation, he had been to a White House affair, escorting his mother to a dinner April 10, 1969, while I was on that trip to Alaska with Sen. Edward M. Kennedy.

That fall I felt optimistic about the conduct of the war in Vietnam—too

Just before his 1969 graduation from Southern Methodist University, I gave my son Rocky the oath as an officer of the United States Marine Corps.

optimistic in hindsight. At a Cuyahoga County Republican fund-raiser in Cleveland, on September 11, 1969, I all but declared victory. "We have stopped the invasion from North Vietnam," I said, "stabilized the government of South Vietnam, furnished supplies to the South Vietnamese, opened up supply routes, and trained the South Vietnamese army. It is time to announce our mission accomplished . . . and withdraw."

Less than three weeks later, though, I took the floor of the Senate to declare that "any hope of military victory was abandoned when we failed to isolate the battlefield—one of the basic rules of combat—and destroy the enemy." My remarks were prompted by an invitation other senators and I had received to attend in Washington the nationwide Vietnam moratorium—a general strike—scheduled for October 15.

Across the country the antiwar protests and demonstrations—some of them violent—swelled to hard-to-ignore numbers. I did not view them as in keeping with what I believed to be the good order of our country. Furthermore, I felt such demonstrations cut the ground from under our troops serving in Vietnam.

"This so-called moratorium indicates an ingenious effort to create a snowballing effect," I told the Senate. "That is, one day in October, two days in November, three days in December, until such time as we would have a week of riots, and hell-raising and national disruption. . . . I want to state unequivocally that I want no part in such an effort as this," I said.

Sen. Charles H. Griffin, D-Mississippi, took the Senate floor to commend me for my remarks that went "right to the point." He called me "a courageous Senator" who "speaks his mind. I do not always agree with him, but I always respect him."

The October 15 moratorium took place without me, of course. Some two hundred fifty thousand protestors marched in Washington alone. Before he went to bed that night, Nixon penned a note to himself: "Don't get rattled—don't waver—don't react."[9]

In February 1970 Rocky was reassigned to Camp Pendleton, California, for ten weeks. While in California he associated with a group of antiwar activists, and even though he was proud to be a Marine, he developed some real misgivings about the war and the unwillingness of Congress and the Nixon administration to end it.

"My friends on the campuses of Ohio State and California became more active, more radical and more militant," Rocky said, "and I sympathized with them. When we went into Cambodia, that seemed to me to be one of the last straws, that Nixon had cast his lot with escalating the war and that was it. I thought it was a big, big mistake."

In one of his most controversial foreign policy decisions, in April 1970 Nixon ordered the bombing of "sanctuaries in Cambodia from which the North Vietnamese were launching hit-and-run attacks on our troops and jeopardizing our withdrawal program," Nixon said. "The Joint Chiefs of Staff unanimously urged elimination of these sanctuaries in order to protect the lives of our forces and those of our South Vietnamese allies."[10]

The 3rd Marine Division was part of the first withdrawal of twenty-five thousand troops announced by Nixon June 8, 1969, during a meeting at Midway Island with South Vietnamese Premier Nguyen Van Thieu. At that time, United States forces in the war zone peaked at 543,000. Now, a year later, the only Marine division there was the First, and Rocky felt he should be there, too.

"I wanted to get out of the United States because I didn't like what was happening," Rocky said, "and I was sympathetic to the people who were protesting the war."

Having volunteered for duty in Vietnam, Rocky returned to the East Coast in the summer of 1970 to begin training in helicopters and small aircraft at New River Marine Air Station, North Carolina. That was just after the May 4 tragedy on the campus of Kent State University at Kent,

Ohio. National Guard troops had shot and killed four students and wounded nine others in an antiwar demonstration that had gotten out of hand.[11]

I wasn't very sympathetic to the people demonstrating there. I'd been in the National Guard a long time and in the army, and I knew damn well that when you've got a bunch of half-scared kids out there with loaded rifles, most of whom have never even shot a rabbit, you'd better keep away from them.

You never send a boy to do a man's job. You send men out with shields and clubs; you don't send them out with loaded rifles. But the real mistake at Kent State was not shutting down the school. If the students didn't want to go to school and the professors didn't want to teach, who gave a damn? Let them go home.

Nixon issued a statement from the White House: "This should remind us all once again that when dissent turns to violence it invites tragedy."[12]

It also invited Rocky to write what undoubtedly was his most widely read letter and for Bart to charter a plane filled with his associates at the Peter Bent Brigham Hospital, Boston, where he was in residency. My office helped about two hundred of them meet with their Washington representatives to voice their objections to the invasion of Cambodia and the Kent State shootings. Bart was not the activist Rocky was, but he told me how "stupid" he thought both events were. "Invading Cambodia was just pouring sand down a rat hole," he told me, "and the Kent State business was just pouring more and more kerosene on the fire."

Rocky decided to write a letter instead. He had been to the theater to see *Dr. Zhivago* with some of his Marine buddies. In the film there is a scene in which a mother's march is put down by force. "I saw the parallel between that scene and what was happening on the campuses, and when I came back to my quarters on base I wrote a long letter to my dad. I dropped it in the mailbox and felt better about myself."

Rocky's letter did not surprise me; I knew how he felt. It was a good letter. It is worth sharing portions of it once again.

Dear Dad:

It may seem trite to speak out on what's happening here in the U.S. and what I say won't be new to you. I'm not trying to be original, just sincere.

Being in the Marines, I feel I have a strange perspective on the confusion here in the country. I'm going to have to risk my life in Southeast Asia within the next year . . . in a war that hasn't been declared, can't be fought and can't be won. What's more, a war that is contrary to everything I've been taught to believe about America.

Sure, I am not unique. Thousands have already gone, with their minds doubting the purpose of it all. More than 50,000 have died. It's not that I am reluctant to go. I'm actually intrigued by the thought of having to do something exciting and dangerous.

The problem is that in the past year I've come to the realization that our country has fallen so very short of its ideals—not necessarily through unfortunate naive blundering, but because of a conscious effort by a large number of stubborn, uncompromising traditionalists who fear any interference with their projected mission for the United States. . . .

Well, you say, these observations and criticisms are all fairly true, but what do I plan to do about it all? The fact that I can offer no solutions that would satisfy all concerned interests is not important. For the last decade Americans have been electing men who said they had the solutions. You were one of those men.

Going through the campaign, you and many others promised to go to Washington and see that the war was ended in as long as it would take to get the troops out. President Nixon pledged to put an end to the insanity and the war, fight inflation, promote continued social reform and bring us together.

Promises have been compromised, the war has been expanded as it was in 1964 and 1968, the economy has gone to hell, racism has been ignored, and the government has made a strong effort to polarize the country into two hostile camps with no middle ground. The people who have seen the enormity of the problem and have taken to the streets to protest the duplicity of the Administration's words and actions have been ignored by the man in the White House while his internal security forces have been unleashed to beat, maim and kill those who dissent.

The people who are demanding the peace they were promised for 10 years are being portrayed as traitors in order to alienate them from the "silent majority."[13] . . .

The old generation gap concept is no joke anymore. The Indochina war is a war your generation started and continued to preserve your generation's concepts of world order and America's role. My generation is being used to fight that war. Old soldiers never die, just the young ones.

A large number of people are directing all their energies at resisting the war they regard as unjust and unnecessary. The Nixon administration labels them as cowards and traitors. It sends out troops to repress them and even kill them. . . . .

If the war doesn't end soon, I see an underground development that would seek to disrupt the country with arson, sabotage, and assassination. The development is difficult to imagine, but just stop to listen to the words and songs played on current radio programs. No more singing about peace and flowers, but about tearing down walls and killing cops. It's very much for real.

If it comes to a civil war it would, of course, be a slaughter, but the movement is being pushed and radicalized to the point of no return. What else can you expect the youth to do when the alternatives are to go to Vietnam and get blown away? . . .

Hopefully, people like you, Dad, will prevail and get the U.S.A. back on the right track. People like you can save America, but you'd better get busy, because I think the Administration is rapidly destroying the relative harmony that the schools teach kids always existed in the U.S.A.

I love you and Mom very much and hope you can understand what I have tried to say.

I realized the letter represented a deep conviction on Rocky's part, and I told him so in my reply letter to him dated June 11, 1970. I also assured him that "many in the Senate share your concern, and I further assure you that we are determined to do the many things that are on the national agenda." But, I warned that frustration was not sufficient grounds for "even thinking about violence. . . . Disgruntled minorities always have the opportunity to become victorious majorities . . . but if the disgruntled take to the barricades and abandon their legal and constitutional role, they will assure the election of those they feel unresponsive and perhaps pull the whole structure down on their heads with disastrous results to the whole of mankind."

Although I had been relatively silent on Vietnam since my chat with the president, I had to agree with Rocky that the administration had been dragging its feet in bringing closure to the war. As I wrote in my letter to him: "I am convinced that the President does want to end the war. Perhaps he does not feel the urgency that you and I do. I am distressed when he says or intimates that we can both get out of Vietnam and win the war. I do not believe this possible."

Three days later I delivered the commencement address at Ohio Wesleyan University in Delaware, a small Ohio college not unlike Kent State. I told the graduates that provoking confrontations at home, in the neighborhood, or on campus doesn't change our value system.

"You don't do it by burning buildings, no matter how much you might detest or distrust what that building stands for. You don't disrupt the institution because the minute you do, you are disrupting, even destroying, some of the basic values [of] tolerance, compassion and understanding. And finally, you don't cop out because you don't like what is going on."[14]

I urged the graduates to lead by example and by participation in the process. I concluded by saying, "Those who wish us to behave with greatness and generosity as a nation should believe we are capable of exhibiting such qualities. We must believe we can replace brutality with reason, inequity with justice, ignorance with enlightenment."

I was very proud of Rocky's letter and, as any proud father would, I showed it to a number of my colleagues on the Hill, including my friend, Democrat Sen. Alan Cranston of California.[15] Unbeknownst to me, he elected to enter both letters in the *Congressional Record*.[16] The letters, Cranston said, "dramatically point up the conflicting emotions this war has aroused." He identified the authors only as "a fellow member of Congress . . . [and] his son, a 23-year-old officer in the Marine Corps."

Well, it took the news media less than twenty-four hours to figure out who the authors were. After all, not many members of Congress had a twenty-three-year-old son in the corps, if any, besides me. Rocky found out about it while eating breakfast with some fellow officers, one of whom piped up, "Rocky! You can't say this!" There, in the local paper, was the story of the letters.

"All hell broke loose," Rocky said. "All of a sudden I am getting calls from all over the country. I am getting calls from Marine Corps colonels who are telling me they have been assigned to assist me with handling the press. I was surprised the letter was released. Quite frankly, I was a little angry. I said, 'Hey, I want out of here; I've got to get out of here.'"

Pro and con letters also poured into my Washington office. A lady in Oberlin thought it was "a terrible thing . . . to make your private correspondence with your son public. To have it inserted permanently in the *Congressional Record* is outrageous! You have lost my vote!"

A retired Army officer in Columbus asked: "What the hell has gotten into you, Bill?" He called Rocky's criticism "immature and undisciplined" and me "an ex-colonel who should know better." He was wrong there. At the time I was still active as a National Guard officer.

A Gallipolis voter took another tack. He praised Rocky for his "courage, lucidity, and prevision. . . . Surely he is a patriot in the classic sense [performing] a commendable service to the republic by ripping the curtain cast over our grave national situation and stating the facts with singular clarity."

A physician in Sidney wrote: "Thank god for our young people, and your son in particular. It took courage and conviction, but I'll wager he'll be muted in some form." Rocky wasn't.

In August of 1970 Rocky got his wish and was shipped out to Vietnam where he was at first an air observer officer, flying around the Far East in planes. As a matter of fact, they were ov-10 Broncos, a twin-engine turboprop built right in Columbus. Later he was transferred to an infantry outfit until the Marines pulled out of Vietnam. He returned to Camp Pendleton in June 1971, followed by another tour at Quantico before being discharged in August 1972.

The last of the U.S. Marines left Vietnam that same month, but earlier in the year Nixon had ordered the resumption of the bombing of Hanoi and Haiphong harbor after a four-year lull. Nevertheless, it seemed the war was finally winding down, at least as far as our forces were concerned.

After the peace talks in Paris stalled in December 1972, however, North Vietnam was pounded anew by our air force.[17] I thought that was just about the dumbest thing the administration had done up to that point. I had remained relatively silent on the conduct of the war, such as it was, but this time I couldn't be silent.

"The president has taken leave of his senses," I said in an interview that was widely reported but not always very accurately. This is how that interview came about.

The "Christmas bombing" began on December 18. I was home in Mechanicsburg for the holiday when I received a call from a network television affiliate in Washington that wanted to talk to me on camera. I suggested they fly into the county airport at Marysville, about a dozen miles from home, and we'd do the interview there. I drove over, wearing a plaid shirt like I had been working on the farm, and did a five-minute interview. In my opinion, I said, "The president has taken leave of his senses." I thought the president had done something a reasonable man would not have done, and I couldn't find an explanation for his action, which was arrogant and irresponsible.

I also gave a telephone interview on December 28 to Havel of the *Cleveland Plain Dealer*. He quoted me as saying that Nixon "appears to have left his senses."[18] Subsequently, others have put other words into my mouth, sometimes adding an expletive or two, but I never said them.

In any event, Nixon's action, taken without notifying any member of the Senate Armed Services Committee, on which I served, was the height of arrogance. I believed then, as I do now, that my outburst had an impact on the bombing halt later that month. It took strong language to get it done.

A month later the peace agreement was signed in Paris and the cease-fire began on January 27, 1973.[19] That pretty much wound up the war as far as I was concerned. Certainly Nixon and I never had another reason to talk about it.

A Couple of Votes for Justice

The resignation of Supreme Court Justice Abe Fortas in the summer of 1969 gave President Nixon the opportunity to fill a second seat on the court.[1] Earlier in the year, his first nominee, Warren Burger, was confirmed and seated as chief justice. To replace Fortas, Nixon's choice was Clement F. Haynsworth Jr., chief judge of the Fourth Circuit Court of Appeals, from Greenville, South Carolina. Nixon heard the name suggested by several people, but Attorney General John N. Mitchell is credited with proposing the nominee after sifting through a list of more than 170 candidates. At the time, Mitchell was the administration's Southern strategist, and the nomination of a Southern conservative was designed to bolster Nixon's vote count in 1972 in traditionally Democratic strongholds where Humphrey and George C. Wallace had run so well in 1968.

From the outset, it became evident that the administration was going to have to rally the troops if Haynsworth was going to be confirmed by the Senate. "Nixon was advised to withdraw the nomination, but he took this sort of political combat far too personally to contemplate such a surrender," writes Jonathan Aitkin in his 1993 biography of Nixon. "'If we cave in on this one, they will think if you kick Nixon you can get somewhere,' he [Nixon] said furiously, instructing his White House aides to twist every available arm in the Senate."[2]

Pressure was applied to those of us who were not committed to voting for the nominee, as evidenced by a series of memos from within the White House staff. They point out what I always maintained: that the White House was cutting and branding, which I did not like very much.

As I was to discover, a number of senior executives in Ohio from such companies as Republic Steel, Phelps Dodge, and General Tire and Rubber were contacted. Each indicated "a strong willingness to help out," wrote Jack A. Gleason in a memorandum to his boss, White House political strategist Kevin Phillips. Gleason went on to write that the support of the executives "stemmed as much from their discontent with Saxbe as any particularly strong interest in Haynsworth. Uniformly, these people seemed almost eager to pin Saxbe down."[3]

A day later Harry S. Dent, special counsel to the president, received a detailed memo concerning my position from Gordon S. Brownell, administrative assistant to the special counsel to the president. It read:

I talked at length this afternoon with John Andrews, Ohio GOP chairman, about Saxbe's vote on Haynesworth [sic].

As of 11:00 A.M., Saxbe told Andrews he is "firmly uncommitted" on Haynesworth [sic].

Saxbe is getting pressure from labor and Negro groups who were behind him in his campaign to come out against Hayesworth [sic]. He personally feels the President has a right to make this appointment and even though he has doubts about several of the Bayh charges, he does not want to go against the President.

Saxbe is miffed because the Attorney General has spoken to him only once since he came to Washington—briefly over the telephone. He has also heard that the Deputy Attorney General has publicly "popped off" against Saxbe and doesn't like this. His queries to Justice have generally gone unanswered and he is not satisfied with most results of his dealings there.

I pointed out how Saxbe could gain back points he lost over ABM by coming out for Haynesworth [sic] and getting behind the Administration. I used Sen. Marlow Cook as an example. Andrews agreed and said he would try this approach with Saxbe.

Andrews, who is pro-Haynesworth [sic], thinks Saxbe will wait and see who needs his vote and how things are when the show-down comes. He doesn't think Saxbe is lost if he is properly handled.

The key seems to be his relationship with the Attorney General.[4]

It may be true that Mitchell and I had spoken but once at that time, but I don't recall being particularly upset by that. I had plenty to occupy my time, and so did he. But we were not bosom buddies, either. I recall the night Dolly was seated next to him at a small dinner party at the British Embassy. He leaned over to her and said, "You know, that husband of yours is kind of an S.O.B., isn't he?" Dolly never missed a beat: "And he speaks well of you, too," she replied.

The White House solicited everyone it could to gain my vote for Haynsworth. A day after Brownell reported that Andrews felt I could be turned if "properly handled," Gleason was advised that Andrews wanted the White House "to stop the pressure on Saxbe." Gleason got that message through Columbus developer John W. Galbreath, one of my good friends and solid supporters, who told Gleason that I was "presently favorable to the President's position."[5] In the same memo, Gleason reported that M. G. O'Neil (unidentified) said I was "indecisive" on my Haynsworth position and that I had expressed "certain strong opinions about the Justice Department and their failure to make his law partner a judge."

That is true—almost. The reference is, I believe, to Ohio Supreme Court Justice Lewis Schneider, but he never was my law partner. I recommended his candidacy for the U.S. Sixth Circuit Court of Appeals. Then Deputy Attorney General Richard G. Kliendienst let it be known in the press that Schneider didn't stand a prayer of being appointed.

Perhaps the "law partner" reference in Gleason's memorandum was to Bob Boyd of Columbus, my former law partner. I believed Boyd to be an excellent attorney, and in February 1969 I submitted his name to Attorney General Mitchell for appointment as U.S. Attorney for the Southern District of Ohio, which included Columbus. His was one of seventy-five names I submitted for various federal posts, but by early spring of 1969, not one of my recommendations had been accepted. As I told the *Cleveland Plain Dealer,* the administration certainly had failed to touch off a "brain drain" from Ohio. In the first three months of my term, only two of the sixty recommended appointments were made.

In any event, on May 28, Boyd asked me to withdraw his name from consideration because, as he said in his letter to me, he had learned "others who were interested in the candidacy of other applicants were making a determined political effort to thwart my attaining this position. . . . I do not feel that I can in good conscience allow myself to become associated with political controversy."

In a letter July 23 to Bryce Harlow, special assistant to the president, I complained about the lack of attention to Ohio's requests. The Boyd case was just one instance in "a number of cases involving patronage where our expressions of interest has [sic] received little attention. In almost every instance our efforts are to no avail, the end result being a lot of wasted time, effort and a feeling of frustration on both our part and the individuals applying for federal positions."

As the leaves began to fall, the administration turned up the heat to gain support for Haynsworth. Gleason sent a confidential memorandum to

Kevin Phillips, stating that my former first assistant when I was Ohio's attorney general, Jerry Donahue, "felt it now possible to get Saxbe to at least begin to think in terms of leaving town rather than vote 'no.' Donahue felt that having Preston Wolf [*sic*] contact [Saxbe] was likely to be productive, but that in the end, if we wanted his vote, it would require Presidential stroking."[6]

Nine days later Dent reported to Mitchell and Harlow, the administration's Capitol Hill liaison, that my vote in favor of the nominee was "doubtful."[7] Obviously the White House crew was confused as to where I stood, for within a week, Gleason dropped another note on Dent's desk: "According to a contact from Bell Telephone, who had been in touch with Jerry Donahue, there are some indications that Saxbe is still available to us. Nonetheless, the report was pretty much contingent upon the willingness of the President to call Saxbe. This does not, however, guarantee that a call from the President will produce the vote."[8]

Dent reported to Mitchell and Harlow that "Nobles Lowe, counsel and vice president of the West Virginia Pulp and Paper Company, [said] his contacts indicate Pearson, Cooper, Saxbe, Packwood, Dodd, Prouty, Jackson, and Spong are okay."[9]

So much for Lowe's contacts, and so much for those who obviously were pretty naive about Ohio politics and me.

Of course, I was hearing from Ohio voters, both pro and con Haynsworth. Many threatened to withdraw their support if I didn't vote for the nominee. At the time, I said they had the wrong sow by the ear if they thought that ploy was going to work. I just don't fetch and carry when some fat cat calls me up. On the other hand, I don't jump through a hoop when some labor guy calls me up and says Haynsworth is antilabor.[10]

One letter in particular I remember from the several hundred my office received. It came from my long-time political ally Fred E. Jones, a Columbus attorney and insurance-company executive. He was upset with me, as you may be able to discern.

Dear Bill:

Permit me to say a few words as your county campaign manager in three different campaigns. For God's sake, do not vote against the confirmation of Haynesworth [*sic*]. You are already in enough trouble in Ohio.

I cannot possibly imagine a tobacco chewing country lawyer not liking this man. Furthermore, you owe *some* loyalty to our President and his party. Best regards.

P.S. I will see you at the Van Darby Club[11] on December 6, assuming you vote to confirm Haynesworth [*sic*].

I voted against Haynsworth, *and* I saw Fred at the club December 6.

Haynsworth was defeated in a fifty-five to forty-five Senate vote on November 21, 1969, the first presidential nominee to fail to be confirmed in more than thirty years. I was one of seventeen Republican senators who voted against Haynsworth, siding with GOP leaders Sen. Hugh Scott of Pennsylvania and Robert P. Griffin of Michigan. I found Haynsworth's judicial record was blemished with antilabor decisions, some questionable stock trading, and a waffling on school desegregation issues. In general I did not think him suitable for the high court nor did I believe him capable of restoring public confidence in the Supreme Court. Of course, that stirred up the folks in Ohio because I sided against the administration and with the Democrats, led by Sen. Birch Bayh of Indiana.

The defeat angered the White House, too, of course; Nixon was reported to be furious at those of us who opposed him on that and on the ABM debate. "The liberals' opposition to Clement Haynsworth rankled and itched," John Ehrlichman wrote. "It was inevitable that the President would try to scratch the itch."[12] And scratch he did. The president was determined to get revenge, outlining a seven-point plan of attack in a memorandum to Haldeman, Ehrlichman, Harlow, and Henry Kissinger. Nixon wrote, in part:

> Since several Senators like Jordan, Saxbe, Schweiker[13] et al have complained about 'White House pressure,' I think the best line to follow in the future with them is not to discuss anything with them and if they complain, simply say we didn't discuss it with them because we wanted to honor their request that we not exert White House pressure.
>
> It goes without saying that those who are in this group should be given completely proper treatment so they cannot have anything obvious to complain about but none of them should get in to see me until I have gone through the list—one by one—of seeing all of those who supported us on these issues. I anticipate that this will take me several months![14]

As a result of my "transgressions," I didn't make the guest list for Nixon's Thanksgiving eve love feast at the White House. The president embraced the faithful—namely the twenty-six Republican senators who cast their vote for Haynsworth—and denounced to the lucky diners those of us who didn't. Nixon told the turkey eaters he was taking our rebuke of his nominee personally.

The second nominee was G. Harrold Carswell, a newly appointed Fifth Circuit Court of Appeals judge and a Southern conservative from Florida. Once again Mitchell was handed the name to give to the president, this time by Gov. Claude R. Kirk Jr. of Florida. In a letter to Nixon, Kirk described Carswell as "a man for all 'regions' as well as for all seasons." I thought Carswell was a better choice, and so did Senator Scott, now minority leader, and the American Bar Association Committee on the Federal Judiciary. Bayh again led the opposition, commenting that "the president has, unfortunately, confronted the Senate with a nominee who is incredibly undistinguished as an attorney and as a jurist."[15] Opponents brought up evidence of racism in Cars-well's background and what some perceived as a lack of judicial stature.

As the debate continued, I wasn't sure which way I would vote. Early in March 1970, I told members of the press that I was inclined to support the nomination, even though I called Carswell "an inconspicuous type of jurist without any striking qualities."[16] But then, I was tired.

I had just returned from two weeks in Nepal—with stops in New Delhi, Hong Kong, and Guam, also—where Dolly and I were Nixon's personal emissaries to the royal nuptials for His Royal Highness, Birendra Bikran Sha, the Crown Prince of Nepal, and Princess Aishwarya Rajyalaxni Rana. I was decked out in a morning suit and top hat—with my chewing tobacco in my pocket—and five or six service ribbons from World War II and the Korean War on my chest. Some of the guests wore medals as big as dinner plates.

The wedding in Katmandu lasted an exhausting yet festive five days, but inasmuch as the actual ceremony was held at 3:00 A.M., when I suppose the moon and stars were just right, we didn't see it. Nevertheless, I wrote the president, "I believe that I was able to carry off this assignment with dignity and responsibility." Why Nixon chose me to represent him halfway around the world, I don't know. Perhaps—as some suggested—he felt that from that distance I could do little damage to the Carswell cause.

Upon my return, however, it clearly was evident that the opposition to Carswell was growing, as were my doubts. I wrote a letter to Nixon, expressing my concerns. Among them was the matter of "his candor, or rather his alleged lack of it, in connection with his testimony [before the Senate Judiciary Committee] on his part in forming a racially segregated country club." I also suggested that perhaps the president's support for his nominee was "less than wholehearted."[17]

"The charges against Judge Carswell are specious," Nixon replied in his letter to me of March 31. He also laid to rest any lack of support on his part. Carswell "has my total support," he wrote. Then he approached what was for him the nub:

What is centrally at issue in this nomination is the constitutional responsibility of the President to appoint members of the Court— and whether this responsibility can be frustrated by those who wish to substitute their own philosophy or their own subjective judgment for that of the one person entrusted by the Constitution with the power of appointment. The question arises whether I, as President of the United States, shall be accorded the same right of choice in naming Supreme Court Justices which has been freely accorded to my predecessors of both parties.[18]

It was a remarkable letter—reportedly drafted by Presidential Assistant Charles W. Colson—in that neither he nor Nixon recognized the constitutional balance between the executive and legislative branches of government. The president can only nominate, the Senate gives or withholds its consent and both share in the appointment. In an editorial, the *Washington Post* described it as "an arrogant assertion of power. . . . The Senate's best response to this attack—this insult, if you will . . . would be an outright rejection of the nomination of Judge Carswell," the *Post* concluded.[19]

I voted with the administration on that one, but Carswell was defeated by a vote of fifty-one to forty-five on April 8, 1970. Not in seventy-six years had the Senate rejected two successive Supreme Court nominations.

In retaliation and probably in a fit of pique, Nixon sicced GOP House Minority Leader Gerald R. Ford on Associate Justice William O. Douglas. In a speech on the floor of the House, Ford urged that Douglas be impeached for a wide variety of activities linked to liberal causes. Ford used secret FBI files on Douglas, which he secured from Mitchell. That, I believed, was a violation of the public trust. Although there was a House Judiciary Committee probe, the effort died when Mitchell informed Ford that Nixon no longer wanted to pursue that course.

On both the Haynsworth and Carswell nominations, I voted my conscience with the support of Senate Minority Leader Scott, who recommended that I vote the way I did. He also voted against Haynsworth and for Carswell. The other two Republican leaders in the Senate—Griffin and GOP Conference Chairwoman Margaret Chase Smith of Maine—also voted against Haynsworth. Only Smith voted against Carswell. The White House certainly should have had made better use of Scott's leadership on the nominations; he should have been the one carrying the ball for the administration.

I also felt Mitchell had let the president down and said as much a few days later. There would be no great furor in the Senate if Mitchell were to be fired, I said in a speech at American University. In fact, I thought both John and his wife, Martha, exhibited a naivete about government that I found astounding.[20]

My biggest regret in the entire Carswell matter was that it became so partisan. The American people were short-changed because the debates over the president's nominees degenerated into all-consuming, time-wasting partisan political arguments. That was unfortunate.

In their book, *The Palace Guard,* Dan Rather and Gary Paul Gates note that the White House battles over the Haynsworth-Carswell nominations "did much more than end the 'honeymoon' with Congress. It created the atmosphere of distrust and enmity which, from that time forward, would define the administration's relations with Capitol Hill."[21]

12

The Finishing Touches

"Well, ladies and gentlemen, I suppose it won't be any surprise to you to know that I am not going to be a candidate for reelection in 1974."

That was my opening comment at a press conference I held in my Senate office on October 9, 1973. Dolly, in her Red Cross auxiliary uniform, was there, as was my entire staff. It was an emotional time for me, retiring from public office after serving for more than a quarter of a century. It was even longer than that if you count my election as eighth-grade class president in Mechanicsburg.

Dolly urged me not to quit, but it was something I had to do. I had hinted at it for more than two years, and by October 1972 I had decided definitely I would not seek a second term. I informed Ohio GOP Chairman John S. Andrews, Jim Rhodes, and others whom I trusted as being able to keep a confidence, but my decision was not made public at that time. It was important to the party that it have time to approach qualified party members willing and able to run for my seat. But, early in 1973, the word began to leak out that I had made a decision. I continued to stonewall, telling the press I had made a decision without making an announcement. In July, the *Cleveland Plain Dealer* carried a front-page banner headline, "Saxbe to Run Again, Ohio Republicans Say,"[1] but the story was based on the wishful thinking of some of my supporters.

As I mentioned before, one of the reasons I didn't want to continue in the Senate was because I didn't want to have to go out and raise money for another campaign. It was getting more and more expensive to run state-wide; it just was not worth it. Every time you took a dollar, somebody would want two dollars in return in the form of a favor. I didn't like that.

Those who joined my campaign worked vigorously for my election to the Senate. Kyle Brooks, a Cincinnati attorney who ran my campaign in Hamilton County, was one. No one worked harder than Kyle in my 1968 race for the Senate against Gilligan. Through Kyle's efforts, I was able to win Hamilton County by eighty-seven thousand votes, which represented almost a third of my statewide majority. But after I took office, Kyle didn't like the way I was voting nor those with whom I was aligning in the Senate. To air our differences, a campaign associate arranged for us to have lunch in Cincinnati, but Kyle never showed, and he never spoke to me again. I thought, if this is the way you lose friends in politics, I'm not interested in politics.

Robert B. Reich described political fund-raising as an exercise of power by association. "Inevitably, as the politician enters into the endless round of coffees, meals, and receptions among the networks of the wealthy, his view of the world is reframed. . . . The access that the politician provides the wealthy and the access that the politician thereby gains to the ever-expanding network of money reinforce each other."[2]

I went so far as to introduce legislation limiting campaign spending for all candidates for federal office, but the bill died. It never had a chance. Money never was a great interest of mine, especially when it related to political fund-raising. I like money, and I like to live comfortably, but I don't gamble. I'm not even in the stock market. I've never been interested in being a captain of industry, and it doesn't make a bit of difference to Dolly. She'd live in a tent if need be and be happy if we did.

The press asked me why I decided to retire. "Why not?" I replied somewhat flippantly. "I have been everywhere. I've taken every free trip I could." I made no bones about my travels, although others did. I like to travel, and at the time thought it would help me, as a freshmen senator, get a better understanding of international affairs—and it did. As a member of the Senate, and particularly as a member of its Armed Services Committee, I had the opportunity to visit India twice, most of Europe, Vietnam, Laos, Japan, Russia, Thailand, Africa, Argentina, Israel, and almost all the states in the union. Between January 1969 and August 1973 I visited more than fifty countries. It was a great life, and Dolly enjoyed accompanying me on many of my trips.

Shortly after Election Day in 1971, Dolly and I departed for India as guests of the Indian government and Air India, which was inaugurating some new jet service out of Washington. My legislative assistant, Michael H. Gertner, and Sen. Frank Church, D-Idaho, and his wife, Bethine, also were on the trip. In May Church and I had sponsored an amendment for the Foreign Assistance Act that endorsed India's position that aid to Pakistan should be withheld until a political solution to East Bengal, later Bangladesh, could be found.

I only got as far as London where I got a call from the White House, urging me to return to Washington to support the administration's $24 billion tax-cut bill. I did, leaving Dolly, Mike, and the Churches to continue without me. I caught up with them in New Delhi just before Thanksgiving, which we spent at the U.S. embassy as guests of Ambassador Kenneth Keating. The following day we visited a war refugee camp near Calcutta, then met with Prime Minister Indira Gandhi and members of Parliament. On December 1, Dolly and I flew to Lahore in West Pakistan and then on to Islamabad, capital of Pakistan. The Churches did not have visas, and Mike felt poorly, so they returned home. Pakistan President Agha Mohammad Yahya Khan granted me an audience on December 2. He told me, "That woman [Mrs. Gandhi] is not going to cow me." I'll never forget that statement.

I had hoped I could talk some sense into Khan and Mrs. Gandhi to avoid war, but I failed. The following day, while I was flying to Bombay and on my way home, Khan ordered an air assault against air bases in India, which responded by sending troops into East Pakistan to join the Bangladesh liberation army, the Mukti Bahini.

In view of the outbreak of hostilities in the subcontinent, I expected upon my return to Washington that I would be asked by the White House to report on what I had seen and heard in India and Pakistan. Surely, I thought, somebody there would be interested in that, but the administration seemed not to care.

My own interest in the subcontinent never waned. I returned to Bangladesh in August 1973 with Dolly and Bill and Sue Hoiles. On that trip we tried to get visas to enter China, but Kissinger was reserving those for himself and Nixon. While in Bangladesh, we were the guests of Hossain Ali, Bengali ambassador to the United States. I had private audiences with President Abu Sayeed Chowdhury and Prime Minister Sheikh Mujibur Abdul Ramen, and I presented Education Minister Yusuf Ali with forty-six thousand textbooks, a gift from the State Department. On the way home, we stopped in Thailand and Hong Kong.

Three times I traveled overseas as President Nixon's representative, the last time to Argentina in May 1973. The first such trip was to Nepal in 1970, and the second came in October of that year when Dolly and I were in Bermuda for the 350th anniversary celebration of parliament there. On that trip, we met Prince Charles.

Secretary of State William P. Rogers and his wife, Adele, and Dolly and I attended the inauguration of President Hector S. Campora in Buenos Aires in May 1973. Campora was just a figurehead for the Peronistas following the death of Eva Peron. It was pretty wild our first night there. The Peronistas were beating drums and parading around the Palace Hotel where we stayed. We heard shooting, and we were asked not to leave the hotel. The U.S. Secret Service was running around like a bunch of Chicken Littles.

During the inauguration parade it got a little dicey. An angry mob pounded on our limousine, and a couple of people were killed in the rioting. What really frightened me, though, were the two armed security guys we had with us. We called them Henny-Penny and Cocky-Locky because every time they received a negative report, they would come running and say the sky was falling. But it was serious. When we attended the inaugural speeches in the House of Parliament, an anti-Peronistas mob stormed the doors, and we had to escape through the back. There, a helicopter picked up Rogers and me and flew us to safety.

A month later, I spent five days in London, participating in a joint foreign relations conference with members of the British Parliament. And so it went. Every few months there would be an opportunity to travel again, so I'd pick up my suitcase and go.

Not all the trips I took were on Senate business. I often would take off on fishing or hunting trips with friends. For example, a particularly memorable fishing trip was for Atlantic salmon on the Saint Jean River in Quebec, Canada, with John Galbreath of Columbus and Bing Crosby. The crooner was a great sportsman and good company. He later surprised me by sending me a limited edition—very limited—of a Columbia Records recording he made; it was entitled, "On the River St. Jean." To the tune of "On the Road to Mandalay," he warbled the following verse:

> In this wide and brawling river,
>> There are salmon large and small.
> Senator Saxbe from Ohio,
>> He took the biggest of them all.
> He had cast upon the waters,
>> Every fly his box contained.
> He'd done everything he oughter,
>> Only one thing remained.
> With tobacco juice his fly he stained,
>> Then he made his final cast.
> And he got a strike at last–
>> Twenty pounds of fighting salmon
> And his line was dwindling fast.
>> Down the rapids twice they went

'Til this mighty fish was spent.
'Twas the nicotine that killed him
Above the Establishment.

That salmon did weigh twenty pounds, and I did use tobacco juice on my fishing fly, which caused great merriment in camp.

Galbreath, of course, was a good friend, and he and I and his son, Dan, often hunted and fished together. I remember one trip up to the Arctic Circle, Baffin Island, with Dan and a bunch of industry titans, such as Edward N. Cole, president of General Motors; Edwin H. Gott, chairman of U.S. Steel; W. F. "Al" Rockwell Jr., chairman of Rockwell International; Sheldon Coleman, chairman of the Coleman Company, Inc.; and others. Once we got there, though, we couldn't fish because the ice jams were so bad.

In Washington, Nixon faced an ice jam of his own in Congress. Following the defeat of his Supreme Court nominees and the battle over the ABM and other issues, he "began to see the Congress as yet another in the list of enemies." And he mapped out a legislative agenda that included "vetoes, impoundment of funds, use of administrative discretion and executives orders, *and* secrecy."[3]

Columnist Jack Anderson revealed that Nixon's chief of staff, H. R. Haldeman, maintained for the administration a list of "enemies," or as they called it at the White House, "the shit list."[4] Certain GOP congressmen who did not fetch and carry for the administration were snubbed socially, denied patronage appointments, and subjected to petty political reprisals. I had suspected all along that was the method of operation at the Nixon White House.

Having Nixon's henchmen on my tail didn't bother me. Following the November 1970 elections, my seniority rose ten places in the Senate, from ninety-sixth to eighty-sixth. That gained me a seat on the Armed Services Committee. Later I gave up my seat on the Select Committee on Small Business to sit on the Veterans Affairs Committee. Those were in addition to my responsibilities on the Government Operations Committee and the Special Committee on Aging.

Much to the dismay of a few party conservatives in Ohio, I supported the liberal, seventy-year-old Hugh Scott for Senate minority leader when the vote came up in January 1971. In turn, Scott named me one of his five regional minority whips. I became responsible for the twelve senators of six Midwestern states, protecting party interests on the floor and assisting Bob Griffin, minority whip

The post brought me closer than ever to my colleagues, and I discovered that all of them had their idiosyncrasies. Senators Talmadge, Williams, and I chewed tobacco, of course. Others were heavy drinkers. Sen. John Sherman Cooper, R-Kentucky, was deafer than a post, and Sen. John J. Sparkman, D-Alabama, suffered from narcolepsy. As chairman of the Foreign Relations Committee he often hosted visiting heads of state. During a meeting with the king of one of the African countries, Sparkman fell asleep on the king's shoulder. Another time he slept during a meeting in Japan with the prime minister. Fritz Hollings and I kept jabbing him to keep him awake. Sen. George Murphy, R-California, the former Hollywood actor, had had his larynx removed in a cancer operation, so they gave him a speaking device. Until then the Senate had no amplification on the floor. Now everybody has a mike. Poor old Sen. Clinton P. Anderson, D-New Mexico, a fine old guy, had Parkinson's disease so bad. He would try to talk but had great trouble in doing so. Sen. Margaret Chase Smith sat right in front of me, and she couldn't see for beans. She would make notes in letters about two inches high, or higher. She would get two or three words on a sheet of a paper.

I visited Rocky in Da Nang, during an April 1971 tour of South Vietnam, while I was a member of the Armed Services Committee. The war appeared to be winding down at the time, and U.S. troops were being withdrawn. Upon my return, Nixon telephoned to ask about Rocky's welfare and to thank me for the comments I made in support of the administration's withdrawal plan. We also had a private meeting in the Oval Office on May 11, after I had met with his national security adviser, Dr. Henry A. Kissinger. In our forty-five-minute conversation, Nixon told me, "If we turn our back on our Asian commitment we will never again enjoy their trust." Complete withdrawal obviously was not in the cards at that time.

The president also wanted to be sure he had my support for the 1972 presidential campaign, and I did indeed agree to work for his reelection. As a delegate, I attended the party's national convention at Miami Beach in August, which proved to be as dull as dishwater, as I thought it would be. I played as much golf as possible.

I've always enjoyed a round of golf. While in Washington, I was a member of the prestigious Burning Tree Country Club, in Bethesda, Maryland. That led to an amusing incident. A newspaper reporter called the president of the club, Hubert "Red" Schneider, to ask, "I understand that Senator Saxbe has been suspended for urinating in the fairway last week. Is this true?"

Schneider replied, "Of course it isn't true! Saxbe has never been in the fairway!"

Another golfing story developed when Nixon returned from his May

1972 summit meeting in Moscow. I was in Florida, playing golf with Senator Murphy and Vice President Spiro T. Agnew. We got the word to be at Andrews Air Force Base to greet Nixon when his plane landed, so the three of us flew right back to Washington on the vice president's air force jet. Dolly was home in Washington with her friend Billy Smith, and I called and told them to meet me at Andrews. They became very excited at the prospect of greeting and meeting Nixon and all the VIPs who would be there. They gave each other facials, did their hair, got all dressed up in their Sunday best, and headed for Andrews in the limousine. Billie kept saying, "Just think; we'll probably be on television. People in Columbus will see us!"

They waited for us in the VIP Lounge, ogling the "celebrities" gathering there. Neither Murphy nor I had any change of clothes with us; we still were in our golf clothes. I had no interest in participating in the festivities anyway, so I sent Dolly's driver to get her and Billie and drive us all home. They were really upset. They kept saying, "We don't believe it! We don't believe it!" I had ruined their television debut.

That fall, during the presidential campaign, I was one of thirty-six "surrogates" (ten of them senators) for Nixon on the campaign trail, making speeches primarily in Midwestern farm states. Afterwards I received another "Dear Bill" letter from Nixon:

> As I look back to our victory on November 7, I realize how much you contributed to one of the greatest landslides in American political history. Many fine reports came back to me about the extensive travel and speaking which you generously did on our behalf—and your efforts paid off handsomely, especially on your home ground in Ohio.
>
> It would be impossible for me to repay you adequately for all the work you did for our cause during the campaign.
>
> I can only assure you that over the next four years I shall do everything I possibly can to make a record which all Americans, regardless of party, will be proud as we celebrate America's 200th Birthday in 1976.[5]

Personally, I thought it was a lonely landslide for Nixon, because the Democrats maintained control of both houses of Congress and picked up two seats in the Senate. The poor GOP showing rested on Nixon's failure to campaign in states where Republican candidates were challenged. As I recall, he ventured out of the White House only three times for campaigning.

Rocky married Susan Paula Sloan of Columbus in Washington on March

25, 1972. Shortly thereafter, and soon after his discharge from the Marine Corps, he entered law school at The Ohio State University.

That spring I also had an opportunity to make history. On April 19, 1972, Sen. Sam J. Ervin Jr., D-North Carolina, and I became the first senators to argue before the U.S. Supreme Court. As friends of the court, we vigorously defended the constitutional powers of the Senate, the immunity of its members, and its right to discipline one of its own. The case involved Sen. Mike Gravel, D-Alaska, and an aide. Gravel used a midnight session of an obscure subcommittee to read aloud passages from the classified Pentagon Papers. Subsequently, portions of the papers were published and a Boston grand jury wanted the aide's testimony regarding that. Even though I felt Gravel had abused the spirit of rules of the Senate, I argued that neither the executive nor judicial branches should be allowed to dictate the bounds of Congressional privilege if a meaningful separation-of-powers doctrine was to be retained. Ervin and I agreed with Gravel that his aide was covered by legislative immunity and need not testify, but the court voted five to four against us.

In the months following the discovery of the June 17, 1972, break-in at Democratic National Headquarters at the Watergate complex, I was unconvinced that the White House or the Committee to Re-Elect the President (CREEP) had anything to do with it, and said so. I was critical of Ervin's Watergate Committee, viewing it as a "rump court" and an attempt to embarrass Nixon or the jerks he had around him.[6]

My opinion slowly changed, however, as more and more facts were brought to light. I became what *Time* magazine described as an "outspoken" critic of the administration and, as a result, made the cover of the magazine's issue of January 15, 1973, along with nineteen other members of Congress.

At a press conference on April 13, 1973, at my Senate office in Washington, I decried the stance taken by the White House that it knew nothing about the break-in and took no responsibility for it. That, I thought, was like the piano player in a house of ill repute claiming not to know what was going on upstairs. I found it hard to believe.

By mid-September 1973 I had had just about enough of Washington, what with Watergate swirling all around and the foot-dragging and procrastination of Congress. John Galbreath and I took off on a duck and pheasant hunt in Tipperary, Ireland. For me, it was a long, long way from there to Washington, and I needed some time to think through my options. As I later revealed to David Hess, a reporter for the *Akron Beacon*

Journal, I weighed making a run for the 1976 GOP presidential nomination.

I actually thought about throwing in my hat and running for it, but I knew I'd never be able to raise the kind of money and support it would take to make a respectable showing. . . . Even if I hadn't been able to win the nomination, perhaps I might have influenced the thinking and policies of the person who would have gotten elected. . . .

I weighed the impact I was making [on public policy] and discovered that what I was selling, the country wasn't buying. Perhaps I am simply out of touch with the mood of the times.[7]

We had more than four hundred roll calls in the second session of the ninety-second Congress. That was a ridiculous number. The record might show that you made them, indicating you were right on the ball; what it really meant was that you were sleeping in the cloakroom until the bell rang, and then you ran out on the floor like a fireman and voted.[8]

As I told Glenn Waggoner of *The Journal* in Lorain, Ohio, in Washington you are rewarded by the absorption of minutia, but it bored me. I just couldn't seem to force myself to really get down to detailed study, and as a result, I gave things a lick and a promise rather than become the real expert on matters of importance.[9]

Much was made of my voting record, how often I voted, whether I sided with the president, whether I supported the party's position, and so forth. In 1972 I sided with the administration 61 percent of the time, with the conservative coalition 59 percent, and on the side of the GOP 54 percent. My votes agreed with the majorities of voting Republicans *and* Democrats 64 percent of the time.

There were some key votes that year. For example, I voted for the Equal Rights Amendment, the Omnibus Education Amendments of 1972, the minimum wage increase, and general revenue sharing. I opposed the $22 billion Military Procurement Authorization bill because many of the weapons systems in it were just not cost effective. Also, it would have authorized funds for more nuclear carriers than even the Navy said it needed.

Agnew resigned the day after I announced I wouldn't seek another term. A journalist collared me the following day in Columbus after a speech I gave to the Mississippi Valley Tuberculosis Association. "Would you say, senator, that the Nixon administration is one of the most corrupt in history?" he asked. I replied that I didn't know whether it was the most corrupt, but "it's one of the most inept. You couldn't get that ridiculous without a plan. If it keeps on they're going to have to get 'em clown suits. Ineptness is

"You're absolutely right, Bill . . . we'll get rid of the piano!"

My comment about President Nixon's Watergate role captured a lot of press, including this political cartoon by Paul Conrad. © 1972, *Los Angeles Times.* Reprinted with permission.

one thing, but stupidity is something else."[10]

Nixon's administration was coming apart at the seams with each thread of evidence that it was somehow involved in the Watergate break-in and subsequent cover-up. What lay just ahead was a turn of events that would impact President Nixon and his administration even more severely. The press called it the "Saturday Night Massacre." I called it astonishing.

Elliot L. Richardson took over as attorney general in May 1973, replacing Richard G. Kleindienst. At the time, Nixon described Richardson as "a hell of a fellow," but the euphoria soon evaporated. Almost immediately the former secretary of the Departments of Defense and of Health, Education, and Welfare became embroiled in Watergate affairs and those surrounding Agnew's resignation. As attorney general-designate, Richardson named Harvard law professor Archibald Cox as special Watergate prosecutor. Richardson and Cox were sworn in the same day, May 25, 1973, but in separate ceremonies.

At first Nixon agreed to release nine Watergate tapes as directed by federal judge John J. Sirica. I wondered out loud why he hadn't done that earlier. I was convinced that had there been anything incriminating on the tapes, Nixon would have destroyed them long before. I was naive to have such thoughts.

After such high hopes for his new attorney general, Nixon barely reached July before he began to express misgivings about Richardson's ability and willingness to restrict the focus of Cox's Watergate probe, which the president felt had degenerated into a "political vendetta." From the Western White House in San Clemente, California, Nixon wrote to Chief of Staff Alexander M. Haig Jr.: "Instead of following up on the Watergate investigation and either bringing indictments or indicating that there is no ground for indictment, [Cox] is deliberately going into extraneous issues. He cannot be allowed to get away with this. Richardson should take him to task on it but we know, of course, that Richardson will be a relatively weak reed in this respect."[11]

As the summer wore on, Richardson's indecisiveness continued to bother Nixon. Also, the White House staff sniped at the Boston Brahmin for his supercilious attitude and harped on the conduct of his office. Geoffrey Carroll Shepard, associate director of Nixon's Domestic Council, described the "growing displeasure" with Richardson's performance, suggesting the attorney general circumvented the chain of command and failed to be responsive to the administration's pet projects. "The Attorney General's staff clearly feels no need to work with the White House on the *development* [Shepard's emphasis] of policy positions on a multitude of issues," Shepard complained.[12]

Cox pressed the White House for the tapes, which the president had decided not to turn over to the prosecutor. Instead, the White House proposed a "reasonable" compromise, the Stennis Plan, whereby the seventy-two-year-old chairman of the Senate Select Committee on Standards and Conduct, John C. Stennis, D-Mississippi, would alone authenticate the accuracy of the transcripts without turning over any tapes to Cox. Richardson endorsed the plan, although he disliked the idea of firing Cox if the prosecutor didn't go along. Nixon stood firm: "Either Cox takes it or Cox is out," he told Haig. "There is no negotiation with Cox."[13]

Cox rejected the compromise plan, going public about the pressure he was under at a press conference at the National Press Building October 20, 1973. Later that day Richardson resigned rather than fire Cox, setting in motion the "Saturday Night Massacre." Deputy Attorney General William D. Ruckelshaus also refused to dismiss Cox and then quit, leaving the task to Solicitor General Robert H. Bork.

Nixon knew he had made a costly error in judgement. "Looking back over the year (1973) . . . certainly the first major mistake was the appointment of Richardson as Attorney General. Richardson's weakness, which came to light during the Cox firing, should have been apparent."[14]

What was apparent at the time was the administration's need for a new attorney general.

13

Desperate Times

Why? That was my first question. Why would Nixon be interested in me for attorney general? My nomination was, in the eyes of author Frank Mankiewicz, "a measure of White House desperation . . . *somebody* had to be nominated who could be confirmed, and Saxbe was the man."[1]

I'd like to think my selection wasn't quite as desperate as that, but perhaps it was. In October 1973, Nixon certainly had a slew of problems on his hands. War in the Middle East broke out as Soviet-backed Arab troops attacked Israel (October 6); Vice President Agnew resigned after pleading no contest to tax evasion charges while governor of Maryland (October 10); Gerald R. Ford was selected to replace Agnew (October 12); the first indictments in Watergate came down; the so-called "Saturday Night Massacre" stunned the nation (October 20); two Nixon tapes were discovered missing (October 23); U.S. troops went on worldwide alert as Soviet intervention in the Middle East loomed (October 25); and the House Judiciary Committee began a review of impeachment procedures (October 30).

In that tumultuous time, my name surfaced, and I was surprised. Early in October, I made official what many had known for some time: I would not seek another term in the Senate. I was heading home to Ohio. Dolly and I had sold our eighteenth-century Harbour Square townhouse in the spring and moved temporarily into a two-bedroom apartment. You might say we were "downsizing," with the intent of returning to Mechanicsburg. I also had begun the construction of a house in Costa Rica for a winter vacation home.

One time around the ring of that Washington circus was enough for me. The deck was stacked against accomplishing anything of significance. The Senate Democrats held at least a ten-vote majority during the ninety-first, ninety-second, and ninety-third Congresses, and the administration had its own agenda that was difficult to buck with independent thoughts.

I also discovered what I suspected had been true all along. The majority in the Congress spends more time figuring how they are going to get re-elected than in determining the future course of the nation through legislative action. I just didn't like that idea at all.

Furthermore, I didn't want to be any part of a community filled with social planners like Walter Mondale (Democratic senator from Minnesota), and that's the direction we were headed. Nixon had a chance to put businessmen back in the saddle and make the free enterprise system respected again, but he blew it.

Some years earlier I had had a shot at working for the Department of Justice. After I lost my bid to be the party's senatorial candidate in the 1954 Ohio primary, Deputy Attorney General William Rogers approached me. He wanted "a young, personable attorney with public affairs experience" to be liaison between Washington and all U.S. attorneys in the field. I turned him down. Now it looked like I could head up the entire shooting match.

Over the years I have heard many names mentioned as having a hand in my nomination; a few would like to think that if it hadn't been for their divine intervention, my name never would have come to the attention of the White House. Many, though, offered their support—Senators James O. Eastland, D-Mississippi, and Howard H. Baker Jr., R-Tennessee in particular—and I was grateful for that. But it was Rep. William J. Keating, a Republican from Cincinnati in his second and final term, who had as much to do with my nomination for attorney general as anyone—more, in fact.[2] During the week following Richardson's resignation as attorney general, Keating tossed my name out to his White House contacts. His message received no favorable response until he collared former Procter and Gamble lobbyist Bryce N. Harlow, then Nixon's counselor.

Keating's office was across from where a GOP House caucus was being held on Thursday, October 25, 1973. Just before it began, Keating pulled Harlow aside in the hall.

"You're not going to be able to get confirmation [for attorney general] except for one person—Bill Saxbe," Keating told Harlow quietly. "He's the only one with the qualifications, the independence, the integrity—and he can be confirmed."

Harlow's eyes widened. "Bill, he wouldn't take it!" he replied. "He wouldn't want to be a part of this administration!"

"I think he would. Bill Saxbe is a friend of mine. I'll call him and ask. Okay?"

Harlow agreed, and while Keating's secretary put in a call to me in my Columbus office, Harlow quickly called Haig to report the conversation.

"Bill," Keating began, "I just finished talking with Bryce Harlow, and I told him I thought you should be nominated as attorney general." He then launched into a pitch as to why he thought I should.

I laughed. I told him that I didn't think the administration would ever accept me.

"Bill, they just told me that you'd never accept them! Would you be willing to serve if nominated?"

"I'd not only do it, I'd enjoy doing it," I replied.

Keating said he would relay that to Harlow. I walked into the adjacent office of my press secretary, Jim Duerk. "What do you think," I asked after filling him in on the telephone call. "Do you think I should take it if it is offered?"

"Why not?" said the usually loquacious Duerk.

I thought to myself, Hell, why not. Quite frankly, I was flattered that my name should be mentioned.

Keating immediately reported our conversation to Harlow. "Is that right?" Harlow said with more than a hint of surprise.

"That's the gospel," said Keating.

"Okay. I am heading over to the White House to talk with Haig," Harlow said, and the wheels began to turn—quickly.

I had not met Haig at the time he called me in Mechanicsburg late in the afternoon of that Friday. The White House operator reached Dolly, who told her I was attending a black tie dinner at John Galbreath's lovely Darby Dan Farm. Galbreath had invited me to make a few remarks to the football coaches from both The Ohio State University and Northwestern University, whose teams were to meet on the gridiron the following day in Columbus. Business and community leaders were there, too.

I was seated on the dais along with others—a bunch of penguins on an iceberg—when Galbreath was handed a note. "You have a phone call from Washington," he said to me quietly. Haig was on the line. "The President has asked me to discuss with you the attorney general's post in his cabinet. Will you come talk to me about it?" I said I would. When I got back to the dais, I told everyone what had transpired. I felt like a rooster on the roof of the henhouse.

Early the following morning I drove to the airport in Springfield and boarded a U.S. Air Force Jetstar assigned to the White House. I was the lone passenger. I thought about the nomination: I wanted it. Attorney general of the United States is the highest position an attorney can hold. I was tired of the Senate anyway and wanted a challenge. If you bitch about the way things are—and I had bitched as much and as loud as anyone on the

Hill—you should take the opportunity to change them. But first I wanted some answers from the White House.

Upon arriving at Andrews Air Force Base, I was whisked by limousine to the White House for my meeting with Haig and Harlow. The White House was quiet; Nixon was at Camp David. For more than an hour and a half the three of us talked about the possible nomination; some of the events that led up to it, such as the firing of Watergate Special Prosecutor Archibald Cox and Richardson's role in that; and my background, experience, and interest. I said I thought I could get the Department of Justice up and running again. Uppermost in my mind, however, were the concerns I had about Nixon himself. I said I wanted a meeting with the president before reaching any decision

Haig remembered the whole "Saturday Night Massacre" as "a fiasco. So, what we wanted was an honest guy with the reputation of calling it as it is, and Bill Saxbe sure as hell had that reputation. He was so goddamned outspoken that when the White House did something dumb—and we did a lot of dumb things—boy, he'd crack us. He was a remarkably blunt and straight talking guy, but he also was an attorney with a lot of political experience and savvy."[3]

At one point during the discussion with Haig, he asked if I wanted to be considered for special prosecutor, replacing the fired Archibald Cox. I quickly said no.

An interesting sidelight to all that behind-the-scenes activity was a note from William E. Timmons, who succeeded Bryce Harlow as congressional liaison in late 1969. In effect, he was a lobbyist for the administration, keeping his eyes and ears open on the Hill, lining up votes for or against legislation favored or opposed by the administration.

The Timmons note turned up in the National Archives where Nixon's presidential materials are kept. It was attached to a *Detroit Free Press* news story analyzing Nixon's ability to survive impeachment. I was quoted in the article, correctly, as having said that "Nixon is through, finished, in terms of his effectiveness over the next years" and that the harm done to his reputation (by the firing of Cox) was beyond repair.[4]

Dated October 31 and addressed to Haig, Timmons added his comment: "Ha-Ha Hee-Hee." Apparently Timmons found amusing my comments on Nixon, coming as they did from someone soon to be nominated as attorney general. At the time Timmons penned the note, I had met with Haig twice, had a long meeting with Nixon that very morning, and was one day away from Nixon's announcement of my selection.[5]

After my first meeting with Haig, I flew back to Columbus on the air force jet, arriving in time to attend the second half of the Ohio State-Northwestern football game. Already word was leaking out that I was under consideration. Before the game ended, in fact, two FBI agents called me out of my press box seat for a brief discussion. Within hours they had people in the field checking into my background.

For my part, I sought the advice and counsel of family and friends. Dolly, of course, knew from the beginning that I wanted the job, so once again she was willing to postpone our return to Mechanicsburg. She always has been my biggest supporter and always was willing to go anywhere, try anything with me, but I know she was looking forward to going home.

"Some of the things Bill does are unexpected," she said. "Everything that's happened to us is unexpected, which is nice. In fact, none of our children were really planned on; they just happened."

In an interview with a Columbus newspaper, she said, "What this country needs in the attorney general's job is someone with common sense and a good sense of humor. This country is in bad shape and somebody had better get down to business right now. And that's my Bill."[6]

She also described the attorney general's revolving door and the machinations in the Nixon administration as "a bucket of worms."[7] Despite some misgivings among her friends about my climbing into that "bucket," she admitted to being "kind of excited" by the prospect of being the wife of a cabinet officer.

Our houseguests that football weekend were Gen. E. R. "Pete" Quesada and his wife, Kate, two of our closest friends. Both were most supportive, as I knew they would be.

I called Rocky and asked him and his wife, Suzy, to join Dolly and me for Sunday dinner at the Neil House in Columbus. Gene D'Angelo had a Dixieland jazz group that performed there Sunday nights, and I liked to go for the music. As I remember, Ralph Waldo also joined us for dinner.

When I told Rocky what was going on, he said, "Don't do it, Dad. They [the Nixon group] are scoundrels, bad people. I don't want to see you get caught up with them."

"Well, somebody has got to do it," I told him.

Juli and her first two children, Charlie and Carey, were living in Pinedale, Wyoming, at the time, in a one-room cabin about eighty miles from nowhere. I had to insist that a phone be installed there so her mother and I could talk to her now and then. As for the attorney general's job, she was supportive. "To me, I always thought he was the right man for the job, whatever it was," she said.

Bart knew nothing about what was going on. He was working as chief of surgery at the Albert Schweitzer Hospital, in a remote region of Haiti where there was no telephone and no radio or television. "Some guy came down from the states and brought with him a ten-day-old copy of *The New York Times*," Bart said, "and there was Dad on the first page."

In any event, I returned to Washington Sunday evening and received another call from Haig's office, setting up a second appointment for Monday afternoon, October 29. When I arrived at the White House, Haig and Harlow were waiting, along with Melvin Laird, the president's domestic adviser, and J. Fred Buzhardt, special White House counsel for Watergate. Buzhardt was a former Department of Defense counsel and, like Haig, a West Pointer. It also crossed my mind, fleetingly but not without some amusement, that here were the two men who replaced those two Nazis, Haldeman and Ehrlichman. Haig replaced Haldeman as chief of staff and Laird assumed Ehrlichman's duties for domestic affairs.

Again the discussion centered on the job at the Department of Justice, some of the major concerns there, and, of course, Watergate. I wanted to know who was going to be Cox's replacement as special prosecutor and what his role would be. For example, I certainly expected the White House to offer up to the prosecutor any and all information concerning the Watergate affair. But the bottom line for me again was hearing those things from Nixon himself.

By the following day, the press had learned that the FBI was checking into my background, and the White House was polling key senators to determine if I could be confirmed if nominated. I particularly like the comment Sen. Daniel K. Inouye, D-Hawaii, gave the press. He said of me: "He comes across as Mr. Integrity and Mr. Independence."[8]

The press wanted interviews, and I began to get calls at the office and at home. About the only thing I could say was that I was interested, but the matter was not on the front burner until I met with the president.

The news also stirred up the politicians in Ohio. The *Cleveland Plain Dealer,* for instance, quoted Cuyahoga County GOP Cochairman Robert E. Hughes as saying I would be "a potential candidate for president or vice president in 1976" if confirmed as U.S. attorney general. The paper also quoted Montgomery County GOP Chairman Charles D. Ross as saying the appointment could "catapult" me into presidential politics.[9]

To me they were just blowing smoke. Over the years, people told me that I should run for president, but I never took it seriously. On the other hand, I probably would have enjoyed it. It was something I thought I could do, certainly. But frankly, I had had enough of Washington. The money-raising thing for campaigns always embarrassed me; that is one of the reasons I didn't run for the Senate again. All those people who had given me money would come in and try to tell me what I should do.

Ohio's GOP politicians also were all in a lather about my resigning my Senate seat and then being nominated to the attorney general post. It meant, of course, that Gov. John J. Gilligan, a Democrat, had the opportunity to appoint a loyal party member, which he subsequently did: Howard J. Metzenbaum, a Cleveland attorney and businessman. In 1970, Metzenbaum beat John H. Glenn in the Democratic primary but lost the Senate race to Robert Taft Jr.

Rep. John M. Ashbrook of Johnstown was among those upset by the turn of events. "I think the president has taken leave of his senses," he said, cleverly swiping my criticism a year earlier concerning Nixon's decision to bomb North Vietnamese cities.

"It's going to be trouble enough electing a Republican senator because of Richard Nixon," he said, echoing the feelings of virtually the state's entire GOP congressional delegation and its concern for the 1976 elections. "Now he's trying to rehabilitate his sagging image at the expense of the Ohio Republican Party."[10]

Ashbrook was a director of the American Conservative Union, which was three footballs fields to the right of Barry Goldwater. It urged Nixon "to think twice" about nominating me. "This is not an anti-Saxbe move," ACU Executive Director Ron Dear maintained. "We will not oppose his confirmation. But we are shocked that the president would nominate Saxbe and thus permit him to be replaced with a left-wing Democrat."

Then Dear really cut me down to size. He said, "Saxbe is not our kind of Republican, but the point is, we don't want to give up that seat to a left-wing Democrat."[11]

Actually, some of the GOP leaders in Ohio were miffed because the White House didn't consult with them on the nomination. I suspect what they really wanted was the ability to brag that "Nixon conferred with me before nominating Saxbe."

Tuesday evening I received an unexpected call from the former attorney general. I always regarded Richardson as colder than a mother-in-law's kiss, but he was cordial enough and wished me well. I told him I would be back in touch once the nomination became certain.

Apparently Nixon was struggling with having me as his attorney general. Many years later, he wrote: "The political situation created by Richardson's resignation dictated that in order to get my nominee confirmed, I would have to select someone who would not have to contend with charges of excessive personal loyalty to me. Senator William Saxbe of Ohio had long ago established that he was a man without that problem, and as my father would have put it, he was 'as independent as a hog on ice.'"[12]

My meeting with the president came Wednesday morning, October 31. Not wanting to be too conspicuous, I drove up to the front of the White House in my bright red, 1967 Cadillac convertible. On the seat next to me was a pack of Mail Pouch tobacco. Only later did I remember that in the trunk was my waterfowl shotgun because over the weekend I was going goose hunting near Easton, Maryland, on the Eastern Shore, with my friend, Marshall Coyne. Before I left the office for the White House I told Rakestraw that if the attorney general's job interferes with my hunting, I didn't think I wanted it. But I did.

Haig joined us in the Oval Office. Nixon was so friendly I thought he was going to hug me! As we were served coffee, the president began with small talk, laughing about some of the differences we had and some of the comments I had made. He assured me he had not "lost his senses," but that some of his advisors thought I shouldn't be nominated because of remarks the administration found abrasive.

"Mr. President, I am afraid you will have to take me, warts and all," I said.

"Well, this is not of interest to me," he replied, smiling broadly. "We are looking forward from here. I think you can do the job, and we are not going to look back."

Then, with no prompting from me that I can recall, he launched into Watergate affairs. It came out as a stream of consciousness, almost nonstop. He avowed no knowledge of any illegal activity. I asked him point-blank if he was involved in a cover-up of any kind, and he replied, "No." We know now, of course, that from the beginning Nixon knew about the so-called "plumbers" and their break-in at Democratic National Committee headquarters at the Watergate complex June 17, 1972.[13]

Still, as he professed innocence, he tried to make me understand the issues that surrounded the tapes and the taping process. It was all Roosevelt did this and Kennedy did that and Johnson taped so-and-so and "these sons-of-bitches" taped, too. He said Kennedy and Johnson even had microphones under the beds in the White House.

Nixon later recounted this in greater detail for Monica Crowley, author of *Nixon Off the Record*. "Johnson was so obsessed with all of that recording crap," Nixon told her. "I will never forget the day he had me to the White House after I won the election. We had so much to discuss—the

[Vietnam] war, the Soviets, and all that. But one of the first things he did was to take me upstairs to show me the . . . recording contraptions that [John] Kennedy had installed under the beds. Johnson got down on the floor, lifted the bedspread, and waved his hand under the bed. 'Dick,' he said, 'they are voice activated.'"[14]

In February 1969, Nixon ordered that the existing taping system be deactivated, but he had a more elaborate system installed two years later. As it turned out, that was the beginning of the end of his presidency.

The more he talked to me about Watergate, the less plausible it all seemed, but I was willing to accept him at his word. At that time, there was the presumption of innocence. I wanted him to be innocent. When the president tells you he's innocent, you are inclined to believe him or you wouldn't take the job, and I wanted the job. Only after my confirmation did reality creep in, and I learned that he was up to his ears in Watergate—and Haig knew it. I also discovered later that Nixon really thought he could get, in me, a patsy to rubber stamp what he wanted. He was wrong.

After nearly two hours of presidential palaver, I left the Oval Office with the understanding that I had the job. The press, having somehow spotted my red Caddy in the driveway, was waiting for me. I told them that the offer of a job was implied when I met with Nixon, and that I was "relatively sure" the job was mine. The president and I had a frank and candid discussion, I added, and in my opinion Nixon had "acted honorably in all the situations since Watergate."[15]

That comment engendered ire among some of my colleagues on the Hill. It was indiscreet, they said, because as attorney general I could be called upon to investigate the president's involvement. I thought that highly unlikely. It didn't take long, though, for the wheels on the Nixon bandwagon to wobble. Later that day I learned that two tapes, covering key talks Nixon had with then Attorney General Mitchell and former White House counsel John W. Dean III, were missing from among nine the White House had promised to U.S. Chief District Court Judge John J. Sirica. I was upset that the president failed to mention that to me.

That afternoon Haig called me back to the White House to meet with him, Buzhardt, Acting Attorney General Robert H. Bork Jr., and Leonard Garment, special assistant to the president. Laird and Harlow also dropped by. The prime purpose of our two-hour conference was to meet Leon Jaworski, who had arrived at the White House for the first time only that morning, while I was in with Nixon. The sixty-eight-year-old Houston trial attorney, a former president of the American Bar Association, was to be named Watergate special prosecutor, although at that point he hadn't accepted the post. I suppose we were all there to affirm his independence should he accept the job.

I know now that initially Haig didn't see me as a candidate for attorney general. That's why he asked that I come to the White House three times. "I wanted to be able to size him up," he said. "I saw him as a confident, very intelligent and very decisive guy. I wasn't sure of him, but I was impressed by him, and I liked him personally."

Later, when he met privately with the president, Haig told Nixon, "You know, you're not getting a guy who is necessarily on your wave length."

"Look, I don't want to politically nominate a straight shooter. Because a lot of people disagree with me, that has never been a problem with me."

Would Nixon have picked me, all things being equal? Haig was unsure: "I would suspect probably not, because he didn't know Saxbe well enough. He wanted, I think, Herb Brownell.[16] Herb was then old [sixty-nine], and he's one of the guys that we looked at, but he wasn't well enough, and he didn't want to come back into government at that stage in his life."

Nixon never came to any decision easily, Haig recalled. "He anguished over it for long periods and tried to get all of the points of view he could hear and then made his decision, and usually made it alone. In this case, he made it alone."[17]

The president's formal announcement of my nomination came the following day, Thursday, November 1. Before a large group of media in the White House briefing room, Nixon said that not only was I "eminently qualified, but he is an individual who wants to take this position and who will do everything that he possibly can to serve the nation as the first lawyer in the nation." He also made light of the fact that after the Senate I wanted to practice law. "So," Nixon said, "I have given him the opportunity . . . to head the largest law firm in America—the Department of Justice."

In response, I said that I believed I could handle the job and "the problem," which I described as "a crisis of leadership." I had no idea how much of crisis it really was. In my opinion, "Everyone in this country wants to get back to routine affairs and the very difficult things that we have to settle, both nationally and internationally. . . . I am anxious to take this job; I have no reluctance." I also stated that I hoped that Bork, who was to serve seventy-six days as acting attorney general, would continue as the nation's solicitor general.

After shaking my hand and Bork's, Nixon turned on his heel and left the room without ever mentioning Jaworski, who was back in Houston. As

Nixon headed for Andrews Air Force Base and Key Biscayne, Florida, Bork announced the Jaworski appointment. "There will be no restrictions placed on his freedom of action," Bork said.

I didn't see my nomination as a reward to be passed out like the post-mastership of Podunk, I told a reporter. I said I would rather be sitting on my front porch in Mechanicsburg than in the attorney general's office in Washington. But destiny beckoned, and I was ready to follow it—on the run.

A Constitutional Question

When news of my nomination as U.S. attorney general reached the traffic light in the center of Mechanicsburg, there was unbounded joy and rejoicing.

"He's a hometown boy," declared Margaret Emory, for many years the community's postal clerk. "Why, he was just a little fella, no more than ten, when he'd come in to talk to me. When I didn't want to be bothered, I'd give Bill a box of nails, a hammer and a board and send him in the back office to drive nails. He was a nice kid."

Down on Main Street, at George Kratky's dry cleaning emporium, he proudly displayed a picture of "me and Bill" that was snapped during an early state campaign. "He's as common as can be," Kratky said. "He'll give advice to anybody!"

That was true. I was a sluice of information, but it quickly became obvious later the day of my nomination that I didn't have all the answers.

At my Senate office, also, everyone was in a celebratory mood after President Nixon's announcement in the morning. Then, late in the afternoon, the bloom fell off the rose. My press secretary, James A. Duerk, received a telephone call from a rewrite man at *The New York Times*.

"Hey, Vince," Duerk said. "There's a guy from the *Times* on here who says Bill can't be seated as attorney general because of a provision in the U.S. Constitution."

Rakestraw rolled his eyes and picked up the phone. Of course, he knew zip about any such provision.

The rewrite man repeated his story. "Our sources tell us that Senator Saxbe cannot be seated because in 1969 he voted for a pay raise for the cabinet, of which the attorney general is a member. Under the Constitution, he cannot be confirmed and his nomination is therefore null and void."

"His words were like arrows through my heart," said Rakestraw, who scrambled for his Constitutional law books, "because I had no clue about anything he said. So, I told him, 'Oh, yeah, we know about that, and we've considered it.' Well, of course we hadn't."

Rakestraw found the cited passage. There it was, Article I, Section 6, Clause 2 of the Constitution. It states: "No Senator or Representative shall, during the time for which he was elected, be appointed to any civil Office under the Authority of the United States, which shall have been created, or the Emoluments whereof shall have been increased during such time." In a nutshell, it said I couldn't be attorney general because on February 14, 1969, five weeks after I was seated in the Senate, I voted to increase the pay of the cabinet as well as the Congress and certain members of the executive branch. Hell, I was just trying to be generous—and frankly, I needed the money.

Rakestraw found a precedent for remedying the conflict, however. In 1909, Sen. Philander Chase Knox of Pennsylvania was nominated by President William Howard Taft to be Secretary of State. Knox had voted on a pay hike for the cabinet, but Congress passed legislation that enabled him to be confirmed at the salary before the vote.

Rakestraw came into my office, looking pretty forlorn. He told me my pay as attorney general, if confirmed, would be $35,000, or $25,000 thousand less than I thought it would be just a few hours earlier. As a senator, I was making $42,500 annually.

"Well, I'll take the job for free," I told Rakestraw. "I might have to sell the team and log chain, but we'll get by." I also recalled that the nation's first attorney general, Edmund Randolph, was paid $1,500 a year, but he got free firewood. Hell, I was going to have to buy my own Presto logs.

The story in *The Times* the following day appeared on the first page, right below the story of my nomination.[1] Thus, a joyous occasion was somewhat dampened for all of us. It was, you might say, the opening salvo fired at me, now that I had stuck my neck out and signed on with the beleaguered Nixon administration.

On November 5, Acting Attorney General Bork submitted the request for legislation to remove the Constitutional impediment to my appointment, and Senators Gale W. McGee, D-Wyoming, and Hiram L. Fong, R-Hawaii, introduced the bill requested. So, that was being seen to, but other shells were fired in my direction.

The first one was lobbed in from Hong Kong, hitting the newspapers in the states on November 5. It concerned a speech I had made on August 23 to an American Chamber of Commerce breakfast in Hong Kong.[2] A reporter covering my talk for the English-language *Hong Kong Standard* reported, erroneously, on my off-the-cuff remarks in response to a question from one of the guests concerning the Watergate tapes. The reporter quoted me as having said that "I personally wish I had never heard of the tapes. If they're incriminating, they should be destroyed, and I am sure he [Nixon] will, but I think he is right in saying that a president cannot be horsed around in our courts."[3]

Obviously I would not advocate any illegal activity, such as destroying evidence. What I said was—and my administrative assistant Bill Hoiles, sitting in the audience, heard it, too—if there was any illegal activity recorded at the White House, I doubted those tapes would ever be forthcoming. After all, who would keep a snake under the bed? I also said that inasmuch as the president and others knew of the taping, I considered it highly unlikely that anything embarrassing would have been said in those circumstances.

Two months later, in comments I made to the press in Columbus, I said that if there were anything on the tapes, they would have been destroyed long before the investigation even started.

Of course, I was wrong on that point, although in April of 1973, when White House counsel John W. Dean III started singing like a canary about Watergate, Nixon did consider destroying the tapes. The thought came to him again three months later, as Senate Watergate Committee Chairman Sam Ervin, who Nixon described as "the old ass," pressed the White House for the tapes and other documents. On July 12, 1973, in what turned out to be the final taped conversation Nixon had in the Oval Office, Nixon told Secretary of State Henry Kissinger:

"The hell with them. I'll sit on those papers, if have to burn them, I'll burn every Goddamned paper in this house. You realize that? Every paper in this house before I hand them over to that Committee."[4]

He changed his mind about destroying the tapes, however. By doing so, he set the stage for the collapse of his presidency and his resignation.

While the process of my confirmation unfolded, life went on at the Justice Department, but many believed it to be crippled and demoralized. After all, in the Nixon years since 1969 there had been three attorneys general—Mitchell, Kleindienst, and Richardson—and one acting attorney general, Bork. When Richardson flounced out in what has been called the Saturday Night Massacre, his deputy, William D. Ruckelshaus, got the boot rather than accept responsibility for firing Watergate Special Prosecutor Archibald Cox.

I was determined I would not flounce at the first confrontation. As I told a Washington reporter, "Once you give up your job, you're a voice in the wilderness. The only time you can fight is when you have the job. You can be fired, but you don't have to quit."[5]

Now it looked like it soon would be my turn at the Justice Department. The *Wall Street Journal* believed I faced "a staggering job." It had no idea how "staggering," given the skullduggery that was afoot by Justice Department appointees loyal to Richardson and Ruckelshaus. This was confirmed by internal White House documents from the National Archives.

The first indication that something might be amiss was revealed in a memorandum dated November 8, 1973, to Kenneth R. Cole Jr., chief of the administration's Domestic Council, from the associate council director, Geoffrey Carroll Shepard. His subject was "Justice Without Leadership." He wrote:

> With all of the publicity and high level White House concern focused on replacing the Attorney General and the Special Prosecutor, the personnel and policy-making authority for the rest of the Department of Justice has been completely ignored.
>
> Acting Attorney General Bork's near total unfamiliarity with the workings of the Department and his desire to be merely a "caretaker" is resulting in this non-Watergate decision-making process devolving to three people:
>
> Jonathan Moore—Richardson's former Chief of Staff who is still Associate Attorney General and who is said to have a list of some 40 policy issues to decide and effectuate before leaving the department.
>
> Gary Baise—Ruckelshaus' former Chief of Staff who has been in the Deputy's office under two months and is presently Acting Deputy Attorney General (by Bork memo of November 2).
>
> Glen Pommerening—the embittered Acting Assistant Attorney General for Administration who was passed over for the top slot by both Kleindienst and Richardson.
>
> ... Before Richardson's tenture [sic], the Department of Justice was moderately conservative. He and his personal staff have sought to "reorient" the Department's policies on social issues. The attitude of the remaining staff of Richardson and Ruckelshaus seems to be that if they can just get more of these projects started and cement in their previous policy decisions, they will later be very hard to turn off.[6]

Those personnel and policy activities clearly were detrimental, pointedly so, to *any* attorney general assuming leadership of the Department of Justice. Shepard also noted several personnel items of concern, including the following: "Richardson's personally designed departmental reorganization started to take affect *[sic]* one week before his departure. There is a near frantic effort to put this into cement before a new Attorney General can alter it."[7]

Shepard recommended to Cole that I put Hoiles, my administrative assistant, in the department "as soon as possible" to ward off those activities, but initially I decided against doing that. After all, my confirmation was still uncertain, given the Constitutional debate surrounding my nomination. He then recommended that Haig urge Bork "to appoint our candidate to be Special Assistant to the Attorney General for the interim."

The following day William E. Timmons, chief of White House liaison to the Congress, wrote Haig on the same subject.

Since it will be a while before Senator Saxbe is confirmed, there is a real danger that holdover personnel are running the Department and not necessarily in the interest of the President.

For example, the White House tried to move a loyalist—Charlie Ablard–into the Deputy Attorney General's office to hold the store, but Gary Baise demoted him and took away his title (Baise apparently is Acting Deputy AG). Rumor has it also that the Richardson and Ruckelshaus people are moving forward on programs and personnel before Saxbe gets there so he will be handicapped.

This situation deserves your immediate attention.[8]

It sure did, and it got it. Haig penned on the bottom of the memorandum that he had talked to Bork "about the problem. He assures me he'll keep on top of the problem." I can only assume that he did.

However, the direction of the department and the implementation of Richardson's reorganization plan concerned me, because I believe the Justice Department is the very heart of the nation. I wanted to reestablish a real, sound belief in our systems of justice and in our country.

Therefore, while the confirmation review was underway, I began assembling my own team. I put in a call to Sawyer, who was in Washington for the annual convention of the National Board of Realtors. He was elected national president in 1973 and was very, very busy, but I got through to him on the telephone in his suite at the Sheraton Hotel. Sawyer was very supportive of my acceptance of the nomination, as I knew he would be.

"Bill, if there's ever a time when the country needed you to be attorney general, it's right now."

"Well, J. D., I'm not going over there by my damn self. Will you come with me?"

"Hell, no! I'm president of the Realtors and we're in the middle of a national convention right now, but if the president asks you to serve this nation, it's your duty to do it—especially now with all of this hassle that he's in."

"You haven't answered me yet. Will you come with me?"

"No. I'm not going. I run a business back in Ohio. I got a wife and kids back there, and I've already spent more money then I can afford down here in Washington."

"What are you giving me all of this patriotic crap for? What about your duty to me?" The arm-twisting became severe.

"You've got a point," Sawyer said, melting. "Yes, I'll come." So, he was my assistant attorney general and a damn good one, too—great at organizing people and a wonderful person.

I also enlisted Hoiles to continue as my administrative assistant and Rakestraw and Michael H. Gertner, Abe's son and one of my Senate staffers, to watch over legislative affairs as assistant attorneys general. Duerk also signed on as press secretary and Frank A. "Duke" Portman II as a special assistant to Sawyer.

I still needed a number two. On November 8, I returned to Columbus to lunch at the Columbus Athletic Club with Jack Chester. I asked Jack if he was interested in joining me in Washington, possibly as deputy attorney general. He said he was.

I also talked with Robert W. Minor, then an attorney with the law firm of Vorys, Sater, Seymour, and Pease in Columbus. Bob and I were undergraduates in the same class at Ohio State University and then in law school together there. He also had Washington experience as assistant counsel to the Senate Investigations Committee in the late 1940s. In the Eisenhower administration, he served as an assistant attorney general under Attorney General William P. Rogers and at the Interstate Commerce Commission. Because he had just joined the Columbus law firm, Bob wanted to stay put for awhile, so he declined my invitation to return to Washington as my number two.

Within a few weeks of my conversation with Chester, I had to tell him that I wasn't going to pick him as my deputy because he would have to sell his stock in the Mid-America Racing Association, of which he also served as president. I didn't feel it would be worth it to him to do so. Chester thought the reason was "hogwash" and said so. I know he was disappoint-ed, and I regret that. He was looking forward to the appointment. My search continued.

It appeared as though the remedial legislation Bork requested and sent to the Senate Post Office and Civil Service Committee would have clear sailing until it stalled in its final days. The House had attached a franking privileges rider that the House and Senate had to resolve. Committee chair, Sen. Gale W. McGee, D-Wyoming, and Rep. Wayne L. Hays, D-Ohio, chair-man of the House Administration Committee, battled until a franking priv-ileges rider attached to the emoluments bill was removed. When it was reported out (November 13), it was referred to the Senate Judiciary Com-mittee by Senators Robert C. Byrd, D-West Virginia, assistant majority lead-er, and Sam Ervin.

Byrd, who ran a corner grocery and was cutting meat before his Senate salad days, led the few who opposed the remedial legislation. In his mind he undoubtedly recalled that I once told him the best thing that ever came out of West Virginia was an empty bus, a remark he found intemperate. In any event, he buzzed around my nomination right from the start, stating that my nomination should be held hostage until the White House gave up any documents sought by the nominee for special prosecutor, Leon Jaworski.

What he was counting on was that Nixon couldn't find an attorney gen-eral because of Richardson dropping out as he did and the mess the Justice Department was in as a result. I think Byrd and his lot became frustrated when I was nominated, which is what I think Nixon had in mind.

Senate Minority Leader Hugh Scott, R-Pennsylvania, came to my aid, upbraiding Byrd in no uncertain terms for his "hostage" stance. "I do not want it said that the Senate would not even let the attorney general be named."

Byrd kept up the fight. On the floor of the Senate, he attacked the pro-posed legislation on constitutional grounds, declaring rather pompously that he believed it was his duty to do so.

The Judiciary Committee voted unanimously on November 20 to send, without recommendation, the legislation to the Senate for a full vote, even though committee member Byrd continued to argue that a Constitutional prohibition could not be so erased. He said Nixon should consider provid-ing another candidate for the job. "The president should have explored this matter further before presenting Mr. Saxbe for confirmation," he said, forgetting that Nixon did not submit my name until *after* the pay bill was passed.

In the Senate debate and under the guise of a Constitutional debate, Byrd continued his attack, dismissing the Knox precedent and denying that the Congress could waive disqualification in individual instances. "I will not attempt to perform a caesarian section on the Constitution," he said, "to bring the senator from Ohio—distinguished as he is and deserving as he is—into the president's cabinet."

Byrd and others suggested that all the work I did as attorney general might later be found to be invalid, thereby placing in jeopardy the Watergate prosecutions. To back him up, he hauled in four college professors, three of whom said that the bill was contrary to the intent and the understanding of those who wrote the Constitution.

On November 28, the Senate passed the remedial legislation by a 75–16 vote. The House stamped okay on the pay bill December 3 by a vote of 261–129. The final bill, minus the franking rider, was approved by unanimous consent of the House on December 7, and Nixon signed it. Finally, after more than a month, he officially forwarded my nomination to the Senate on December 10.

When Jaworski and I appeared together at the Senate Judiciary Committee's confirmation hearings on December 12, only Democrats posed questions of me. Their prime focus was on the independence of the prosecutor's office. In fact, Byrd droned on and on, reading from the charter of the prosecutor, paragraph by paragraph. After each, he paused and asked me to swear that there would be no interference with the prosecutor's responsibilities under the charter, which I did.

I told the committee that I expected Jaworski to operate independently of the Justice Department, unless he sought the department's help, but I refused to go further. The committee wanted me to secure from Nixon a letter stating he would abide by the charter, too, but I told them if they wanted it, they would have to ask for it. I wasn't going to be their gofer. On December 13, behind closed doors, the committee voted fifteen to one in favor of submitting my name to the full Senate for a vote.

Four days later, the Senate took just twelve minutes to take a voice vote, seventy-five to ten, to confirm my nomination. The feeling in the Senate, columnist Mary McGrory wrote, "seemed to be that if a president wishes to appoint a man who has once publicly questioned his sanity and if that man pants for office in an expiring administration, no prudent man should intervene to spoil the match."[9]

Among the ten naysayers were Byrd; Ervin; Adlai E. Stevenson III, D-Illinois; and Edmund S. Muskie, D-Maine. No Republican opposed the confirmation.

Somehow I knew Ervin would be against me. When he chaired the Senate Watergate Committee public hearings, I called it a "kangaroo court" and a "rump court"—and it was. A veritable Roman holiday. I believed Ervin used the hearings for political gain. I was quoted somewhere as having said the nation "was being brought to the brink of financial catastrophe just to embarrass the president or a few jerks he had around him." I am sure Ervin didn't take kindly to that. Yet, he claimed I was a "fine lawyer . . . well qualified." He said he was "horribly upset" that he had to oppose the legislation on Constitutional grounds, "But . . . the language is clear as it can be and there is just no room for interpretation," he maintained.[10]

My biggest concern after the vote was that I would serve for a few months and then the Supreme Court would come along and declare the legislation unconstitutional. Then I'd have to give the money back, and I would already have spent it.

The following day I visited with Nixon at the White House at his request. Again he was cordial. He presented me with a copy of the *Congressional Record*, commenting that "it's the only thing you can get free here; otherwise we would be bribing you." He also noted the Senate vote confirming my nomination: "It's very seldom you get only ten votes against you," he said.

Back in Ohio, Gov. John J. Gilligan moved quickly to fill my seat in the Senate. As expected, he appointed Howard J. Metzenbaum on December 19, overlooking former astronaut John Glenn Jr.

The White House approved my request to delay my swearing-in until after January 3, 1974. By doing so, I became eligible for ten thousand dollars annually in congressional retirement benefits, beginning at age sixty-two, for having served in the Senate for five years.

It was a delightful family Christmas in Mechanicsburg that year, but not without its own excitement. One of our cows ran into the road and was killed near our house. Bart—our son, the surgeon—hauled the beast into our barn and butchered it right then and there, all the while giving a running anatomy lesson to the locals who gathered around. It was a spellbinding performance. As I remember, the meat was excellent, too.

Very Model of a Modern Attorney General

Judge Robert M. Duncan was nervous. As he stood in the Great Hall of the Department of Justice, awaiting the start of my swearing-in ceremony, he thought to himself, "Oh, God, how will I do this?" He didn't hesitate to admit that he was scared to death as he approached his task. Traditionally, a justice of the Supreme Court gives the oath of office to a new attorney general, but I chose Bob Duncan, whom I had known almost all of his life. I knew his father and his grandfather, too. For more than fifty years his grandfather, Harvey Duncan, was a swamper,[1] bellman, and headwaiter at the Douglas Inn in Urbana, a few miles from Mechanicsburg. Bob's dad, Benny Duncan, shined shoes in the hotel's barbershop for a time. Both men were leaders in the African American community in Urbana—and good Republicans.

In the late 1940s I secured a page's job in the state legislature for Bob while he was attending The Ohio State University, although he ended up working in the state treasurer's office, counting receipts and checks in the basement of the statehouse. After he got his law degree and served in the Army, I hired him as an assistant attorney general for Ohio and then as chief counsel.

I remember one day a lady from Akron showed up in Duncan's office. She was mad, so mad she never realized she was speaking to an African American. "Blacks are moving into my neighborhood, and they are ruining it!" she yelled. Duncan replied: "I'm having the same problem. They are moving into my neighborhood, too!"

In 1966, when a vacancy opened up on the Franklin County Municipal Court bench, I urged Governor Rhodes to appoint Duncan, which he did. Two years later he named Duncan to the Ohio Supreme Court bench, at the time the only African American in the nation to hold that lofty post. Paul Brown created the vacancy when he left the high court to accept a

Rhodes appointment as Ohio attorney general, replacing me after I was elected to the U.S. Senate.

I was in the Senate in 1971 when I successfully urged that Duncan be appointed to a fourteen-year term on the U.S. Military Court of Appeals in Washington. It is the court of last resort for the armed forces. When a U.S. District Court judgeship opened up in Columbus three years later, Duncan was elevated to that post.

But on January 4, 1974, it was military court Judge Duncan who administered the oath of office to the nation's seventieth attorney general while Dolly held the Bible. Robert Bork, who had resumed his post as solicitor general after serving seventy-six days as acting attorney general, introduced me to the assembled well-wishers. He noted that I had served as Ohio's attorney general longer than any other, and he quipped, "I find that longevity reassuring." Sitting nearby on the platform, with laughter and applause wafting over them, were Kleindienst and Richardson, the sixty-eighth and sixty-ninth attorneys general, both of whom were short-timers in the job.

When it came my turn for the quips, I was prepared.

Undoing my predecessor's reorganization plan was among my first tasks as United States attorney general.

It turned out that I had to be approved by both the House and the Senate. . . . They felt they had to adjust the pay according to my capacity. . . .

I had a moment of panic this morning when I looked in the mirror. I suddenly realized that I had resigned from the Senate at the close of business last night, and I wasn't to be sworn until this afternoon—and I was off the public payroll. There is nothing that frightens an office-holder more than that!

There was a serious side to my remarks, of course. With one eye on the administration and its problems with Watergate, I detailed the importance of the Department of Justice in upholding the nation's laws. The laws are there, I said "to protect the weak who cannot protect themselves."

In any society . . . there are those who must be protected by the law and by the might of government. Unless it is defended, unless it is respected by people, there is no way that you can keep a society from drifting into anarchy.

Today, in this period of transition, we have lost a great deal of respect for the law. There are those who feel that the law is used by the powerful to see that they get their way, and that it no longer protects the weak and the helpless. They do not realize that law is designed not only to protect the weak and the helpless, but it also is for the purpose of having order within a society. . . . Law is for the purpose of bringing order in our society. . . . A society operating in a manner as to give each individual the opportunity to express himself without fear of Big Brother taking over, without fear of Big Brother doing those things outside of the scope of the law in the name of protection, in the name of defense.

In closing, I recalled the prayer group in the Senate that I regularly attended. I repeated an admonition of Sen. J. Bennett Johnston, D-Louisiana, adapted from the Old Testament prophet, Micah: "The finest direction that could be given to Man, and the one that ensured success, was that they do justice, they love mercy, and that they walk humbly before God.

"This is a big order," I said, "but one that I am determined to do to the best of my ability."

Bart, Juli, and Rocky attended the ceremony, as well as my sister, Betty, her husband, Carl "Sparky" Sparks, and my brother-in-law, Marine colonel John L. Kleinhans. Among those from the Washington scene were Melvin

Laird, White House domestic affairs counsel; four cabinet officers; five senators, including Howard M. Metzenbaum, a Democrat who was sworn in that morning as my appointed successor, much to the consternation of the Ohio GOP; a host of present and former Ohio congressmen, including my good friend, William J. Keating of Cincinnati, who got the ball rolling for my nomination; Watergate Special Prosecutor Leon Jaworski; and Clarence Kelley, director of the Federal Bureau of Investigation.

Several hundred friends and political associates from Ohio found their way to Washington for the occasion, including Jim Rhodes; Jack Chester; Ralph Waldo; former state GOP chairmen Ray Bliss and John Andrews; then chairman, Kent McGough; and a host of other community, county, and state officials.

For me it was heartwarming to see so many friendly faces in the audience. There had not been so many smiles in town since Haldeman and Ehrlichman departed nine months earlier.

As I discovered, the cabinet post came with a number of perks and privileges. I now was seventh in line to the presidency, a daunting thought indeed. As a cabinet officer, I now had a code name—Flivver—to be used when someone dropped the bomb, I assumed. At state functions, Dolly and I would be seated, separately, sixth from the president. A Cadillac limousine with a FBI chauffeur and an on-board telephone was assigned to me: I added a brass spittoon. Two Filipino stewards prepared the food and served it my private dining room—"tastefully decorated" by Martha Mitchell, according to one journalist—that was adjacent to my Justice Department office. On my stand-up desk, which my good friend Pete Quesada made for me, was a direct line to the president. I never could get through to Nixon, so that became a dust-collector.

There was wood paneling everywhere, several stories high. We had a conference room so long that former attorney general Robert Kennedy tossed footballs in it to his aide, Byron "Whizzer" White. My office had an electric fireplace, over which was hung a portrait of another Buckeye, former Ohio governor and former attorney general, Judson Harmon. He served in President Grover Cleveland's cabinet.[2] I also had a small private apartment above my office, but I never used it. I understand Martha Mitchell did, though, when she couldn't make it home.

My office was not as large as Rakestraw's though. As assistant attorney general, he had a huge corner office; he was a pig in silk there. From time to time I would rib him about that. One day Henry Peterson, assistant attorney general in charge of the criminal division, heard this and quipped, "Bill, when you make more money, you get more space." The reference, of course, was to my salary being knocked down by Congress to a level below what my senior staff members made.

When I traveled, which was frequently, either the FBI or the U.S. Marshall's office met me at the airport. Both were under my command, as was the Drug Enforcement Agency, the Immigration and Naturalization Service, and the Bureau of Prisons. And when I left the cabinet, I could leave my painted portrait for hanging in the Justice Department.[3] I did and, as far as I know, it's still there someplace.

Following the swearing-in ceremony, many retired to L'Enfant Plaza Hotel where there was a large reception in the Grand Ballroom for seemingly half of Ohio and most of Washington. "The party turned into something like a mini-inaugural ball," wrote a *Washington Star-News* society reporter. "The ebullient occasion for several hundred persons . . . marked the first happy gathering of Republicans since Watergate."[4]

It was true. We were having so much fun, you'd think we were all Democrats. Terry Waldo, Ralph's son, and his band, the Gutbucket Syncopators, performed, and we all danced in celebration. But the hit of the evening was the eighty-five-carat emerald ring I bought for Dolly in India. On her finger it looked like the bottom of a 7-Up bottle.

Dolly and I left the party in the Cadillac assigned to me. We hadn't gone far before a park policeman halted us. He told my FBI driver that the vehicle bore an outdated inspection sticker, and he was going to write us a ticket. The press said I pulled off "a classic bully-boy act," demanding the officer's name, but that never happened.[5] The driver took the ticket, and we were on our way again.

The week following my moving in, I recommended to Nixon that former Labor under secretary Laurence H. Silberman be named deputy attorney general and my number two in the Justice Department. I wanted someone who knew his way around Washington, and Larry had that reputation. I also liked the idea that on several occasions while at Labor he stood up to White House shenanigans.

Other appointments, all assistant attorneys general, followed. The White House pushed Carla A. Hills, a bright, young attorney from San Francisco. I had met her while still in the Senate and thought she had excellent credentials. She became head of the civil division and the highest ranking woman in the Justice Department. Rakestraw took charged of legislative affairs, and Antonin Scalia became legal counsel. In 1986 President Ronald Reagan appointed him to the U.S. Supreme Court.

It wasn't long after I was seated in my Senate chair—it had been given to me by the Senate—behind my desk at the Department of Justice that I began to get a close view of Nixon's modus operandi. As 1974 unfolded, those close to the president noticed marked changes in his personality: radical, even whimsical, shifts in mood; a general restlessness; and a more combative stance. In notes Nixon made to himself at the time, he determined that he had to stand and "fight" the forces lined up to bring him down. He wrote:

> Fight because if I am forced to resign the press will become a much too dominant force in the nation, not only for this administration but for years to come. Fight because resignation would set a precedent and result in a permanent and very destructive change in our whole constitutional system. Fight because resignation could lead to a collapse of our foreign policy initiatives.... Above all else: Dignity, command, faith, head high, no fear, build a new spirit, drive, act like a President, act like a winner. Opponents are savage destroyers, haters. Time to use full power of the President to fight overwhelming forces arrayed against us.[6]

He began to create a legal defense team. In mid-December, prior to my being sworn in, I sat in the Oval Office with Nixon, White House Chief of Staff Alexander M. Haig Jr., and Kenneth Rush, deputy secretary of state. Rush later became a good friend, after we both retired from government work.

"I have asked Dean Rush to be my special counsel," the president began, having rejected several other names, including Acting Attorney General Robert Bork. Nixon referred to Rush as "dean" because he had held that position at Duke University's Law School while Nixon was a student there. Rush just sat there, looking kind of strange, almost dumbfounded. I don't know whether it came as a surprise to him or not.

Rush, who later became U.S. Ambassador to West Germany, recalled the same meeting. "I told him that I hadn't practiced law in years and had never practiced criminal law....

"I asked Nixon, 'Have you told Henry?' [Secretary of State Kissinger was then engaged in shuttle diplomacy in the Middle East.] The president said, 'Who is more important, me or Henry?' I answered, 'You, of course.'"

Rush told Kissinger, his boss, that he didn't want the job, and Kissinger convinced Nixon that Rush was too important at State to leave. "If I had gone to the White House, it would have been the worst thing that ever happened to me," Rush said.[7]

It wasn't long thereafter that Nixon sought the Justice Department's help in defending him. I told him I couldn't do that. In my confirmation hearings, I had promised the Senate I would not involve the department in Watergate—and he knew that. I told him I would provide anyone he liked from the ranks of the Justice Department, but they would have to go on the White House payroll.

I suggested my friend Jack Chester, a damn good lawyer who could serve as liaison between the White House and the Department of Justice. At fifty-three, Chester had a lot of experience and an excellent reputation back in Ohio. The *Cleveland Plain Dealer* described him as a "lawyer's lawyer . . . [and] known as an indefatigable worker, a shrewd tactician, a savvy politician and a good lawyer."[8] I also recognized Chester's disappointment at not having been my choice for deputy attorney general.

After interviews with Haig, Bork, and others, Chester became special counsel to the president and a member of the Watergate defense team. He set up his office shortly after the first of the year. On the day I was sworn into office, Boston trial lawyer, James D. St. Clair, also took office in the White House as special counsel to the president—to defend the presidency, Nixon told him. He and Chester shared the same title and were the only attorneys in private practice on the fifteen-man defense team; the remainder came from various government offices.

Chester and St. Clair didn't hit it off well. Chester believed he got an early brush-off from St. Clair after he read the "Lawyer's Lawyer" article in the *Plain Dealer*, which closely linked Chester and me. Also, Chester hung a picture of me on his office wall, which undoubtedly irked the Nixonites. "I sorta asked for it," Chester admitted. The more time passed, the less Chester was given to do. On Thursdays, Chester often had Dolly as his luncheon guest at the White House Mess. That was the day when the mess served a Mexican dish—with a side shot of tequila. "It was the only day an alcoholic drink was served," Chester said.

Chester did get a key assignment, though, and I was involved in that. When the Senate Watergate Committee lost its bid in federal district court to force Nixon to turn over five tapes it had subpoenaed, the committee appealed to the Court of Appeals in the District of Columbia. Nixon and St. Clair wanted Solicitor General Bork to argue the case, but I had promised the Senate no Watergate participation by the Justice Department. So, I turned down the White House.

St. Clair was furious at the rebuff. What I learned from Chester later was that St. Clair said he would take the matter to Haig, and that would be the end of it: Haig would force me to comply with the request. Chester recalled thinking to himself at the time: "St. Clair, you dumb son-of-a-bitch. You don't know Bill Saxbe." Chester was right, of course. I didn't cave in to White House pressure on that or anything else that would violate the law, my promises, or my principles.

I suggested that Chester be assigned to the case. He was, and he did an excellent job, winning a decision for the president. Of course, that was like winning at Parcheesi aboard the Titanic. I did file a friend-of-the-court brief, however, urging the appeals court to reject the Watergate Committee's request. That brought Ervin up for air; he thought I should stay at arm's length on the tapes issue. I often thought he and his committee were on a "fishing expedition," and said so even before I became attorney general.[9]

In the scheme of things, that was a minor flap. Trying to get the Justice Department up and running, working long days—and nights—took every ounce of energy I could muster. I was so tired I went to bed three times one night. There was so much to learn, and the fact that the department was in some disarray made me feel like a mule in a horse harness. I quickly discovered I couldn't keep up the long hours. I had to pace myself. Dolly and I seldom had a night at home while I was in the Senate, but as attorney general I cut back on receptions and dinners. I just didn't have time to go to all those rat-killings.

A pair of formal English velvet slippers I had made in Hong Kong during my visit there the previous August made the society pages, though. At a reception for Lord and Lady Cromer, a reporter noted the slippers, with my initials embroidered in silver sequins and what was intended to be the Great Seal of the United States. But the slipper maker placed tiny Stars of David in the Great Seal. They caused quite a stir among the social set.[10]

Meanwhile, in Columbus, attorney Bob Boyd did some important spadework, reviewing Richardson's rather violent reorganization plan for the department. The Richardson plan, implemented on October 22, just before I took office, was designed to "help adapt the Department to its late-twentieth century responsibilities," Richardson said, "and better equip the Department of Justice to foster the full, fair, and efficient administration of justice—now and in the future."[11]

Quite frankly, I didn't understand it, even after he spread it all out on the conference table. He and his boys wanted me to sign it right away so they could get on with it. But if there is one thing you learn as a small-town lawyer, if you don't understand it, don't sign it. The plan may have worked for Richardson, but it didn't work for me. He watered down the power of the deputy attorney general, for example, by operating the department with a two-man team at the top, he and his Deputy Assistant Attorney General Bill Ruckelshaus. I wanted my deputy to be my executive officer, with full authority to run the department. I didn't want every single problem brought to me. I wanted to save my time for the problems that really required my time. So, not only did I not sign off on the Richardson plan, I assigned Sawyer the task of creating a new proposal.

The rush to implement Richardson's plan prior to my taking office, plus the changes I required, resulted in an administrative upheaval. There were a lot of new hires—many were those with whom I had worked previously—and it required time for those folks to get up to speed, too.

It also helped immeasurably when they knew who was boss. Shortly after my arrival, I telephoned one of the Justice Department's top attorneys, a holdover from Richardson's days. "He is too busy to take your call," his secretary cooed, "but he asked me to be sure to get your name."

Sawyer thought the department's problems went well beyond just Richardson. With all the comings and goings in the office of attorney general during the Nixon years, "Reorganization of the Department was either emphasized or deemphasized, depending upon the attitude of the then individual Attorney General," Sawyer wrote in his report to me.[12] "Thus, Department reorganization has been bandied about and has been subject to fits and starts to an alarming degree. In the interim, each Attorney General has operated in his own style and has issued new orders or amended old ones to focus on the modes and methods of operations that he wished to prevail."

I received a cup of coffee and a kiss-off from Richardson when I visited him at his beautiful Virginia home overlooking the Potomac. He remained aloof, wrapped up in his own ambitions and his own agenda. For my part, I already had more hay down than I could get in the barn.

Richardson's plan was not well received by Justice Department staff. Sawyer reported to me that there were "protestations and vigorous objections raised at nearly every level of the entire Department . . . believing that it [was] a step backward rather than a progressive program."

It was apparent to both Sawyer and me that the Richardson plan was disruptive. As I said, I decided to place more responsibilities, not fewer, in the office of Deputy Attorney General Laurence H. Silberman, whom Sawyer accurately described as "decisive . . . courageous . . . and of strong convictions." Silberman became responsible for all agencies of the department, except for the Watergate Special Prosecutor Jaworski, and Solicitor General Bork. I also eliminated the Office of Legal Administration, which Richardson had set up.

Finally, Sawyer proposed, and I accepted, that his job as assistant attorney general be eliminated. "My role is fulfilled," he wrote, and so once again

Sawyer left my side to return to his real estate business in Middletown, Ohio.

In a parting comment, Sawyer noted that I always had functioned "as a problem solver, innovator, top policy maker, all of which requires a daily schedule unhampered by administrative and operational details.

"His natural wit, candor and common sense judgment, coupled with a feel for prevailing public opinion, makes him imminently [sic] qualified to be a great Attorney General."[13]

I appreciated those comments, but sometimes my "candor" was not what people wanted to hear.

Walking on Eggs

"It's awfully hard to shut him up," Dolly told Helen Thomas, White House reporter for United Press International. "He's always been kind of nervy, but I am glad he is. Everyone complains about secrecy and being unapproachable."[1]

I was approachable all right. Shortly after I became attorney general, I began Wednesday morning coffee-and-donuts meetings with the members of the press who regularly covered the Justice Department. I thoroughly enjoyed those gatherings. Often the newsmen brought to my attention matters of concern to the public, issues about which I would not be aware otherwise. I really didn't have a lot of time to carefully read the papers or watch television. Usually I began by bringing the press corps up to date on what was going on in the department, and then I'd let them have their shot on any issue. It was the matching-of-wits part of those somewhat informal sessions that I liked.

On February 14, 1974, I was questioned about the kidnapping ten days earlier of Patricia Hearst by the Symbionese Liberation Army, a small band of violent fanatics. The nineteen-year-old daughter of Randolph A. Hearst, president of the Hearst Corporation and publisher of the *San Francisco Examiner*, was abducted from an apartment in Berkeley, California, that she shared with her fiancé, Steven Weed.

The SLA demanded as ransom some $70 million in food to feed California's needy. I did not favor any compliance with such a vague and unrealistic demand because it was beyond even the capability of the government to meet. Furthermore, it was unlikely to satisfy the SLA anyway. A reporter then asked me if the FBI knew where she was being held captive. "If we did, we'd go get her," I responded. "We'd be subject to a dereliction of duty charge if we didn't."

My remarks brought a strong rebuke from Randolph Hearst. "Mr. Saxbe is not the father of the prisoner," he said angrily. "I am going to do what I can to get her out." He described my comments as "irresponsible" and "antagonistic" and said they had "no place in the kind of negotiations that we are involved in."

Frankly, I was upset and contrite, and said so. My immediate response was to assure the Hearst family that I did not want the FBI to pursue any action that would in any way "jeopardize the life of the young victim in this case." I went on to admit publicly "I was wrong in stating my personal views in such a manner as to cause distress to an already overwrought family."

The following week I asked FBI director Clarence M. Kelley to accompany me to Los Angeles where we held a press conference at the Beverly Hilton Hotel. The room was jammed with reporters. I made it clear that the SLA was involved in terrorist acts that must be met head on, and amnesty for Patty Hearst's kidnappers was not in the cards.

"I personally feel that kidnapping and crimes that usually result from kidnapping are heinous crimes that should be covered by the death penalty," I stated. "The deterrent to crime is the apprehension and prosecution of criminals, and I personally feel nothing should stand in the way."[2]

This is a view I have long held, even when I was attorney general in Ohio. Furthermore, I believe it to be the duty of every citizen to support their laws and the legal system that administers them. All too often, I am afraid, the public abandons this responsibility as citizens.

I caught a lot of flack for my comments on the Hearst case, of course. Back in Ohio, for instance, the Akron *Beacon Journal*'s editorial headline said, "Now Saxbe Should Learn to Button His Quick Lip." The newspaper concluded that I was "absolutely wrong" in expressing my opinion. It made no difference to them, or to others, that I clarified my position within a few hours. I believe that in conducting the public's business, the public has a right to know what you are doing and thinking, and if they don't like what they see and hear, they should let you know. But I recognized at the time that in my job as the nation's top law officer, I had to be more guarded about what I said. I was naive, to be sure, and probably deserved the criticism. At one point Sen. Jacob K. Javits, R-New York, wondered aloud if I hadn't been taking "dumb pills."

Two months later, however, I found myself in the thick of the Hearst case again. On Monday, April 15, the SLA robbed a San Francisco bank. Patty Hearst, now "Tania," was photographed by security cameras, holding an automatic weapon on the bank's customers. A bank guard said she told them she would "shoot the first S.O.B. who moved." The robbers escaped with $10,690.

At my press conference two days later, I had nothing to announce, so we went to questions. "What about the bank robbery?" a reporter asked. I said we would catch the armed robbers. "What about the kidnap victim, Miss Hearst?" She is a wanted person, I replied, adding that it appeared to me "that she was not a reluctant participant in the robbery." [3]

I went on to say that the entire SLA group was no more than "common criminals," and "Miss Hearst is a part of it."

Well, they came out of the woodwork in droves. Randolph Hearst—and his wife, Catherine—attacked me once again. The head of the American Bar Association criticized me. The news media had a field day. John W. Hushen, public information officer for the Justice Department, suggested to reporters that I would cut back on the Wednesday press conferences. I guess you would call that "damage control."

Even my son, Rocky, took a shot. At the time he was a second-year law student at The Ohio State University Law School and running for the GOP nomination for a seat in the Ohio House. That is the first political office I had sought in 1947, and I gave Rocky the same assistance my father gave me: None.

"I am not sure what he said was appropriate," Rocky said of my Hearst comments, "but at least it is refreshing to have someone give you their opinion when asked. . . . I don't think he was trying to hurt anybody." [4]

I realized what I said in Washington would be fed back to Rocky in the form of a question on the campaign trail. "What do you think of your father's statement about such-and-such," reporters would ask him. I tried awfully hard not to put him on the spot like that, but I had no intention of abandoning my meetings with the press.

Following the "Hearst" press conference on April 17, I had lunch at the office with my staff and my friend from Columbus, Ralph Waldo. I had invited him to Washington for a round of golf that afternoon at the Burning Tree Country Club. He said I was in one of my "non-talking moods."

"Bill hardly said a word," Waldo recalled. "We played 18 holes; it was cold and wet and nobody else was on the course. When we finished, Bill decided to go another nine, so off we went again, with two FBI agents trailing us. Never had what you might call a conversation, not even through dinner afterwards. He dropped me off at my hotel where I picked up a newspaper and saw the Patty Hearst 'common criminal' story. Old Bill knew that he'd put his foot in it and that was the reason he was just grunting and wasn't talking."

Well, Waldo was right; I was quiet. What was on my mind was the call I had received from Nixon after my Patty Hearst comments. The president was upset and minced no words in saying so. Apparently he had received a call from her father, whose name cut a goodly swath in White House circles. After our ten-minute conversation—Nixon did most of the talking—I knew where he stood and he knew where I stood. I still think she was a common criminal.[5]

In April 1974, FBI agents were assigned to Dolly and me because of the wave of terrorist activity around the country and, more specifically, "threats" made by the Symbionese Liberation Army "to bring harm to the attorney general." I liked to walk to my office, about thirty minutes away, until the threats; then three FBI agents met me every morning with a limousine and a chase car. I also was issued a .38-caliber Smith and Wesson pistol.

One of the FBI agents assigned to me, Phil Kerby, later wrote a book about his years in the bureau. About the threats against me, he wrote: "If terrorists really were after Saxbe, I concluded they were far more likely to try something in Washington than out here [in Mechanicsburg], where any strange face would instantly be noted and reported by the townsfolk. . . . The most dangerous thing about the job was trying to avoid sitting in any of the little Styrofoam cups full of tobacco juice that Saxbe left all over the place."[6]

Dolly remembers another humorous time in the Denver airport with the FBI agent assigned to her, Sheila J. Regan. Before boarding any aircraft, Sheila always had to tell airport security that she was armed. She did so and mentioned that she was escorting the attorney general's wife.

"Is she shackled?" the security officer asked.

"No, it's the attorney general's wife," Sheila explained.

"Well, is she shackled?" the officer asked again.

"No, she's not shackled."

"Shouldn't she be shackled?" The officer seemed unable to fathom the situation.

During those early days at the Justice Department, there was a lot more occupying my time than the Hearst case, of course; a lot more. To put it frankly, I was swamped. But one of the pleasant interludes in the first few hectic months at the Justice Department came upon my return to Mechanicsburg on February 3 for "Bill Saxbe Day." I was so proud of my community. On a cold, blustery day, the town turned out, and I knew virtually every name in the crowd. I dedicated the new $144,000 municipal building and was given a Lion's Club-sponsored dinner in the cafeteria of Mechanicsburg High School, my alma mater.

Prior to the dedication, I held a press conference to discuss the most pressing issue of the day—the violence that had broken out following the start of a nationwide strike of independent truckers in mid-December. In Ohio and Pennsylvania, gunfire erupted, and vandalism ensued. After one death in Pennsylvania and more acts of violence, I requested that the FBI launch an investigation into violations of federal laws.

"This handful of truckers [participating in the violence] is not going to bring this nation to its knees," I said in Mechanicsburg. Shortly thereafter, I sent wires to all ninety-four federal district attorneys, notifying them that the Justice Department would crack down on those who committed acts of violence.

Nixon wanted to make sure he got the credit for ending the strike, which involved but 20 percent of the total number of truckers, most of whom were Teamster members. Perhaps that stemmed from knowledge Nixon had that the AFL-CIO was prepared to support his impeachment. In any event, I was reminded of his wishes at an Oval Office meeting on February 8 that included Secretary of Transportation Claude S. Brinegar, Federal Energy Office Administrator William E. Simon, Special Assistant to the President William J. Usery Jr., Haig, and me.

Nixon wanted me to be the administration's "tough guy" on preventing violence. He asked what I was doing in that regard. I said I was preparing legislation that would make it a crime to interfere with motor vehicles engaged in interstate commerce and that I would send it up to the Hill in response to Congressional demands for such legislation. Nixon amended that: "You should say you are sending it up at the *direction* of the President," he said. He also told all of us that when we talk to the press, we should indicate that he personally had been spending a lot of time on the issue.

What he was spending a lot of time on was Watergate-related matters. At my first cabinet meeting, on January 23, 1974, Nixon encouraged us to make a "sustained effort" to speak out in favor of the administration and its policies, thus diverting attention from the tide of Watergate, which was by then lapping at the White House door. Nixon wanted us to accept as many speaking engagements as possible and "to use these forums to discuss how this administration is alive and well."

I believed Nixon's cabinet meetings to be largely a waste of my time. There was very little of substance discussed. The president just was not focused on anything—except how to get out from under the Watergate cloud. Even on the rare occasions when I met with him in private to discuss some of the pressing issues facing the Justice Department, such as the American Telephone and Telegraph antitrust suit, he would ramble on,

At this 1974 meeting with Nixon in the Oval Office, he wanted me to be the administration's "tough guy" with the striking independent truckers. Seated around the desk are Nixon; me; Secretary of Transportation Claude S. Brinegar; White House Chief of Staff Alexander M. Haig Jr.; W. J. Usery Jr., special assistant to the president; and William E. Simon, administrator, Federal Energy Office. White House Photo.

almost incoherently at times, about his family, his predecessors, and all his troubles.

As the Watergate investigation proceeded and the White House tapes became an issue, Nixon spent hours listening to them, over and over and over again. He didn't have time for me or for any other member of his cabinet, for that matter, except for Secretary of State Henry Kissinger. Kissinger always seemed to have the president's ear.

When it came to Watergate matters, I tried to remain on the sidelines. I told *U.S. News and World Report* that an attempt by Congress to impeach the president, "Especially a bitter, partisan impeachment, which it would have to be if no further crimes of a great nature are developed, would tear this country apart. . . . The nature of the evil deeds that are alleged to the President are not of an impeachable nature."[7]

The whole Watergate business smelled worse than a Mississippi hog farm in July, and it reflected badly on Nixon, but at that point nobody knew anything with certainty that directly linked the president to a cover-up.

The president was being beaten over the head with a bag of wind, I initially believed. The White House maintained that Nixon was not made aware of the break-in and cover-up details until March 21, 1973.

My predecessor, Richardson, agreed. "The evidence won't show direct criminal involvement in a criminal act, that he [Nixon] knew in advance of the Watergate break-in or participated in the cover-up," he told the *Washington Post*.[8]

There was no question that there were numerous disturbing revelations, including the erasure of eighteen and one-half minutes of a Watergate tape. Experts indicated that the erasure of an Oval Office conversation between Nixon and his chief of staff, H. R. Haldeman on June 20, 1972, probably was deliberate, which is what I expected as well. Somebody had to be fooling around with it, but I did not believe it had been the president himself.

I already had made it clear that should Nixon be impeached for political reasons, the Justice Department would defend him, but if accused of high crimes and faced with trial in the Senate, then he would be on his own.

In the *U.S. News and World Report* interview, I probably didn't endear myself to Vice President Ford when I observed that Congress would "rather have a crippled Nixon than a healthy, sitting Jerry Ford." That was true, of course. Those in Congress opposed to the administration were enjoying Nixon's agony. When Agnew resigned, the hounds bayed even louder, because now the president was left without a buffer between him and his critics.

Agnew was long gone by the time I joined the Nixon cabinet. In fact, Agnew was a political liability to Nixon long before he was forced to resign. Nixon wanted to dump his vice president, force him out of office, and sail into the 1972 presidential elections with former Texas Governor John B. Connally, a Democrat at the time, as his running mate. That scenario had been in Nixon's mind for some time. When Supreme Court Justice Hugo Black retired in 1971, the president thought of nominating Agnew to the court, just for the chance at getting Connally as vice president, but it was a fleeting wish. Nixon realized the Senate never would confirm Agnew, and the two made up the 1972 GOP ticket once again.

Even though Ford was the appointed vice president when I joined the Nixon administration, Agnew came back into my life when I became attorney general. I say "back" because I had known Agnew first when he came to Ohio during the 1968 campaign. I thought he was a crude son-of-a-bitch, devoid of moral character. To say I didn't like him would be slathering my thoughts with molasses.

Many people remember Agnew's political attacks on the media and the opposition, but few recall that in a commencement address at The Ohio State University on June 7, 1969, he made his first reference in a speech to an "effete" society. Later he expanded on that theme and won nationwide attention with a speech in New Orleans on October 9, 1969, in which he referred to "effete snobs."

Agnew's Ohio State University remarks came amidst considerable campus unrest in protest to the Vietnam War. The worst of it—the Kent State killings—was still a year away. He noted that the graduates' generation was not the first "to aggressively challenge the fundamental values of a society. Such challenges are normal, proper, and the basis for human improvement." The nation was in "trouble because my generation has apparently failed to define and defend either its achievements or its inheritance from past generations of Americans.

"A society which fears its children is effete," he continued. "A sniveling, hand-wringing power structure deserves the violent rebellion it encourages. If my generation doesn't stop cringing, yours will inherit a lawless society where emotion and muscle displace reason."

Prior to his resignation, Agnew plea bargained with anyone and everyone, trying to cut the best deal he could for himself, including asking for an ambassadorial post. What he did end up with from Nixon were a number of minor perks—including an office, secretary, car, and driver—perks to which he clearly was not entitled. The General Accounting Office ruled early in 1974 that those perks were improper.

Nixon, primarily through Haig, put a lot of pressure on me to overrule the GAO and restore the perks for Agnew. Haig called several times, each time saying, "The president wants this done" or words to that effect. I knew Haig was speaking for the president. Nevertheless, each time I refused. Even if it had been proper to do so—and it wasn't—I had no intention of lifting a finger to help a crook like Agnew.

One weekend Jack Chester came over for a Sunday night dinner with Dolly and me. As Chester accurately recalled, Haig telephoned yet again while we were having dinner. He and Nixon were in Key Biscayne, Florida. "The president has decided not to pursue the Agnew matter," Haig said. Nixon had backed down; Agnew lost his perks.

There were many times that the White House applied similar pressure to get me to do this or that for them, particularly in the early going when the White House must have felt they had a patsy in the attorney general's chair. In the first few months the requests centered on the work Watergate Special Prosecutor Jaworski was doing.

I stayed out of Jaworski's way, as I promised Congress I would do—or I tried to do so. I always felt that Richardson and Cox talked too much to each other. It became buddy-buddy between them, as I understand it.

From time to time Jaworski and I would have a need to discuss matters concerning the law and his pursuit of justice. In April 1974, for instance, he wrote me concerning the Internal Revenue Service's recommendation that he, Jaworski, undertake a grand jury investigation into possible violations in the preparation of Nixon's 1969 income tax return.[9] The focus was on Nixon's deduction of a gift of prepresidential papers to the National Archives.

In response, I authorized Jaworski "to investigate and prosecute all violations of law arising out of the preparation of President Nixon's 1969 income tax return and the deductions in subsequent years . . . without regard to the official or nonofficial status of the individuals involved in these matters."[10]

Turnabout is fair play, I suppose. During the early 1970s, the White House created the infamous "Political Enemies" list. Nixon was in the thick of using various branches of government, including the IRS, against his "enemies."

But Nixon was disappointed in the administration's failure to effectively employ the power it held. The efforts of the White House staff were "half-hearted and ineffective," he said. In his diary at the time he noted, "This has really been a shameful failure on our part, and it is hard for me to understand it, in view of the fact that I had so often pointed out that after what they [the enemies] did to us when we were out of office we at least owed it to ourselves in self-defense to initiate some investigations of them."[11]

Nixon soft-pedaled the administration's vindictiveness. Author Michael A. Genovese believed that the "Nixon administration made government into an instrument for revenge and retaliation. They attempted not to defeat their rivals, but to destroy their enemies. Along the way they broke the law and subverted the democratic process."[12]

Broadcaster Marvin Kalb came to a similar conclusion. "Critics became enemies, and criticism became treason in the Nixon White House. A pervading sense of arrogance corrupted the president's men. They had power, and they intended to use it against their critics, who they saw as 'enemies of the people,' of the 'silent majority' who supported the president. Like 'enemies' of any authoritarian system, they had to be squashed and silenced."[13]

Internally and externally, then, the battle raged on. Jaworski and I were, it seems, in the thick of much of it. I got along fine with Jaworski, but that doesn't mean we didn't have a difference or two. For example, in response to a Watergate-related question from the press, I said that, in general, I thought ill of plea bargaining agreements. To plea bargain with the Watergate crooks and grant them immunity and coddle the hell out them would only break down our system of justice.

In a speech to the National Association of Attorneys General on June 24, I said that it was "hardly reassuring when one man goes to prison for years of theft while another man involved in a conspiracy to steal our freedoms is in and out of jail in the wink of an eye."

Jaworski believed that my comments, "Whether intentional or unwitting," were tantamount to interference with his office. Through his deputy, Henry Ruth, who discussed the matter with my top deputy, Laurence Silberman, Jaworski registered his displeasure. I wrote him a note of apology, suggesting that he cool down. Thwarting any part of his investigation was not my intent. Nor did I intend to fire him. If Nixon asked me to do that—which he didn't—I was prepared to stand my ground and not resign, like Richardson had.

During my first one hundred days as attorney general, I spent most of my time defining the problems of the Justice Department and fending off the White House, which clearly saw Justice as a weapon with which to thwart the various Watergate probes, and other investigations. One of those at the time involved John Connally, who served as Nixon's treasury secretary between February 1971 and May 1972 and, for a brief time thereafter, counsel to the president.

Nixon believed he still could position Connally for the GOP presidential nomination in 1976. Ford was ready to step aside and let the Texan have it, but I felt that if the party gave a retread like Connally the nomination, they'd put a monkey on the back of every GOP candidate. It was not to be, of course.

In the summer of 1974 Connally's star was falling. Some said he had accepted a ten thousand dollar bribe from the milk producers in 1971 for his part in winning White House favor for increasing milk price supports to 85 percent from 79 percent. A hike like that would mean a $700 million dollar increase in revenue for the nation's dairy farmers. A grateful dairy industry pledged $2 million to Nixon's 1972 campaign. A Justice Department suit against the milk producers was settled with the industry admitting to 1972 election contributions of six hundred thousand dollars, but denying any illegal activity.

Connally was indicted on bribery charges July 29, 1974, the same day the House Judiciary Committee voted to recommend to the House that Nixon be impeached. In addition to the bribery accusation, Connally also faced charges that he obstructed the investigation into the milk lobby fund and lied to the grand jury about it. He told the jurors he had learned of the administration's decision to hike milk supports from the newspapers, not from the White House Oval Office. Nixon's tapes from the Oval Office for March 23, 1971, indicated otherwise.

In the face of everything else that was swirling about him, Nixon was determined to help Connally. He didn't want all of that milk-fund business to come up. He called my office, but I was out west, fishing. He then cornered my deputy, Laurence H. Silberman, raising hell about Assistant Attorney General Henry E. Peterson and his support of Jaworski's probe of Connally.[14] He demanded that Peterson, who headed up the department's Criminal Division, be fired. It didn't take long for Silberman to reach me. Cabinet officers are never out of touch with the administration. He quickly filled me in on Nixon's comments.

"The president wants me to call Haig back and tell him what we have done about Connally and Peterson," a somewhat harried Silberman said. That was so much horseshit, and quite frankly, I was tired of it. "Tell him to go piss up a rope," I replied, referring to the president. Then I went back to fishing. I don't recall that Silberman ever relayed my message to Haig and the president quite that way, but I wish he had. I was mad. Silberman kept his cool, though. He told Haig that neither he nor I were about to fire Peterson.

The following April a Texas federal jury found Connally not guilty of the bribery charge and shortly thereafter the perjury and conspiracy charges were dismissed. Nevertheless, Connally's political life was ended.

Those White House requests, or demands, were not isolated; there were many of them, at least at the beginning of my term as attorney general. I knew Nixon was getting goofy, and he was laying everything off on Haig, bending his ear every day for an hour or two at a time. Do this, do that. Tell Justice to do this; tell the FBI to do that—just irresponsible stuff he kept throwing out. White House Counsel J. Fred Buzhardt, too, would get an earful, and both Haig and Buzhardt would pass along to me the president's daily demands.

Almost from day one as attorney general, I received calls from Haig or Buzhardt that Nixon wanted me to shut down the Watergate investigations. He wanted me to use the FBI to probe the Central Intelligence Agency, which he blamed for all his problems. He thought the CIA was out to get him, although I think that was just a ruse. Nixon knew well the man responsible for the trouble he was in; he looked at him every day while shaving.

One day I was in a meeting with Haig, just the two of us, and he talked about Nixon's wish to have the FBI get after the CIA. I balked once again.

"Well, we always can get another attorney general," Haig said. I didn't take it as a threat, but I knew what he was talking about.

"That's fine, Al," I replied, "but you are going to have to fire me. I am not going to resign and flounce out of here like Richardson did. You would be a lot better off today if he had stuck it out."

That was that. I don't recall that Haig ever brought the subject up again.

Still, there were many other requests, supposedly from the White House, but you didn't know where they were coming from. This is what happened on the "Double D" requests.

Double D was in-depth wiretapping, surreptitious wiretapping. Such taps were perfectly proper, but they were not the ones that required a court order. They were top secret, usually reserved for electronic eavesdropping on double agents and for people suspected of being double agents. It's what they called a "black bag" job. FBI agents would go into a private apartment, put the wiretap under the bed or whatever. It was a completely secret kind of deal. The most we ever had was twenty or so, as I recall, but I had three of them in the first week I was attorney general.

What I thought was improper was the way the White House went about it. They had a practice of getting some GS15 (a middle-echelon functionary) to telephone the Justice Department and say, "This is the White House calling," and everybody at Justice would jump. I guess the procedure was intended to frighten my staff, but I insisted they find out who in the White House was calling.

It was that kind of thing that got Mitchell in trouble when he was attorney general. The White House would call up and say it wanted a tap; Mitchell would sign the request, but the White House initiated it. When the administration got into trouble over them, the White House disavowed any knowledge. They unloaded it all on Mitchell because he had signed the requests. As a result, Mitchell was criticized because it looked like he was arbitrarily laying them on.

I wasn't going to go down that road. I didn't want to put a wiretap on somebody and then have the White House say, "We didn't authorize this." I wanted the head of the department making the request to send me a letter authorizing Double D requests.

Even after Nixon resigned and Ford was president, I still got some of those wiretap requests without a signature. I was having problems with Secretary of State Henry Kissinger in particular. I'd get them from the State

Department, from Kissinger through some GS15, but he never would sign them. So some of them hung fire for two or three weeks—just gathering dust in the department—and that really irritated Ford. Kissinger would ship those things to Ford and get him to sign them.

That was a pattern Kissinger had established long before I became attorney general. When he was national security advisor, prior to joining the Nixon Cabinet as secretary of state, he would ask Haig to request FBI surveillance of people he believed were leaking sensitive foreign policy matters to the press. Among those Kissinger suspected were members of his own National Security Council staff, plus members of the press. In the late 1960s, Haig was a colonel attached to Kissinger's White House office.

"It was very clear to me that [the surveillance] would probably include wiretapping," Haig told a Senate Foreign Relations Committee hearing. Kissinger testified that he assumed the FBI "would conduct an investigation using whatever techniques they deemed appropriate," including wiretaps.

Both Nixon and Kissinger were paranoid about leaks to the press and saw in FBI surveillance methods a way to threaten the perpetrators. But Kissinger vehemently denied that he ordered any wiretaps and, at one point, threatened to resign over the issue.

"To some friends, Kissinger deflected blame for the wiretaps by pinning the excesses on Haig," wrote author Walter Isaacson. "Much of what was 'requested' in Kissinger's name, he insisted, was done on Haig's own initiative.... [But] Kissinger decided that it was in his own interest—and served to enhance his credibility with Haldeman, Nixon and [J. Edgar] Hoover—to let Haig do so."[15]

William Safire, who served as a presidential speechwriter, recalled that "an embarrassed and worried Kissinger and Haig" explained to him the wiretap procedure in April 1969.

"The arrangement was made for Kissinger to supply the names to the Director [Hoover], the conduit being Al Haig to William Sullivan of the FBI. Hoover required that each authorization be signed by John Mitchell, which he thought would make the taps lawful."[16]

In July 1974 Nixon reaffirmed to Senate Foreign Relations chairman J. William Fulbright that he, not Kissinger, had authorized wiretaps of seventeen individuals and that each tap was justified and legal. Kissinger noted later that Nixon thus confirmed that "my account of his roles was 'entirely correct,' and he [Nixon] took full responsibility. Attorney General William Saxbe, FBI Director Clarence Kelley, and other FBI officials gave evidence that sustained my version of events."[17]

That is true. Two days prior to Nixon's letter to Fulbright, I told the Senate Foreign Relations Committee that Hoover might have used Kissinger's name for some of the wiretaps without Kissinger's knowledge. But then, I wasn't attorney general at the time of the wiretaps in question. I only recall firsthand Kissinger's subsequent actions.

As Isaacson points out, the seventeen wiretaps that were carried out in the name of national security were "just the first step down a slippery slope. . . . It was just a short step to the formation of a secret White House unit to bug political opponents"—and to the downfall of a president.[18]

Nixon Bows Out

When transcripts of the Oval Office tapes began to appear, I suspected—but did not know—that Nixon might be more involved in Watergate than he was willing to admit. Still, I couldn't accept in my mind that there was anything on the tapes that incriminated Nixon directly in any wrongdoing. If there had been, I reasoned, any fool would have destroyed them long before any investigation began.

By midsummer, however, I was convinced that he had lied to the American people and to me. I believed that I had been loyal to the president as a member of his administration, regardless of my personal opinions, and I put my trust in him. Then I learned my trust was misplaced. It shook my faith in the political system and those who were running it.

Throughout the summer of 1974, Nixon fought tooth and nail to keep the transcripts to himself, as a matter of "executive privilege." I supported that view, up to a point. I also supported the role of Watergate Special Prosecutor Jaworski and on numerous occasions during 1974 was called upon by Congress and by the press to reiterate my position.

I recall one battle Jaworski had with the White House over the release of sixty-four tapes that had been subpoenaed. In the process, the question of Jaworski's independence from the White House came before the Senate Judiciary Committee, headed by my friend, James O. Eastland, D-Mississippi. The committee reaffirmed the special prosecutor's authority, but it also believed it necessary to write me a letter to remind me of statements I had made, during my confirmation hearings, supporting Jaworski.

In my reply to Eastland, I said I would continue to see that the special prosecutor had all the room he needed to carry out his responsibilities. I also promised to "use appropriate means to support his independence." When reporters asked if I would fire Jaworski, I told them flatly that nobody was going to fire him. Nobody could fire him but me, and I certainly had no intention of doing so.

It was long suspected that somewhere in the hours of tapes there would be found a "smoking gun," a taped conversation that would prove Nixon's complicity in Watergate. In an eight to zero vote on July 24, the U.S. Supreme Court rejected the president's claim of executive privilege and ordered the White House to give up the sixty-four subpoenaed tapes to U.S. District Court Judge John J. Sirica. On the heels of the court's decision, the House Judiciary Committee voted articles of impeachment. It was over for Nixon, and everyone knew it.

Nixon certainly knew all along there was a "smoking gun." It was hidden in the sixty-four subpoenaed tapes. The fatal "bullet" was fired on June 23, 1972, in a conversation he had with his chief of staff, H. R. Haldeman.[1] Furthermore, Nixon had listened to that particular tape in May. "When I first heard it, I knew it would be a problem for us if it ever became public," he wrote in his memoirs.[2] In his own book, Haldeman wrote that Nixon "was involved in the cover-up from Day One, although neither he nor we considered it a cover-up at that time."[3] I don't know what you would call it then: A stroll in the park?

In his opinion, Haldeman believed the "cover-up collapsed because it was doomed from the start. Morally and legally it was the wrong thing to do—so it should have failed. Tactically, too many people knew too much. Too many foolish risks were taken."[4] I shudder to think what might have happened had fewer people known less and had the crooks not been so "foolish."

On August 1, even before the June 23 tape had been revealed publicly, Nixon told Haig that he planned to resign, but over the next few days he waffled as to whether he should or when he should. Haig put Nixon's top speechwriter, Ray Price, to work drafting a resignation speech, which Price completed on August 4. Ford and Haig met several times to discuss the succession that appeared imminent. A transition plan already was in the works.

The following day, Nixon released three transcripts, which included the June 23, 1972, conversation he had with Haldeman, just six days after the Watergate break-in. Here was irrefutable evidence that Nixon had lied to protect his presidency. He had covered up illegal acts, and he had obstructed justice. Following a discussion of how to limit the FBI in its probe, Nixon told Haldeman to tell the CIA that "'the president [believes] . . . they should call the FBI in and say that we wish for the country, don't go any further into this case.' Period." He emphasized how hard he wanted Halde-man to push the matter. "Play it tough," he said. "That's the way they play it, and that's the way we are going to play it."[5]

The following morning, August 6, a somber cabinet gathered for what everyone expected to be the final meeting of the Nixon administration. It was customary during times of crisis in the administration to applaud the president as he entered the cabinet room, but no one clapped that morning. Everyone seemed a little nervous, on edge, expecting Nixon to finally announce his resignation and relieve the nation of its agony. Ford later described the tension as "unbelievable." George Bush, there by invitation as chairman of the Republican Party, described it as "a kind of carnival atmosphere . . . unreal." To me it was like being in Wonderland with Alice; it seemed so illusory. The Nixon presidency was collapsing all around us; the wolf was at the door.

I took my customary seat to the left of Vice President Ford, who sat at the oblong table directly across from Nixon. I think everyone noticed how tired, even pale, the president looked. He had been up during the night, unable to sleep. Resignation stared him in the face, but he had decided to "play the role of President right to the hilt and right to the end. . . . I was determined not to appear to have resigned the presidency because of a consensus of staff or cabinet opinion or because of public pressure from the people around me."[6] Actually, Nixon knew that he would be "going in two days time, but if I said that it would have leaked."[7]

Nixon launched into the first of his "talking points" from the agenda drafted that morning. Point A concerned "the most important issue confronting the nation and confronting us internationally, too—inflation." I was stunned. I think we were all stunned. I thought I heard Ford suck air next to me.

Like all of us, the vice president had believed "this was going to be a momentous occasion, that Nixon was going to come to grips with the threat to his presidency, that he was going to tell us about his future plans.[According to Haig, Ford already knew Nixon planned to resign.[8]] Instead he was talking about something that was totally irrelevant to the circumstances that confronted him and the nation as well."[9]

Perhaps Nixon sensed our surprise. He observed our faces—"intent, sober, noncommittal"—and turned to the crisis of the presidency.[10] He was going to tough it out, convinced that "the constitutional course must be adhered to" in order to preserve the presidency and "the principles that give our government legitimacy."[11]

After two or three minutes Nixon paused briefly, as if to get some sign of support, perhaps even a rousing cheer. Nothing. Continuing, he told the cabinet, "You don't have to talk about Watergate. I suggest you talk about the good things the administration has done."[12]

Ford caught Nixon's eye; he had something to say, and Nixon allowed the interruption.

"First, everyone here recognizes the difficult position I am in," he began. "I am a party in interest." He expressed sympathy for the president. But, Ford said, "Had I known and had it been disclosed to me what has been disclosed in reference to the Watergate affair in the last twenty-four hours, I would not have made a number of statements that I have made, either as minority leader or as vice president of the United States."

Ford backed away from the president as gracefully as he could under the circumstances, adding: "I expect to continue to support fully the administration's foreign policy and fight against inflation."[13]

Nixon seized that as his cue to return to his discussion of the economy. He mentioned the agricultural appropriations bill, which he said he intended to veto.[14] He then took up the inflation issue again and plans to stage in six months or so an economic summit meeting between the executive branch and Congress.

I couldn't sit there in silence any longer. The barn was on fire and nobody appeared to be paying any attention to it. I interrupted the president. "Mr. President, I don't think we should be talking about a summit conference six months from now. I think we ought to be talking about next week!"

Nobody said a word. The cabinet sat there, looking down their noses. What happened next comes in a variety of packages, depending upon whose recollection of history it is. I recall that Nixon picked up his papers and walked out of the cabinet room. Others don't remember it that way. Some remember Bush speaking next and suggesting speedy resignation was the only route to save the presidency and the Republican Party. Haig recalled that he was "so God damned offended" by Bush's remarks "that I almost got up and threw him out of the room. . . . Right then and there I decided George Bush had no business ever being president of the United States."[15]

In his book, *Years of Upheaval*, Kissinger also wrote about that last Nixon cabinet meeting and the comments that were made. "It was cruel. And it was necessary. For Nixon's own appointees to turn on him was not the best way to end a Presidency. Yet he had left them no other choice."[16] Kissinger told the cabinet, "We are not here to offer excuses for what we cannot do. We are here to do the nation's business."[17]

Now, whether those statements were made in Nixon's presence, I don't recall. What I do remember, and Dean Burch recalled it, too, is that Nixon left the cabinet room shortly after my comment. Burch was political counselor to the president and former chairman of the Federal Communications Commission.

In any event, Nixon realized he had no choice but to resign. He did so in a nationwide television address from the cabinet room on the evening of August 8, 1974. That day I was in Mechanicsburg when I received a call at the farm from Nixon. "Bill," he said somberly, "I wanted you to know that I have decided to resign tomorrow." He said I was the first cabinet member he had called. That, I thought, was a lie. Then, he briefly mentioned he would speak to the nation that evening. At noon the following day, Ford took the presidential oath of office.

I next saw Nixon in the White House East Room on Friday morning, August 9, with Pat and the family. The mood was like attending a funeral. More than a few of the three hundred members of the Nixon White House assembled there already were blubbering, even before he and the family entered the room. The cabinet members were in the front row, seated on the most fragile of chairs. Suddenly, just before the president arrived, I felt my chair give way, and I ended up flat on my ass. I mean, it was a total collapse. That old chair just became kindling. It was the only comic relief we had that day.

Nixon, struggling to maintain his composure, spoke of his father, "a streetcar motorman first" in Columbus, Ohio, and of his mother, "a saint." It was a strange, rambling farewell, particularly the passage in which he urged others to "never be petty. Always remember, others may hate you, but those who hate you don't win unless you hate them, and then you destroy yourself." I thought that rather ironic for him to say, given that his entire political career was marked with pettiness and vindictiveness.

Everyone stood and applauded as Nixon ended his speech and left the White House for the last time as president. I thought it was high drama, like someone had choreographed it. Under the circumstances, I believed it was a little over the top, a little overly dramatic, as he turned on the steps of *Marine One,* the president's helicopter, and waved farewell. He should have just folded his tent and quietly slipped away.

Standing around under the portico of the White House, I felt like a bastard at a family reunion because all of these other guys were so loyal, and I felt I wasn't. It was a bizarre and unique experience, to be sure.

I never saw Nixon after that, and didn't want to. When he opened his library in Yorba Linda, California, in July 1990, he wanted me to be there, along with other members of his cabinet. On one occasion he called and said he would send a plane for me, but I refused to go. Afterwards, he sent me a note: "Sorry you couldn't be here."

While I was in India for two years, I often thought of Nixon and his crew. It reminded me of a big scandal out in Colorado in the 1870s. A guy by the name of Alfred G. Packer was missing in the San Juan Mountains for two months in the dead of winter. He survived, but the question was whether he killed the five others in his party or whether they died natural deaths. In any event, he was accused of eating them to survive and was convicted of manslaughter. As wags tell it, when Packer was sentenced the judge said, "You son of a bitch. You ate up the Democratic majority of this county!"

That was my attitude toward Nixon. He wrecked the Republican Party. He also corrupted some of our highest officials, and for supporting him in that effort, many of them went to the penitentiary—and he consistently said he never had anything to do with it.

Nixon will not go down as a great president because of the things he did in Watergate, but he was not a victim. Many of his problems were because he surrounded himself with a bunch of zealots rather than people who had faced the electorate over the years. When you are president, you can't get by by blaming others. He tried to blame Watergate and everything on other people. When you have clowns like Haldeman and Ehrlichman and some of the other ding-a-lings in the White House, you can't blame anybody but yourself.

When he died, I didn't go to the funeral, either. He had lied to me, as he had lied to everyone else, and he tried to involve me in his lies. I never can forgive him for that.

The Transition

The transition from Nixon to Ford was in the works several months prior to Nixon's departure, although Ford said he knew nothing of that until days before Nixon resigned. Anticipating the change in command, Ford's first law partner, Philip W. Buchen, secretly created a transition team, "A dangerous and questionable undertaking," Ford thought.[1] When he told Buchen the end was near for Nixon, considerable work already had been achieved by what was dubbed "The Ford Foundation" to surround the vice president with the "trusted group of advisors" and other key players he would need during the formative days of his presidency.

Among the myriad issues raised was whether Ford should ask for the resignations of each of the cabinet officers, a tradition at the time of changing administrations. "It will be clear that most of the political types will be expected to leave within a reasonable time," Buchen, now White House counsel, wrote in a memorandum to Ford.[2] There certainly was no love lost between the Nixon holdovers and the new kids on the block. Ford said his transition staff was telling him, "As soon as we get rid of these Nixon appointees, the government will be legitimate again."[3]

The president's decision became known quickly. He convened his first cabinet meeting the day after he took office and four days after we met for the last time with Nixon. It was a much different atmosphere, relaxed and friendly. The seat on my right was empty now, awaiting Ford's nominee for vice president.[4]

Ford told us he neither expected nor would ask for any resignations, citing the importance of maintaining the continuity and the stability of government. "I think we have a fine team here, and I am looking forward to working with each and every one of you," he said.[5]

However, he suggested that changes might be forthcoming in "a reasonable time," without mentioning specifics.[6] I assumed I was on the short list. As I later learned, everyone was on the short list, save Kissinger; Interior Secretary Rogers C. B. Morton, a Ford confidante; and perhaps Treasury Secretary William E. Simon.

The president gave each of us an opportunity to speak. I mentioned that the involvement of the Justice Department in administration politics, such as what had transpired during the previous three administrations, was undesirable. In that regard, I felt it unwise for me to be knee-deep in the campaign, drumming up votes for party candidates. He agreed. I also mentioned that I thought the amendments to the 1966 Freedom of Information Act then pending in Congress were "bad legislation" and probably deserved to be vetoed.

Taking note of that in the *Chicago Tribune* some weeks later, Ford's former press secretary, Jerald F. terHorst, wrote

> On the way out of the Cabinet Room, Presidential counselor Robert T. Hartmann and I . . . exchanged grim glances. It was clear that the attorney general had not caught the spirit of Ford's desire to establish an open administration after years of Nixon isolation. We immediately sought out Ford and pointed out to him that a veto of the Freedom of Information amendments would make his pledge of openness ring hollow.
>
> Ford agreed and . . . suggested that the Senate and House chairmen be asked to hold up the amendments so his administration people could work out an acceptable compromise.[7]

As the discussion moved around the table, Ford eyed each speaker intently, sizing us up. Later, in his autobiography, he noted that his staff found me to be "garrulous, and he tended to shoot from the hip, but his independence made him credible, and I was delighted when he agreed to stay."[8]

Political cartoonist Gary Trudeau, I believed, captured my situation perfectly in a four-panel *Doonesbury* strip. Each panel depicted only the White House, with the "voices" of Ford and his political counselor, Robert T. Hartmann, coming from within.

"Sir, if you don't mind me saying so, letting the entire Nixon Cabinet stay on could be a move we're going to regret."

"Bob, as you know, during those first days it was important to stress continuity."

"Yes, sir, but the whole Cabinet?"

"Yeah, I know. It's just I didn't want to embarrass Saxbe in front of the others."[9]

Cartoonist Gary Trudeau found humor in my service in the Ford Cabinet.
Doonesbury © G. B. Trudeau. Reprinted with permission of the Universal Press
Syndicate. All rights reserved.

Getting the green light from Ford that I was, in fact, part of his team
didn't really come until the following Tuesday, August 13, when Ford and I
met one-on-one for the first time. As is the custom before any meeting, the
president was briefed on the subjects to be discussed. In that instance, the
briefer was Kenneth R. Cole Jr., executive director of the Domestic Council, who began his memorandum to Ford: "He [Saxbe] has learned that
you called some Cabinet Secretaries before assuming the Presidency to ask
them to stay, and that you personally asked other Cabinet Secretaries to
stay when you greeted them in the receiving line after taking the oath of
office. Saxbe is fearful that he is the only Cabinet Secretary who has not
been personally and directly asked to stay on, and is most likely seeking
some form of clarification of his own future tenure."[10]

"With Mitchell leaving, Richardson leaving, Kleindienst leaving and Bork
taking over and then Saxbe taking over, that was a pretty unsettled situation in the attorney general's office," Ford explained in an interview later.
"Because of all that turmoil, I decided right early that we had to get somebody totally outside of the political arena. It was nothing personal against
Bill Saxbe; it was just that we wanted no politician in the office."[11]

He's right in saying the Justice Department had been in disarray. When
I took over in January 1974, it was. I turned it into a working department
again, which is what I was supposed to do. That's what I said I was going to
do, and that is what I did. It was never a political issue with me; I just was
not Ford's man. I never was close to Ford. When he became vice president,
he visited all the departments, including Justice. We had lunch together.
He didn't know anything about the Justice Department, and I am sure he
left that day thinking I didn't know anything about it, either.

Ford began our August 13 meeting by following the agenda Cole drafted. He reassured me that he wanted me on his team as attorney general and to run the department as I had been running it—clean and fair. I discussed the problems I had had with Nixon, trying to get him to focus on some major issues before the Justice Department. Among those were the flood of illegal immigrants, primarily from Mexico, and my plans to combat the problem with the aid of some five hundred additional Immigration and Naturalization Service officers. I saw it as a problem that only was going to get worse, and I was right.

We talked briefly about wiretaps. I assured him that the government was no longer engaged in illegal wiretaps or other lawless electronic surveillance operations. Also, we reviewed pending legislation, including the proposed amendments to the Freedom of Information Act, which I opposed. I felt it opened too wide the drawers to FBI files. Contrary to ter-Horst's opinion, I did understand Ford's desire for an "open door" administration, especially after what the country just had been through.

Ford admitted that most of the cabinet opposed the act, "But early on in my congressional career, I had favored it, so I wasn't going to change just because I went to the White House. Presidents and attorneys general don't always agree, but the boss is the president, not the attorney general."[12] He concluded our hour-long talk by saying he did not intend to interfere in matters involving litigation, prosecution, or law enforcement.

Ford's presidency of 895 days was but hours old when it was confronted with the issue of Nixon's papers and tapes, which soon would involve the Justice Department and me, as well. On Friday, August 9, the day he left the White House, Nixon wasn't home five minutes in San Clemente, California, before he called Haig and demanded that everything be packed up and shipped to him forthwith. "The following day Haig circulated a memorandum for the White House staff. 'By custom and tradition . . . the files of the White House Office belong to the President in whose Administration they are accumulated.'"[13] Haig asked that they be kept separate from Ford's files.

Nixon's documents, some 950 reels of tape and 46 million pieces of paper, were stored in the White House and the Executive Office Building. Ford said the Secret Service, in a confidential memorandum, expressed concern that the Executive Office Building's fourth floor might not be able to withstand the extra weight.[14]

Late in the afternoon of August 10, Benton L. Becker, an attorney volunteering his services with the transition team, discovered several military trucks at the West Wing of the White House being loaded with file cabinets and boxes that appeared to be stuffed with Nixon documents. The air force officer in charge said Haig had ordered them shipped that night to San Clemente.[15] Becker immediately went to see Ford, who summoned Haig. Haig denied any knowledge of the shipment, saying it apparently was a misunderstanding, Becker recalled.[16] The shipment was halted, much to Nixon's consternation.

After wrestling with the problem for a week or so, Ford asked me, "Bill, who owns these documents? I need you to give me an official opinion before we do anything."[17] He followed up with a letter dated August 22. Two weeks later I sent Ford my opinion.

> To conclude that such materials are not the property of former President Nixon would be to reverse what has apparently been the almost unvaried understanding of all three branches of the government since the beginning of the Republic, and to call into question the practices of our Presidents since the earliest times.
>
> . . . Moreover . . . the 1955 Presidential Libraries Act, which serves as the permanent basis of the Presidential Library system, constitutes clear legislative acknowledgment that a President has title to all documents and historical materials—whether personal or official—which accumulate in the White House Office during his incumbency.
>
> . . . Because the principle of Presidential ownership of White House materials has been acknowledged by all three branches of the Government from the earliest times; because that principle does not violate any provision of the Constitution or contravene any existing statute; and because that principle is not inconsistent with adequate protection of the interests of the United States, I conclude that the papers and materials in question were the property of Richard M. Nixon when his term of office ended.[18]

Ford was anxious to rid himself of the tapes and documents issue and of the specter of Nixon—both of which became oppressive for the Ford presidency. "I can't run this office while this [Nixon] business drags on day after day," Ford told House Majority Leader Thomas P. "Tip" O'Neill just before the pardoning of Nixon. "There are a lot more important things for me to be spending my time on."[19]

Ford reviewed my opinion with Becker, Buchen, and Hartmann, all of whom "strongly advised me it would be dangerous to let those papers out of the White House until the courts decided who had control and jurisdiction," the president explained. After numerous and vigorous court challenges by Nixon and his family, the bulk of the materials remain in the hands of the Archivist of the United States under the Presidential Recordings and Materials Preservation Act of 1974 and the Presidential Records Act of 1978.

Earlier in the year I undertook what the press described as "an unprecedented speaking campaign . . . preaching a homespun, common-sense philosophy designed to restore the nation's faith in its system of justice."[20] In the month of June alone I gave thirteen speeches, protesting what I saw as shortcomings in the nation's morality.

I received a standing ovation from state attorneys general meeting in Williamsburg, Virginia, when I described Watergate as "the greatest cloud in the nation's history." At the Cleveland City Club, I vowed that the Justice Department would not engage in illegal electronic eavesdropping. Before a regional meeting of the International Association of Police Chiefs in Indianapolis, I decried those federal officials who would undermine the justice system through the illegal collection of evidence. To the graduates at The Ohio State University Law School, I said the Watergate scandal must become a "watershed" for morality in public life. "We are either moral or immoral, and it really doesn't take much soul-searching to know which is which." And at the Urbana (Ohio) College commencement, I told the graduates, "If we want better days, it all comes down in the final analysis to individual responsibility and morality."

I have believed and lived by this philosophy all my life, and at the time I thought it was important for somebody in the administration to get out of Washington and say those things to the people. We all had been battered and bruised by those who chose to play fast and loose with the law of the land.

In July, Nixon had expressed to me his concern for the rising crime rate; it had risen 15 percent in the first quarter of 1974 following a 16 percent increase in the final quarter of 1973.

"The fifteen percent increase . . . troubles me deeply," Nixon wrote in his memorandum to me July 16. "This crime rise *must* be dealt with . . . I want this done as quickly and as professionally as your Department is able to compile it and look forward to a full report by the end of this month."[21]

The statistics were harsh, bitter, and dismaying, and only supported what I had been saying in my speeches. In fact, the administration's efforts had been a dismal failure. In my report to the president I outlined a number of options to attack crime: massive funding; "jawboning" by public officials to focus on the problem; pinpointing federal assistance for training, advance information systems, and special task forces; and congressional funding for Law Enforcement Assistance Administration (LEAA) programs aimed at youthful offenders.

In conclusion, however, I admitted that "none of these programs, nor all of them in combination, nor any other program that we can devise is guaranteed to result in a dramatic decrease in crime in the foreseeable future. . . . Any dramatic increase in law enforcement effectiveness will have to be at the state and local level and must result from a genuine demand from the people that criminal activities be reduced."[22]

In submitting my report to the president, I sent a copy to Haig with a covering note:

> What we are saying in this report is that there are no more rabbits in the hat. Massive amounts of money would disappear into the present law enforcement structure without materially affecting basic statistics. The L.E.A.A. impact city effort has not produced a commensurate decrease in those selected cities.
>
> . . . The grand scale overhaul of our fragmented law enforcement structure is not now a practical solution but would, in my mind, be the only dramatic way to tackle the problem. I hope to propose it again when the climate is right.[23]

Nixon never responded, but Ford did, after a fashion. I read with some dismay the following passage in his autobiography, published in 1979:

> Too often the Nixon Administration's response to [the rising crime rate] was a lot of rhetoric about the need to maintain "law and order." In addition, the Law Enforcement Assistance Administration . . . an agency of the Department of Justice, funneled billions of dollars' worth of hardware to police departments in almost every community. The result was a public perception that Washington felt the federal government—and only the federal government—could do something about crime. . . . Clearly, a new approach was necessary. . . . I felt it was time for us as a people to change the way we *thought* about crime.[24]

During my tenure as attorney general, both in Ohio and in Washington, I hammered away at strengthening *local* law enforcement. To suggest that a new approach was required clearly demonstrated a lack of understanding and awareness on Ford's part.

19

Telephones and COINTELPRO

One of the major issues before the Justice Department when I took office as attorney general was whether to file an antitrust suit against the nation's largest privately-held corporation, American Telephone and Telegraph Company. I didn't initiate the action—quite frankly, I don't know which of my predecessors did—but it fell on my watch to deal with that behemoth.[1]

The task was imposing, to say the least. Here we had a corporation that was second only to the federal government in the number of people it employed; it boasted assets of some $67 billion; and it made some $3 billion in profit in the year before I joined the Department of Justice.

What the Justice Department alleged was that AT&T had for years illegally monopolized the telecommunications industry. After all, it had some 90 percent of the long-distance telephone business, more than 80 percent of the domestic business through its twenty-three Bell companies, and owned the Western Electric Company, which manufactured equipment for the Bell System. It also owned and operated Bell Laboratories, the nation's largest industrial laboratory.

So, the case was an extremely important one for the Justice Department and for me. The magnitude of it demanded the attention of the president of the United States. Time and again in 1974 I tried to talk to Nixon about AT&T, but all he wanted to talk about were his problems and how he was being put upon by just about everybody. He was filled with self-pity and not very rational in his thinking. So I would go to Al Haig in an attempt to get answers. He would do what he could, but he was not in a position to give the green light on filing the AT&T case.

The Justice Department's antitrust case against International Business Machines was another big one that had been languishing since its filing in 1969. It hadn't gone to trial by 1974, and I just let it die. By then IBM faced numerous competitors in the computer field, so the suit just ran out of gas.

As for dealing with Nixon on any of those important issues, I finally gave up.

When Ford took office, I sensed it was time to renew our efforts on the AT&T case. An annual inflation rate of 12 percent saddled the nation. Inflation was, Ford believed, "domestic enemy number one." Proudly wearing a WIN (Whip Inflation Now) button on his lapel for the first time, Ford laid out his economic plan to a joint session of Congress on October 8, 1974. In his remarks concerning the "restrictive practices" that spur inflation, the president said he was "determined to return to the vigorous enforcement of antitrust laws," and urged that the penalties for antitrust violations be dramatically increased.

Four days before Ford's speech, I was at the Whiteface Inn, Lake Placid, New York, to address the Associated Industries of New York State, a strong group of industrialists. I took the opportunity to advance the administration's position on increasing the jail terms and fines in antitrust convictions. Doing so would raise the offense from a misdemeanor to a felony.

Those who fix prices, evade income taxes, or violate our antitrust laws "should go to prison," I said. "They are not better than the car thief or the burglar or the robber" who, statistically, receive much stiffer sentences than white collar criminals. "They are all members of the same fraternity. And it's about time that all of the federal judges begin realizing that. . . .

"The pattern today is for the antitrust offender, like so many tax evaders, to receive a suspended sentence and be back on the golf course the next day," I said, which drew snickers from the industrialists. I also suggested that the federal courts coddled white-collar criminals. And they did.

I realized that particular audience might not receive the speech with enthusiasm. Just before going to the podium, I told Bob Havel, my new director of the department's public information office, to keep the motor running and the car door open just in case we had to make a quick getaway.

In any event, Ford tacitly gave me the green light for the antitrust division of the Justice Department to bring legal action to force AT&T to divest itself of its Western Electric subsidiary and reduce its monopoly of the long distance business or its operating companies. Most of the work had been done by the fall of 1974, with but a few t's to be crossed and i's to be dotted. News of the renewed effort had been well known for months,[2] and the lobbyists for AT&T and all its subsidiaries busied themselves twisting arms in the Congress to oppose any such action.

The chief arm-twister was AT&T Chairman John D. deButts. He was well-placed in Washington circles, having been with the Washington Telephone Company before heading up AT&T. For some months he had been quite vocal in defending the company's monopoly, maintaining that in the telecommunications industry a monopoly was the far better alternative to unbridled competition. Some of us in the Justice Department didn't see it quite so clearly as did deButts.

I received a call from John Fox, AT&T's Washington-based vice president for legislative affairs, whom I knew in passing as a member of the Burning Tree Country Club. He asked if he and AT&T's corporate counsel, F. Mark Garlinghouse, could come see me. I knew what they wanted: They knew we were getting close to filing our case and wanted to twist my arm, too. I said they could come.

Early Wednesday morning, November 20, Garlinghouse, Fox, and an entourage of attorneys arrived at my office. As I remember, joining me were my antitrust chief, Thomas E. Kauper; his deputy, Keith I. Clearwaters; and Hugh P. Morrison from our litigation division. Garlinghouse did most of the talking, arguing his case against filing the suit or, barring that, for a delay in filing. Breaking up AT&T would only increase telephone rates and lead to a deterioration of service, he said. His prime concern, however, was the financial impact on what was then the nation's largest corporate borrower.

Any antitrust action would have a disastrous effect on AT&T's ability to raise capital, Garlinghouse said, but of immediate concern was the $600 million public offering that had begun the week previous. It was the biggest public financing ever by a corporation, and a suit at that time would place it in jeopardy. "You just can't do this to us!" he said. "It will cost us a fortune! You can't do this to us!"

I listened politely as the AT&T delegation dictated to me and to the federal government what we could and couldn't do, and then I told them the Justice Department intended to bring suit. After the meeting broke up, I told Kauper, "File that damn suit!"

Word quickly spread that the suit would be filed after the close of the markets that day. I made sure the White House and the Securities and Exchange Commission were notified of our intention. White House Counsel Phillip Areeda, whose expertise was in antitrust law, immediately sent a memorandum, to be treated as "highly classified," to President Ford, who was touring Japan. Areeda correctly noted, "The Attorney General recognizes that this may have a short-time depressing effect on AT&T securities and perhaps more broadly."[3]

By 11:00 A.M. deButts and AT&T learned of our intent. At 3:00 P.M. the New York Stock Exchange halted trading in AT&T for an hour prior to the filing of the suit in U.S. District Court. "The [Justice Department] announcement took Wall Street by surprise," Vartanig G. Vartan wrote in *The*

New York Times. The street was "surprised and shocked," *The Wall Street Journal* reported.

"I can't understand why Justice would take an action that could lead to dismemberment of the Bell System," deButts said at a New York news conference later that day. "We are . . . astonished that the Justice Department would take its present action with apparent disregard for its impact on the public."

I maintained that we had, in fact, carefully considered the impact of such action and concluded that the law must be enforced.

Among those unhappy with my decision to file the suit was fellow cabinet officer, William E. Simon, who has been labeled "Nixon's last and worst Secretary of the Treasury,"[4] and who never did get on Ford's bandwagon. DeButts telephoned Simon on the twentieth to voice his complaint about the filing of the suit. DeButts began softly with a report on his success as U.S. Savings Bond chairman. Then their conversation went something like this:

"Well, John, that's just wonderful," Simon told him. "What a tremendous contribution you have made to your country."

"Well, it's got a helluva way of showing its appreciation," deButts said angrily.

"What do you mean by that?"

DeButts told Simon he had just learned that Justice was going to sue AT&T in an attempt to break apart the Bell System and that trading had been suspended in AT&T's stock. Simon was surprised and upset.[5]

In a memorandum to Ford, Simon decried the timing of the suit, stating that it had forced the cancellation of the $600 million debt offering and raised "serious questions" as to how AT&T could operate without capital for construction and improvement programs.[6]

That, of course, was the deButts argument all over again. Simon pointed out to the president that the New York investment firm of Salomon Brothers was the manager of the underwriting for AT&T. Previous to his government service, Simon had been the director of Salomon's municipal and government bond department, so he had more than a passing interest in the matter.

Simon believed the suit should have been discussed with the Economic Policy Board, chaired by him and run by William L. Seidman as executive director. The EPB had been "assigned responsibility to review governmental decisions affecting the economy," he wrote to Ford, and the suit certainly would have "substantial impact on the economy."[7]

Well, that was true. The AT&T monopoly in the telecommunications industry was busted in 1982, and under court order, its Baby Bells split up into regional telephone companies. Since then, many people have made a lot of money. What was not true was the predicted demise of mankind, as delineated by AT&T executives in 1974. Two days after the suit was filed, AT&T withdrew its $600 million offering, stating that investors needed time to assess the situation in what was described as an unstable market. DeButts told a national television audience that the company would return to the bond markets at a later date, which it did.

The AT&T suit was big, all right, but we had a lot of other balls in the air. I felt like a short-order cook, first shaking this pot, then another one. On Monday of that same week, I issued a report critical of the FBI for its damn near illegal activities against those suspected of being subversives.

Shortly after I became attorney general in January, I discovered in a closet just off my office several filing cabinets. Each was securely chained with padlocks as big as a fist. Nobody seemed to know anything about them. I couldn't get a straight answer as to why they were there and what they contained, other than they were top secret FBI files. When I was told I couldn't open them up, I picked up the phone and called FBI Director Clarence M. Kelley.

"Clarence. We got these damn files over here in my office, and I am told they belong to you. What the hell is in them?"

"I have no idea," he told me.

"Well, I want to see them."

"So do I," he said, and he promptly dispatched a couple of agents to my office to open them up.

When we got looking at that stuff, it all related to J. Edgar Hoover's counterintelligence operations, known collectively as COINTELPRO—counterintelligence program. For fifteen years Hoover personally had directed a secret campaign to track, infiltrate, and discredit seven major protest or hate groups.[8] Among them were the Ku Klux Klan and the Minutemen; the Socialist Workers and the Communist parties in the United States; the Black Panthers, the Nation of Islam, and the Southern Christian Leadership Conference; and the "new left," such as the Students for a Democratic Society and its radical wing, the Weathermen.

The workings of COINTELPRO came to a halt shortly after March 8, 1971, when a group of activists burgled those counterintelligence files from the FBI office in Media, Pennsylvania.[9] A year later NBC news reporter Carl Stern learned of such files and requested them under the provisions of the Freedom of Information Act. Kleindienst, attorney general at the time, denied the request, but Stern acquired two documents fourteen months later under a court order. Subsequently, he and other journalists acquired additional documents.

I was floored by what was in those secret files. To my way of thinking, Hoover and the FBI clearly had conducted operations well beyond the scope of the law. (Kelley didn't agree with me.) There seemed to be no limit to Hoover's "dirty tricks," and apparently he carried those out independently, without any authority.

I felt that the nation's security could be adequately protected without resorting to tactics of disruption. I deliberately took that message to the June 20, 1974, graduating class at the FBI's academy at Quantico, Virginia. "The dirty tricks are over," I told them, "not only in campaign tactics but in law enforcement as well."

Then I set my sights specifically on Hoover, who for a generation had built up an independence for the bureau. He didn't feel he had to answer to the Congress, the president, or the people. "There is no person who should be immune from criticism and no practice that should be shielded from healthy skepticism," I told the graduates. "Those who would like to march to a dictator's drum will find themselves walking into an abyss."

Shortly after discovering the COINTELPRO files I alerted the White House and Sen. James O. Eastland, chairman of the Senate Judiciary Committee. I asked to meet with the committee. "I've discovered this rotten stuff; now, what do you want me to do with it?" I asked. "I can go out and announce it tomorrow, but I am asking the committee what it thinks I should do." It was a bombshell, for sure. They came back and asked that I sit on it, which I did.

Subsequently, I appointed Assistant Attorney General Henry E. Peterson, who was in charge of the department's criminal division, to head a committee composed of Justice Department and FBI representatives to review the files and make a report on COINTELPRO. That was in June 1974. Kelley, Sam Ervin, and others wanted the report sealed, but I thought it should be public. I knew Ford wanted it out in the open, and the press already had pieces of it through the Freedom of Information Act. It was only a matter of time before they dug out the whole story.

Before the release of the twenty-one-page COINTELPRO report, Peterson announced he would resign at the end of the year, after thirty years of federal service. It probably was just as well. I inherited him from Kleindienst's days as attorney general. Peterson really had outlived his usefulness because he was so tainted with Watergate. During the probe into the Watergate affair, for instance, he passed on to Nixon confidential grand jury information. That was understandable because Nixon was Peterson's boss after Kleindienst had removed himself from all Watergate matters. But Nixon passed the information to John D. Ehrlichman and H. R. Haldeman, and they used the intelligence to try to block the investigation of Watergate.

On June 7, 1974, Kleindienst became the first U.S. attorney general in history to be convicted of a crime. He received a suspended sentence of thirty days and a one hundred dollar fine for refusing to answer questions of the Senate Judiciary Committee about his conversations with the White House concerning the 1971 International Telephone and Telegraph antitrust case.

Peterson vigorously defended his actions. He told me he never would have passed along grand jury information had he known what Nixon was doing with it. But a cloud hung over Peterson, and Congress was on his case. His days were numbered, so the White House announced his resignation on November 5.

On Monday, November 18, an edited version of the COINTELPRO report was released, noting that of the more than twenty-three hundred COINTELPRO cases, the FBI may have engaged in illegal activity in but a handful. Still, I directed Assistant Attorney General Stanley Pottinger to determine whether any civil rights had been violated. His review determined that such was not the case. However, in winding up its investigation of COINTELPRO, the Senate Select Committee on Intelligence Activities concluded it had seen "a pattern of reckless disregard of activities that threatened our constitutional system."[10] That was true. It was a sorry time for the country and its system of justice.

One of the more interesting assignments I had from the White House was to work with Secretary of Defense James P. Schlesinger on a report to Ford on what to do with an estimated fifty thousand citizens who evaded the draft or deserted during the Vietnam War. I felt quite strongly that those people should not be welcomed back as heroes. I thought they should serve the nation in some capacity as a condition of amnesty. That was much the same position the president took when he announced his amnesty program on September 16, 1974, although the demands on the deserters were greater than on those who dodged the draft. A few days later Ford sent me an official copy of his amnesty proclamation and a pen he signed it with "as tokens of my appreciation."

Despite all the work that had yet to be done, it seemed to me it was time for me to perhaps move on. The Ford team and I never really hit it off; I always had the impression they would prefer that I would just fade away. Quite frankly, the job wasn't much fun. It wasn't for Chester, either. He left as counsel to President Nixon on August 23, 1974, after vegetating there for some months under James St. Clair.

Ford dropped a bomb on me, and on Jaworski, by announcing in a nationwide address on September 8 that he had pardoned Nixon for "all offenses . . . [he] has committed or may have committed" during his term as president. It was time, Ford said, to write an end to "an American tragedy." To allow a year and perhaps longer to elapse between the indictment of Nixon and the trial would be "to prolong the bad dreams." It was time to move on.

I always have felt that pardoning Nixon was a cut-and-dried deal at the time Nixon left the White House, although Ford vigorously denied that. "There was no deal, period, under no circumstances," he told the House Judiciary Subcommittee. I was not privy to the decision to issue a blanket pardon. I was unaware he was going to do it until thirty minutes before his speech, and yet Ford had been weighing his decision for a week or more, discussing it with others.

For the most part I kept my thoughts about the pardon to myself. However, I addressed the matter, and the coddling of Agnew, in that previously mentioned speech before the Associated Industries of New York in October. I told them that a reporter had asked me how I could be advocating tougher sentences for white-collar criminals when Richardson worked out a no-contest plea for Agnew. "I cannot second-guess my predecessor's decision. The country probably agreed he did the right thing, for it would have been an agonizing ordeal if a vice president under indictment or appealing a conviction would have succeeded to the presidency. But I will add one thing today. I am tired of exceptions in the process of justice— tired of persons being exempt from its sanctions—and I believe the country is equally tired of exceptions to justice. It is time the exceptions were stopped, and one place to begin is with the white-collar criminal."

At the time Jaworski was deep into his Watergate probe, which was destined to get Nixon indicted or impeached or both. When the pardon was announced, he wrote to me to express his view of the Constitutional correctness of Ford's action. "For me to procure an indictment of Richard M. Nixon for the sole purpose of generating a purported court test on the legality of the pardon would constitute a spurious proceeding in which I had no faith," he wrote. "In fact, it would be tantamount to unprofessional conduct and violative of my responsibility as prosecutor and officer of the court."[11]

Convinced that the bulk of his work had been accomplished, Jaworski tendered his resignation to me, effective October 25. In his letter, he expressed his appreciation to me "for having permitted me to proceed with my responsibilities as I saw them." I thought he had done a helluva job and said as much in my reply. "Your dedication and success in pursuing many difficult problems and your great personal sacrifices deserve the praise of all Americans," I wrote.

Soon word began to leak out that I might be leaving the Ford administration also.

In Kipling's Footsteps

Ford and his crowd from Michigan—they were a sorry bunch—were determined to rid the White House of "Nixonites" as quickly as possible, and speculation concerning my departure from the cabinet began almost on day one of the Ford administration.

The rumors began to circulate in earnest in October 1974. Columnist Jack Anderson was the first to publish what eventually became true, at least in part. He reported:

Charles Goodell, the former (NY) Republican senator who was ridden out of office by the Nixon administration because of his antiwar views, has now been tentatively chosen as the next Attorney General by President Ford.

. . . Saxbe dearly loves the job, however, and has told us he came away from a meeting with Ford a few weeks ago with the understanding that he could keep it.

At the White House, Saxbe is admired for his tough stands on crime, which have also won him popularity with the average American. But Saxbe is outspoken and often is caught with his foot in his mouth. In addition, his deputy, Laurence Silberman, is handling most of Saxbe's day-to-day duties already. Ford, therefore, has decided that Saxbe eventually must go.[1]

Two weeks later, *New York Times* reporter John Crewdson chased another rumor across the White House lawn, namely that a decision had been made to replace me after the November elections. Through Larry Speakes, press secretary to White House Counsel James St. Clair, Crewdson was told that "the president has indicated the cabinet would stay." *The Wall Street*

Journal reported that Chicago attorney John Robson, a confidante of White House transition team leader Donald Rumsfeld, may be named attorney general "in early 1975."[2]

Even some of the editorial writers found grist for their mill, to wit the following editorial in the *Toledo Blade:*

> It is disappointing to take note of periodic speculation that in the otherwise laudable process of giving the Administration a fresh "Ford" identity, the President might replace the attorney general.
>
> Most Americans probably look upon the squire from Mechanicsburg, O., as one of the few refreshing figures in the federal Cabinet.
> . . .
> When additional Cabinet shake-ups come, it would be our hope that President Ford's ax fall someplace other than at the Justice Department.[3]

Rocky, who was a state representative-elect,[4] told the *Akron Beacon Journal* he thought it would be a "grave mistake" for Ford to replace me.[5]

So it became obvious that Ford was going to make changes, no matter what he was saying publicly. You can't keep a secret like that secret for very long in Washington. Taking note of the talk, Sen. James O. Eastland, D-Mississippi, asked me one day what I was going to do. "You know you are not going to stay there" (in the Ford cabinet), he said. I confided that *if* the ambassador's post in India was up for grabs, I would have an interest in being considered for it. "Well," he said, "if you do go to India, that will solve a problem for the president," who didn't want on his hands the appearance of another Saturday Night Massacre. I also had an eye on Costa Rica, where a year earlier I had invested in some residential property, but India was my first choice.[6]

I knew the ambassador's post in India would be opening up. In the summer of 1974, weeks before submitting his resignation on the same day Nixon resigned, Daniel Patrick Moynihan was making noises about leaving India. He lobbied to be named Librarian of Congress. "He is most definitely interested in such an appointment," Leonard Garment, counsel to the president, informed Nixon. "He does not view his return to Harvard and the academic world with a great deal of enthusiasm."[7]

Moynihan and I did not have a lot in common, and I knew he did not hold me in high regard. In his book, *A Dangerous Place*, written a few years after he left India, Moynihan notes that "The man who was to succeed me as Ambassador, Attorney General William Saxbe, was not much interested in my theories. [He was correct there.] I had in fact proposed that a career officer replace me."[8] As I understand it, he considered me as "sort of a farmer."

What I remember most about my pompous predecessor is that he left behind in India a fistful of unpaid personal bills. He had a three thousand dollar personal liquor bill, a "gift" of a piece of furniture for the Embassy that he still owed money on, an upaid account at the commissary, and charges for airline tickets for his wife and family going back and forth to the states.

In 1975 Moynihan hosted a two-day visit to New Delhi by Secretary of State Henry Kissinger. They went crazy with the preparations. I remember the purchase of a million dollars worth of generators (as a back-up to the state power system in case it failed, which it did all too often), fancy Cuban cigars, a wine list that would choke the best restaurant in Paris, and who knows what else, all charged to the commissary.

The Embassy had to absorb those charges, but I was damned if I was going to also absorb nearly ten thousand dollars of his personal expenses. So when he came up for Senate confirmation as ambassador to the United Nations in the spring of 1975, I got in touch with Sen. John J. Sparkman, D-Alabama, and asked him to get Moynihan to pay those personal debts before confirmation by the Foreign Relations Committee. He did, and Moynihan paid up in full.

But I am getting ahead of my story. I was trying not to dwell on my future fortune with the Ford administration. There was plenty for me to do yet as attorney general. I attacked the problem of the one million aliens who held U.S. jobs and mocked our justice system. In my talk to the Cameron and Hidalgo Counties Bar Association in Brownsville, Texas, for instance, I warned that the Immigration and Naturalization Service soon would be unable to cope with the flood of illegal aliens, or gate crashers, principally from Mexico. I sent Ford a recommendation to beef up the INS by increasing its budget by $50 million and adding more than two thousand men and women, mostly border patrol officers. Before a meeting of the Grocery Manufacturers of America, I disclosed a Justice Department antitrust investigation into suspected price-fixing in the food industry. Speaking at the dedication of a new federal prison in San Diego, California, I stirred up the justice system by calling prisoner rehabilitation largely a myth. And, of course, I filed that massive antitrust action against AT&T.

Meanwhile, Dolly was making her own news. Reporters discovered that for several months she had been on the FBI's indoor firing range, sharpening up her marksmanship with her .357 Colt Python pistol. She was a pretty good shot, too, but I didn't want it to appear that she was receiving any special favors, so I put a stop to it. Besides, one day she hung on the door of my office elevator one of her silhouette targets on which she had posted a good score. I felt she had had enough practice.

Speaking of the FBI, the two agents who were always with me became quite upset with me one evening at the Ohio Theatre in Columbus.[9] We were at a benefit concert given by Terry Waldo and His Gutbucket Syncopaters, the same group that performed in Washington after I became attorney general. Eubie Blake, then well into his nineties, was to be the star performer, but illness forced him to withdraw. I was in the audience, waiting for the show to begin, when Terry sent word that he'd like me to "fill in" briefly. I agreed and went backstage, with the two FBI guys protesting all the way. They were going crazy. They were scared to death that I'd be on that stage, unprotected. I told them not to worry about it, that everyone in the audience was a friend and probably that was very close to the truth. I gave them a warbling rendition of "Ace in the Hole" to thunderous applause.[10]

The White House asked me to give a talk December 6 in New York to the National Association of Manufacturers, a twelve thousand-member organization that was the strongest big business voice in the land. It was an important antitrust speech, and I had worked hard preparing it. Bob Havel and I were in my suite at the Waldorf-Astoria, getting ready for the black tie affair, when a knock came at the door. A delegation of four NAM officers entered: Donald A. Gaudion, chairman; E. Douglas Kenna, president; David B. Meeker, chairman-elect; and William H. McGaughey, senior vice president for public relations. McGaughey had in his hand an advance copy of my talk. "It seems, general, there's been a little breakdown in communication here," he said, explaining that perhaps the speech was a little "heavy" for the affair and the audience, which was to include women and young people.

"This is more of a gala occasion, not a regular business dinner," he said, thinking that a tough antitrust message would bomb. "Couldn't you put this speech aside and talk about other things?" The "other things" he had in mind included no-fault insurance or the nation's problems with organized crime, drugs, and immigration. He and the others recalled an off-the-cuff speech I had made to a NAM group in New Orleans a year or so earlier and, in his words, "It was just as entertaining as it could be." They suggested something "funny" like that would be fine.

That did it! I had heard enough.

"I didn't come here to be a stand-in for Bob Hope!" I said, trying to control my anger. "If you don't want me to give that speech, just say so and we'll pack up and head back to Washington!"

I have to admit I was not in the best of moods. Dolly was in California that night, attending funeral services for Sheila J. Regan. Sheila was the FBI agent assigned to Dolly and one of the very first female agents. On December 1 she had been killed in a plane crash while returning to Washington. That weekend, in Mechanicsburg, she had seemed so pleased. Dolly had painted her portrait and had given it to her. Her loss hurt us terribly. Both of us admired and respected her so much.

In any event, the NAM show went on. The other guests on the dais (it was five tiers high) and I marched into the Grand Ballroom to the tune of "Stouthearted Men," which I thought was rather a nice, ironic touch, given the spineless performance I had just witnessed.

At the appointed hour, I launched into my address on the enforcement of the nation's antitrust statutes, suggesting that in the past the Justice Department had been soft on big business and on those operating "at the adventuresome edge of the free enterprise system." By doing so, the violators "claim thousands of victims . . . and pile up millions in illicit profits as well."

I noted that in 1974 criminal cases filed by the Justice Department exceeded civil cases for the first time in many years.

> This is happening because we are mystified how in 1974 some businessmen can still engage in price-fixing and other predatory practices that have been clearly illegal for years.
>
> But merely bringing criminal cases will not accomplish much unless adequate penalties are imposed by the court upon those who are convicted or who plead no contest. . . . During the past fiscal year, there were 26 persons who could have been sentenced to prison for antitrust violations, but only five actually received jail terms—and each case the sentence was only 30 days. That situation must be changed and more appropriate sentences must be imposed. . . . We are urging jail terms in virtually all criminal cases involving hardcore price fixing.[11]

Investigations into price fixing on sugar, beef, eggs, dairy and bakery products, beer, seafood, and other groceries were underway, I revealed, as well as "deadly serious" reviews of the auto, steel, tobacco, coal, earth-moving, and newsprint industries. "I will tell you bluntly that I expect that some of the studies will lead to antitrust investigations." To be sure I got the attention of my entire audience, I also mentioned Justice Department reviews of doctors, lawyers, real estate agents, pharmacists, dentists, accountants, engineers, funeral directors, and veterinarians. Indian chiefs were spared.

"We will not have a free enterprise system if our economy becomes dominated by a few robber barons who can dictate price and quality," I concluded.

Bob recalled the speech was met with thunderous silence. I thought I heard two Democrats clapping. Both were waiters.

Five days later I attended the funeral in Columbus of my longtime friend and supporter, Fred E. Jones. Six weeks later I received more shocking news. Three more very good friends—Edgar T. Wolfe Jr.; Frederick W. LeVeque, president of Tower Parking Company; and Carlton Dargusch Jr., my former law partner—died with two pilots in the crash of their private plane.[12] The three Columbus men, all forty-nine, were approaching Washington, on their way to an Alfalfa Club banquet honoring Senator Taft, when the plane struck a radio tower on the campus of American University. Wolfe, publisher of the *Columbus Dispatch* and chairman of the Dispatch Printing Company, shared my avid interest in hunting and cattle raising, and we had spent many an hour discussing and doing both. I served as an honorary pallbearer at his funeral January 28.

The curtain went up on the final act concerning my future with the Ford administration on Monday, December 9. I met privately with Ford in the Oval Office. He detailed his recollection of the meeting in his book, *A Time to Heal:* "Initially, I didn't plan to replace Saxbe, and he didn't tell me that he wanted to leave. Then I heard indirectly that he wanted to climax his career as our ambassador to India. Our man in New Delhi at the time was Daniel Patrick Moynihan, and as luck would have it, he wanted to return to his teaching post at Harvard."[13]

"Bill, I am not asking you to resign," Ford told me, "but I have been told by reliable sources that you'd like to be ambassador to India, and if that is true, I'll nominate you, and I am sure you will be confirmed."[14] He also mentioned that the Court of St. James envoy post in London was open, but I quickly deflated that balloon. That was the most expensive posting in the diplomatic corps, especially for the ambassador. After having taken that pay cut a year earlier to accept the job as attorney general, I picked up every penny I found on the street.

Despite the words coming out of Ford's mouth, I heard it as a demand for my resignation. I really was not happy about leaving Justice because I believed I had stabilized the department in times that, for all of us, were difficult at best. Also, I felt there was much yet to be accomplished. At the same time, I saw India as an attractive opportunity and an ambassadorial post as a fitting climax to my political career. As a senator I had been to India five times, met with Indian Prime Minister Indira Gandhi four times (twice in the United States), and had made a number of Indian friends both in Washington and in India.

Inasmuch as I had little choice, I told the president I would accept the nomination. Ford recalled that I was "enthusiastic," adding, "Now I could select my own man to replace him."[15] He saw it as "a nice fit," he would say later. "[There was] nothing back room about it. It was just a sequence of events that was mutually beneficial for Bill and mutually beneficial [sic] for my administration."

Ford did not ask for a recommendation of a successor; he already had chosen, but not announced, Dr. Edward H. Levi, president of the University of Chicago. Assistant Attorney General Laurence H. Silberman thought he should be considered as my successor, and his campaigning for the post became quite unseemly. I had to put a stop to that. I didn't want him running the department while I was still there.

My letter of resignation was dated December 12, 1974, but it became effective upon my appointment as ambassador. The following day, when the White House announced my nomination,[16] I received a personal letter from Ford:

Nearly a year ago you assumed the duties of Attorney General under the most difficult circumstances. At that time you wisely set as your goals the rekindling of public confidence in the law and the rebuilding of morale within the Department of Justice. . . .

The impressive record you have compiled as Attorney General has in large measure brought fulfillment of those goals, adding new luster to your already distinguished career and further testifying to your superb leadership and unswerving devotion to the public good. You have truly earned the admiration of your colleagues in government and the thanks of your fellow citizens throughout the Nation.

It is with these high qualities in mind that I look forward to your continued service to this Administration and to our Nation as my Ambassador to India. I am wholly confident you will bring to your new responsibilities the same skills, energy and dedication to responsible government that you have demonstrated throughout your public life.

Betty joins me in wishing Dolly and you our best wishes for every continued happiness and success.[17]

So, that was that. I was out as attorney general. My nomination was sent to the Senate on December 14, and I was confirmed as Ambassador Extraordinary and Plenipotentiary on February 2, 1975. A day later, Deputy Secretary of State Robert S. Ingersoll gave me the oath of office in the Benjamin Franklin Room of the State Department.

Not everyone was happy with my leaving the Justice Department. Some saw evil forces at work, such as Ford seeing me as a possible threat to his gaining the 1976 GOP presidential nomination. By shipping me off to India, he got me as far away from the 1976 campaign as possible.

I have to admit that after I became attorney general there were those who urged me to make a run for the presidential nomination. There was talk, both privately and in the press. Perhaps Ford heard some of it; I don't know. I thought about it. Even if I didn't seek the presidency, I thought I might have been able to influence some thinking at the convention. But Dolly was opposed to it, and I shut it down. On reflection, perhaps I should have made a run at it, but I have no regrets not having done so.

I have no idea how leaks to the press occur, but the Associated Press got wind that my nomination was a done deal, thanks to one of my friends shooting off his mouth instead of his shotgun. Wednesday afternoon, December 11, I flew into Columbus to attend an afternoon of quail shooting at the Van Darby Club in Mechanicsburg. The way it came out in the newspapers the next day was, "'He's going to India, you know,' said one of Saxbe's quail-shooting associates. 'He'll make a hell of an ambassador.'"[18]

When Columbus attorney and my deputy in the Ohio attorney general's office, Jim DeLeone, saw the report, he fired off a letter to Ford, saying how "troubled" he was by the news. Jim felt strongly that I had been an outstanding, stabilizing attorney general, and he believed my departure would seriously wound the Republican Party in 1976. He stressed this point in his letter to Ford: "I would ask you . . . how many ballots are cast in the United States Presidential election from New Delhi, India. I would ask further how many votes Edward Hirsch Levi can deliver into the Republican column in either Ohio or Illinois [Levi's home state]. I know how many votes Mr. Saxbe can deliver in Ohio, and I would suggest that even with Jim Rhodes being elected Governor . . . this state will go Democratic. If you are a Presidential candidate in 1976 and you cannot carry Ohio or Illinois, you cannot be elected."[19]

DeLeone was right, of course. Jimmy Carter won both Ohio and Illinois in 1976—and the presidency. Senator Taft joined Ford on the heap, so the Ohio GOP ended up without Senate representation and with no national voice.

Philip W. Buchen, counsel to the president, replied to DeLeone's letter, saying that DeLeone had "misinterpreted the circumstances" of my nomination. He believed, he said, that I would "continue to earn the respect of the Ohio voters with a consequent benefit to this Administration."[20]

I mention Buchen because of a letter Jack Chester wrote to Ford on January 8, 1975, copying Buchen, and then a separate letter he sent to Buchen. "The people whom I know and with whom I associate do not understand why you removed William Saxbe as Attorney General when he was doing such a good job," he told Ford. Chester also recommended Buchen for attorney general.

In his letter to Buchen, Chester wrote in part: "President Ford's removal of William Saxbe as Attorney General was dismaying to me, to the lawyers and politicians in Ohio, and to the man in the street in our area of the country. Mr. Saxbe was almost unique among officeholders in Washington in that he was plain, forthright, without guile or pretension. He had guts, political intuition and common sense. He was usually right. He was not a Washington power seeker of the type that I found to be in super-abundance. . . . What a tremendous waste of a real talent to send him to India."[21]

Columbus Dispatch cartoonist Doc Goodwin painted me as having my foot in my mouth as envoy to India. Reprinted with permission of the *Columbus Dispatch*.

In an undated, handwritten note to fellow White House counselor, Phillip Areeda, Buchen commented on Chester's letter to Ford. "Coming from a man whom I eased from the White House legal staff on my arrival, the letter to the President is surprising, as well as ill-advised."[22]

There were many expressions of support when my nomination became known. The editorial writers were, in the main, kind to me, but I don't know to this day if that was because they saw my appointment positively or because they were happy to see me leave the country. The tone of the *Cincinnati Enquirer* editorial was typical:

Mr. Saxbe is often blunt and sometimes intemperate and undiplomatic in his expression of his beliefs. He has, however, proven in recent months that he can be both honest, refreshingly and often idealistically so, and restrain Kissinger himself from publicly expressing personal opinions on controversial matters. He has become an effective attorney general, particularly effective when viewed against the times in which he had to govern one of the key departments of the federal government. . . .

Contrary to the opinion of others that Mr. Saxbe will anger the proud and often overly sensitive Indians by his bluntness and outspokenness, *The Enquirer* believes he can be an excellent ambassador to India.[23]

But you can't win them all, at least not in Cincinnati. The headline on *The Cincinnati Post* editorial said, "Saxbe to India? Oh, No!"

The White House announced yesterday that President Ford is nominating Attorney General William B. Saxbe as ambassador to India.

We urge the President to reconsider.

Saxbe has many good qualities and has done a better job heading
the Justice Department than many had expected. But he is given to
popping off and putting his foot in his mouth, both extremely bad
traits in a diplomat.[24]

Dolly and I planned to spend the Christmas-New Year holidays at our
vacation house in Costa Rica. It was a three-bedroom stucco ranch on the
first fairway at the Cariari International Country Club in San Jose. But
Robert L. Vesco ruined it all for us, and therein lies another tale.

Vesco, a freewheeling U.S. financier who Nixon described as "a cheap
kike,"[25] fled to Costa Rica rather than face Securities and Exchange Commission charges that he looted some $224 million from four mutual funds.
Then former Attorney General Mitchell and former Commerce Secretary
Maurice H. Stans were charged with accepting from Vesco a secret two
hundred thousand dollar contribution to Nixon's 1972 reelection campaign
in return for their influence on the sec case. Both Mitchell and Stans were
acquitted, but Vesco was still on the loose in Costa Rica.

Shortly before closing on the house in the spring of 1973, Dolly and I
had spent a few days in San Jose with Viron P. "Pete" Vaky, U.S. Ambassador to Costa Rica. At his request and upon my return to Washington, I met
with Syd Herlong, sec Commissioner. I conveyed Vaky's concern that there
be prompt pursuit of the sec case against Vesco. To prolong it "could result
in great harm to our country's relations with Central and South American countries, especially Costa Rica."[26] Costa Rica itself was alarmed that
through Vesco it might be swept into the Watergate scandal.

In any event, when I filed my travel plans for Christmas 1974, red flags
went up at the White House, the National Security Council, and the State
Department. Two days before our December 20 departure, the trip was
canceled. A memorandum from Warren S. Rustand, appointments secretary to the president, explained why: "Any visit by the U.S. Attorney General to Costa Rica, no matter how private, would be viewed in Costa Rica as
associated with the Vesco matter. Since the Vesco issue is the focal point of
highly charged national debate in Costa Rica,[27] large numbers of Costa
Ricans would believe—no matter what the facts—that the purpose of your

Hunting pheasant
and other game
always has been a
passion of mine.

visiting Costa Rica at this time is related to the U.S. interest in Vesco and involves an attempt to pressure the GOCR [the government of Costa Rica] to act against Vesco at our behest."[28]

Early in January Dolly and I traveled to Ireland for a few days of pheasant hunting with Dan Galbreath of Columbus. Subsequently I sold the house in Costa Rica for fifty-three thousand dollars or so, which was about double what I paid for it. So, in that regard, I guess we did okay.

Dolly threw herself into packing for India and dressing for cocktail parties and dinners. In our last twenty days in Washington, we attended seventeen farewell parties in our honor. Had I known our departure was going to be that much fun, we would have left earlier.

"Washingtonians, who probably say goodbye oftener and sometimes more artfully than most species, can hardly remember a more intensive departure," the *Washington Post* reported.[29] Humorist Mark Russell, whom Korean millionaire Tongsun Park invited to the party he tossed for us at the George Town Club, noted that "there hasn't been this much sadness in Washington since Millard Fillmore left town."[30]

Kissinger and Moynihan were among the guests at the party given two nights later by Indian Ambassador Triloki Nath Kaul. "You've been feted, have you?" Moynihan asked, peering down his nose at Dolly. Flashing her remarkably quick wit, she replied, "Yes, I am the fatted calf!"[31]

The seemingly endless round of frivolity caused Sen. Gaylord A. Nelson, D-Wisconsin, to quip that if he had to go to one more Saxbe party, he'd have to go by ambulance. Sen. Ernest F. Hollings, D-South Carolina, asked, "How many times do I have to say goodbye? If he doesn't leave soon, I'll be an alcoholic!"

It's true, I guess, that I went through Washington in a helluva hurry—just over five years—but some have a habit of hanging around too long. I didn't want to hang on. We left Washington for good on February 5, and nine days later we were winging our way to India, via Tokyo.

21

Tiptoeing into India

As Dolly and I flew across the Pacific toward Tokyo, our first stop on the way to India, I thought about what Secretary of State Henry Kissinger told me about my duties and responsibilities there. "The less I hear from you and the less I hear about India, the happier I will be," he told me in a private meeting shortly before I left Washington. "You are on your own." That is just about all he told me.

Clearly he didn't like India, nor its prime minister, Indira Gandhi, whom he and others called the "Empress of India." Because of her statesmanship, Mrs. Gandhi annoyed Nixon "both as a leader and as a woman," columnist Jack Anderson wrote.[1] Nixon referred to her as "the bitch," and worse, and directed that U.S. foreign policy be tilted against India and toward India's border rival, Pakistan. As Nixon's national security advisor, Kissinger delivered the "tilt" policy to New Delhi in July 1971.

According to Kissinger, "Nixon ordered a diplomatic tilt toward Pakistan to prevent a forcible dismemberment of West Pakistan and to show China that we would resist Soviet-backed military intervention. The State Department representatives at daily interagency meetings argued passionately that India was a more important country than Pakistan—a judgment we did not challenge. But, at that moment, our incipient China policy was more important than Indian goodwill."[2] The following month Kissinger secretly used Pakistan as his stepping stone into China.

"Kissinger's anti-India zeal troubled some subordinates," Anderson maintained. When it came to India, a member of Kissinger's staff told Anderson that Kissinger would act "like a wild man. . . . His animus toward India seemed irrational."[3]

Ford made an effort to get off on the right foot with India less than two weeks after he became president. He and Kissinger met briefly on August 21, 1974, in the Oval Office with Indian Ambassador Triloki Nath Kaul, a sixty-one-year-old career diplomat. At the time, though, Congress looked askance at direct aid to India (a modest $75 million) in the face of India's nuclear tests in May that cost more than $170 million. The administration also was concerned over "India's very friendly and cooperative political-military relationship with the USSR."[4] That was in reference to Mrs. Gandhi's 1971 visit to Moscow at the time Kissinger was visiting China. There she signed the Indo-Soviet Treaty of Peace, Friendship, and Cooperation (renewed in 1991) to provide India some protection against China, which sided with Pakistan over the Bangladesh issue and was secretly arming Pakistan.

Nevertheless, Ford told Kaul that he hoped relations between the world's two largest democracies would continue to improve and serious dialogue toward this end would begin.

Mrs. Gandhi resented the Nixon administration's position against India and in favor of Pakistan. She "understood, of course, that this 'tilt' was intended to offset the military, political, and economic closeness between India and the Soviet Union. Still, bitter wars had been fought between India and Pakistan—wars that Mrs. Gandhi felt could have been avoided had the United States not fattened Pakistan's arsenal so relentlessly."[5]

Both President Ford and Secretary of State Henry A. Kissinger seemed glad to ship me off to India. White House photo.

{ I'VE SEEN THE ELEPHANT }

I felt Kissinger had done me a favor by not giving me a large agenda in India. Hell, it was no agenda at all! But I knew I had to be even more careful about what I said as a diplomat than as attorney general. No more crushing ice cubes with a sledgehammer.

As soon as it became known in India that I would be the ambassador, India's local and national press published every comment of mine. *The Statesman* (Calcutta) reported on my long-standing support of Bangladesh, the former East Pakistan:

> Mr. Saxbe's sympathy with India's role in the Bangladesh crisis, however, came not from his visits as a U.S. Senator, but rather from the concern expressed to him by a Harvard University Medical School classmate of his son's [Bart], who had been a hurricane relief worker in the then East Pakistan and had first-hand accounts of the shooting of students at Dacca University.[6]
>
> With his son's friend proceeding to keep him informed from refugee camps, Mr. Saxbe started speaking out on the Senate floor in criticism of the Pakistani suppression. He wrote to Mr. Nixon for a change in America's "tilt" policy, and he was instrumental in getting Mr. Nixon to recognize Bangladesh and approve the appointment of an U.S. Ambassador there.[7]

The *Indian Express* cartoon, *Private View,* also took note of my comments concerning India. It depicted one Indian reading a newspaper to another. "Saxbe says Indians are the most hard-working people in the world."

The other man replies, "The Ambassador has started lying even before he's abroad."[8]

I read John Kenneth Galbreath's book, *Ambassador's Journal,* and several other books by former ambassadors.[9] Quite frankly, I didn't think any of them were worth the candle. But Galbreath and several other U.S. ambassadors to India were messing in Indian politics, which I didn't think right. I told the press that I intended to treat India as a strong country and keep out of its affairs. I said that "the day we have an arms shipment or massive dose of righteousness to answer every crisis is gone."[10]

In his book, *A Dangerous Place,* former ambassador Daniel P. Moynihan admitted that the CIA had "interfered in Indian politics twice" on behalf of Mrs. Gandhi's Congress Party.[11] One time money was given to her by the CIA, Moynihan said, a claim she dismissed as "absolutely baseless."

Moynihan warned me that India would soon come apart at the seams.

Bart, Juli, Dolly, and Rocky joined me at the Department of State when I was sworn in as ambassador to India.

"It's going to fly apart, Bill. There's no way they [Mrs. Gandhi's administration] can hold this together with all these divergent groups and states and so on."

For me it started to fall apart early. When we arrived in Tokyo I got word from the State Department that we should hold up our arrival in New Delhi for a few days because the administration was about to announce it was ending the ten-year arms embargo. As a result India was not looking kindly on the United States. There were demonstrations, threats, and strong feelings expressed against the United States, all fanned by Mrs. Gandhi. At issue were the spare parts Pakistan needed for its U.S. military equipment. Because of Kissinger's breakthrough into China via Pakistan, a grateful United States was supplying that equipment for free. That set the Indians against the United States because they thought it was preparing Pakistan for another war against India.

We spent a week twiddling our thumbs in Tokyo at the U.S. Embassy residence. James D. Hodgson was our ambassador there at the time. But Tokyo was cold, nasty, and expensive, so on February 21 we flew to Bangkok where it was at least warm. I had my counsel, Vince Rakestraw, who already had arrived in New Delhi, fly to meet me in Bangkok. He brought news of the political climate as well as my golf clubs.

I had been scheduled to arrive in New Delhi the following day and present my credentials to the president of India on the February 24, but the administration chose that day to announce the end to the arms embargo. I argued in vain against the decision. It was unwise to get so heavily into the arms business on the grounds that the Pakistanis would only buy arms someplace else, so why not from the United States. But, as I told an Indian reporter while still in Bangkok, since the decision had been taken, "I'll support it. It's the president's decision to go ahead, and it's an ambassador's job to support his position."[12]

There were reports—fostered in Washington I feared—that the delay was due to my being ill, but I quickly dispelled those rumors. The Indian press corps saw through that ruse, anyway. In New Delhi *The Motherland* correctly reported:

It is obvious that the envoy is being deliberately asked to put off the visit after he had started for India by asking him to halt for some days at Bangkok. This is taken to be a method of showing the American displeasure with India in view of the sharp reaction in this country to the resumption of US arms supply to Pakistan.

... In diplomatic dealings even a deliberate absense *[sic]* is normally camouflaged as due to illness or some other inconsequential [excuse]. On the other hand Shri Saxbe took pains to make it clear that he was delayed for political reasons and not for treatment in Bangkok.[13]

Another newspaper in New Delhi, the *Patriot*, reported: "The postponement of Mr. Saxbe's arrival . . . [comes] in the wake of announcement by senior officials in Washington that the US is preparing to go ahead with limited cash sales of military equipment to Pakistan and that the announcement of the relaxation of the arms embargo is expected early next week."[14]

Indians resented the administration's decision, of course. Yashwantrao B. Chavan, the nation's minister for external affairs, canceled a scheduled trip to Washington in protest. Lakshmi K. Jha, India's ambassador to the United States, vilified the Ford administration at a Washington press conference—much to Kissinger's displeasure—and Mrs. Gandhi said the shipments "reopened old wounds."

Those "old wounds" included Washington's 1954 decision to court Pakistan and to the "massive supply" of U.S. arms that secured the arrangement under a mutual security pact. Mrs. Gandhi declared that "we cannot believe that the U.S. administration was unaware that these weapons could be and would be used only against India. . . . The United States openly backed Pakistan at the cost of basic human values."[15]

After spending ten days shopping and playing golf in Bangkok, we finally received an okay to proceed to India. The coast was clear, more or less. My arrival there as ambassador was somewhat less auspicious than on my previous five visits, all of which had been as a senator. Our grand entrance into New Delhi's Palam Airport on March 2 was in the dark of night, as a precaution against rioting. The Indian government didn't want a demonstration against us. At the airport, a group of officials daubed vermilion (a mark known as a *tilak*) on our foreheads, tossed a couple of garlands around our necks and whisked me off in a sedan. Dolly and a government official were left standing on the ramp with all the junk we had bought in Bangkok. They didn't have any transportation for them. Dolly recalled, "I told this woman, 'We better start walking; we'll get run over out here.' We walked into the VIP room and nobody paid any attention to us. So much for women's lib in India. I was extra baggage. I've been left a lot of places, and better places than that."

I arrived at the embassy, but an hour or so later still no Dolly. Where's

Dolly and I arrived
in New Dehli in
the dark of night.

Dolly? Well, she finally arrived, somewhat put out by the "welcome" she had received.

The ambassador's residence, with its fluted tulip columns, was an impressive edifice designed by the noted American architect, Edward Durell Stone. Its splendor earned it the nickname "The Taj" among State Department functionaries. The residence was called Roosevelt House in honor of Franklin Delano Roosevelt.[16] It opened January 29, 1962, while Galbreath was the ambassador.

The artist in Dolly saw right away that Roosevelt House, having been neglected for some time, was in desperate need of redecorating. For instance,

Cleveland Plain Dealer reporter Jayne Ellison, who visited shortly after our arrival, described the bedroom decor as "early motel." Dolly saw to it that multihued walls were painted white, stairs repaired and carpets replaced as needed. Some original furniture that had been in storage was retrieved, repaired, and recovered. She did quite a job restoring the place to its former grandeur.

In the morning the sun beamed on the great seal of the United States in the embassy entryway: very impressive. The embassy itself was built around a rectangular reflecting pool, surrounded by two floors of offices. The architect had not foreseen the extent of wildlife, particularly wild fowl, in India. A wire mesh had to be placed over the pool to keep the birds from landing in it. Once the birds got in there, it was hell to get them out.

The residence and the gardens were fantastic, I told the press, adding that I had heard the gardens had won a prize "for having the biggest pansies in the diplomatic corps." That raised a few eyebrows among the stodgier diplomats.

The ambassador's office was spacious, as were the other offices for various departments. Connected by a tunnel was another office building for the agricultural and the cultural people. On the grounds were the Enclave Apartments for employees, although most of the official people had homes in the nicer parts of Delhi. Underneath the embassy was a spacious garage where I'd just go down by elevator and get in the car. We must have had twenty-five or thirty automobiles, including my personal car, a Ford Town and Country station wagon. It took a couple of months to get it there by ship, and when it arrived at the embassy it was delivered on a cart pulled by two big white oxen.

Our theater seated up to three hundred. We had a commissary, a club, a library, a swimming pool at the club, tennis courts, and a small hospital that I had built.

We had about 1,100 employees there, 230 of which were Americans working in the embassy enclave itself. One of the reasons we had so many Americans working in and around the embassy was because when the State Department had somebody in Africa or someplace else that they had to move out, they temporarily parked them in India until they could be relocated. India was the choice spot because we had plenty of money to pay for them. We'd give them some job to do while they were with us.

New Delhi was a communications center for much of Asia, clear up into the Mediterranean—very top secret operations. That was the prime reason for our large military detail there, which included the usual marine detachment.

We received messages in code, which then would be translated by a security officer from the State Department. We also had a secure room, which is interesting to note, especially when the Russian Embassy was located several hundred yards away. The room was made of plastic and was raised from the floor and lowered from the ceiling. You could walk around the outside of it, a room inside a room. The inner room was completely shielded and transparent so no device or wire could be attached to it. I never used it because I didn't have anything to talk about that was that secret, but many embassies of importance had rooms like that.

David Schneider, a career State Department diplomat, was my deputy chief. He was there under former ambassador Kenneth Keating, I believe, and also under Moynihan, so he was an old India hand—a good man, solid. Later he became ambassador to Bangladesh.

In terms of the pecking order, it was me, Rakestraw, and Schneider. Schneider had the clear hand in running the day-to-day affairs of the embassy and maintaining our State Department contacts, which meant he didn't have whole lot to do in that regard while we were there, given Kissinger's attitude.

Rakestraw had been with me in the Senate and at the Justice Department. Part of his job was to make sure that Americans who came to visit the ambassador saw what they wanted of India and met everybody they wanted to meet, including Mrs. Gandhi. As a result, he saw more of her than I did. Most first-time visitors made it around what's known as the Delhi triangle—New Delhi, Calcutta, and Agra, site of the Taj Mahal, which everyone wanted to see, of course.

O. T. Berkman Jr., my brusque acting deputy assistant for administration at the Justice Department, was in charge of administrative affairs, which included housekeeping and our financial affairs, as well as arrangements for my travel. He was tight-fisted, but good. Dolly would go to him and say, "O. T., I need one hundred rupees" and he'd say, "What did you do with the hundred rupees I gave you yesterday?" That would be twelve dollars. He also was a sharp talker. He had been to State Department schools and could speak Chinese.

The Indian household staff was scared to death of Berkman. The head bearer's name was Kishiri Lal. Berkman would loudly call, "Lal!" and the old man would shake. But Lal ran a tight ship and was honest, or relatively so.

As the embassy's head bearer, Lal held a very important position. He and his assorted, sometimes able, assistants had the not-inconsiderable task of maintaining the smooth operation of Roosevelt House under Berkman's watchful eye. That included the cooks and gardeners and chauffeurs and all manner of other servants, each of whom probably would have given an arm and a leg for Lal's embassy job.

Berkman knew all the servants had their little rackets, selling newspapers, empty bottles, and anything else they could lay their hands on. He let them get away with very little. I asked the Canadians what they did with their trash. They said, "We put it out in the alley, and it disappears." Nothing was wasted. In fact, the garbage dump was picked over so carefully that nothing remained but dirt.

When we'd have a party, Berkman hired the band, got us fresh vegetables, or chickens that were good and fresh. He just ramrodded the whole place. I've always been lucky in being able to get a guy like that.

Officially my duties began on Saturday, March 8, when I traveled to the Rashtrapati Bhavan, the presidential palace. I donned a formal morning suit, with striped pants and tails, but I had to borrow a homburg from the German ambassador. I don't think anyone noticed that it was a half-size too small.

We arrived at the Rashtrapati Bhavan in a black Mercedes Phaeton, the top down. The military secretary to the president received me and escorted me on an inspection of brilliantly garbed lancers, the guard of honor. Then Foreign Secretary Kewal Singh presented me to President Fakhruddin Allison Ahmed, the titular head of India, who accepted my credentials. Without mentioning the lifting of the arms embargo, he seized the occasion to remark that "recent developments . . . cast a shadow" across the subcontinent. The best we could expect, I said in an interview shortly thereafter, would be for each nation to develop "a grudging respect, which these days would be a major accomplishment."

In response to questions from the news media, I went on to explain, "I don't see improving relations between our two governments as my basic role here. I'm here to represent the government of the United States. I believe in our culture and policies, and if the Indians find them acceptable, that's fine. But I am here whether they accept them or not."[17]

In January, India had became the first non-Arab, non-Communist nation to grant the Palestine Liberation Organization diplomatic recognition. I found that disturbing, pointing out at the time that India had "no better friend in the world than the Jewish community in the United States. . . . But this romance with the PLO is going to turn off a lot of them."[18]

That comment, which the government promptly said it had "noted" and would study, brought a rebuke in a number of newspapers, including an editorial in New Delhi's *Patriot:* "US Ambassador Saxbe has a well-founded reputation in his country for opening his mouth too wide too

My first official duty as United States envoy to India was to present my credentials to President Fakhruddin Ali Ahmed on March 8, 1975.

often. He seems to be bent upon maintaining that reputation untarnished while in India. . . . A very disgusting smallness of mind is his reference to the estrangement from India of the Jewish community in the US because of New Delhi's recognition of the PLO. Surely, even a US Ambassador, should be informed enough to know that Indian policies are not decided on the basis of Jew and gentile, Hindu, Muslim or Christian?"[19]

A few members of Mrs. Gandhi's own Congress Party in Parliament got on my case. The national *Times of India* reported:

> Five Left-leaning Congress MPs today described the observations made by the U.S. Ambassador here . . . as "uncalled for, discourteous and a declaration of cold war against India . . . designed to contribute to the tremendous effort now underway through various agencies to destabilise the democratic regime in India in conformity with the CIA's practice."
>
> They said that Mr. Saxbe's "fulmination and arrogance" would not work on India. "Neither U.S. arms supply to Pakistan nor Diego Garcia military base [in the Indian Ocean] terrifies us."[20]

Whether my remarks had anything to do with the delay in my meeting with Mrs. Gandhi or not, I don't know, but it was almost three weeks—a long span in diplomatic affairs—before I secured an audience with her at Parliament House. My "courtesy call" on March 24 was cordial enough and lasted fifteen minutes.

It was easy to understand the delay: She had other things on her mind. India was in turmoil in early 1975. Riots, killings, and many arrests flared up as opposition to Mrs. Gandhi and the Congress Party mounted. The Supreme Court's ruling that Mrs. Gandhi's 1971 election was illegally achieved only heightened the resistance to her and her government. She convinced President Ahmed to declare, on June 25, 1975, a state of emergency because "the security of India is threatened by internal disturbances." Thousands were arrested without warrants, many of them leaders of the opposition parties. As Dolly wrote in her diary, "Anyone who does not go along [with the Gandhi government] gets put in the jug."[21]

Mrs. Gandhi also imposed severe censorship on the press. The electric power to the opposition press was often cut off, halting publication. Some foreign journalists were urged to leave India. Although some of those restrictions were relaxed within a few months and some jailed opposition leaders were released, the emergency laws were not lifted for a considerable period.

Mrs. Gandhi also had been quite forceful in expressing her distaste for U.S. plans to establish a naval base at Diego Garcia in the Masirah Islands, southwest of India in the Arabian Sea. She viewed the move as "a threat" to India. Ford, who indicated during our meeting at the White House that he would like to visit India, gave up that idea August 13 in the face of Mrs. Gandhi's anti-American rhetoric and the state of emergency she had imposed in India. He called her action "a very sad development," which the government viewed as meddling in India's internal affairs once again.[22]

Ford later recalled that another reason the India trip was scotched was that "Reagan challenged me for the Republican nomination. So, I had an obligation, if I wanted to get nominated, to stay and take on Reagan, which I did, of course. That Reagan campaign for the nomination moved aside a lot of things that otherwise would not have been cut off the schedule. There were a lot of things at a higher priority than an official visit to India."[23]

The first India-Pakistan war was in 1947; then they fought again in 1965 and in 1971. Each time India emerged victorious, ending with East Pakistan becoming an independent Bangladesh. I was in India and Bangladesh a few days before the India-Pakistan war broke out December 3, 1971, and visited Mrs. Gandhi as well as Pakistan's president and dictator, Gen. Agha Mohammad Yahya Khan. His troops carried out the genocide in East Pakistan that left some three million dead and forced millions more to seek sanctuary in India.

As a result of the 1971 outbreak in hostilities, "The United States cut off economic and military aid to India while continuing to send supplies to Pakistan. . . . [and on December 9] sent its Seventh Fleet toward Dhaka [Dacca] in an effort to intimidate India. Before the nuclear-powered air-craft carrier U.S.S. *Enterprise* could reach anywhere near Indian waters, Moscow dispatched its own fleet for the same region."[24] Nixon believed India, with Soviet backing, intended to invade West Pakistan after the campaign in East Pakistan.

The month before the 1971 India-Pakistan war began, Mrs. Gandhi had had two meetings in Washington with Nixon and Kissinger. They did not go well. Kissinger described them as "the most unfortunate meetings Nixon ever had with any foreign leader."[25] Thus, the rift widened between her and Nixon. Mrs. Gandhi believed "it was appalling that Nixon sided with Pakistan—the very same Pakistan whose troops had killed more than three million Bangladeshis. . . . She also felt that Nixon had read India wrong. She thought he did not understand that India would never give in to pressure from Washington or anywhere else."[26]

Kissinger carried out Nixon's policy wishes. As the war between India and Pakistan raged, Kissinger met on December 6 with the secret WSAG (Washington Special Action Group) at the White House.[27] He made it clear that Nixon had no intention of being "even-handed" in the subcontinent. He told the assembled members, "The President believes that India is the attacker. We are trying to get across the idea that India has jeopardized relations with the United States. We cannot afford to ease India's state of mind. The lady [Mrs. Gandhi] is cold blooded and tough and will not turn into a Soviet satellite merely because of pique."[28]

Ambassador Jha criticized U.S. naval movements during a press conference in Washington, which brought a rebuke from Nixon, via Kissinger: "The U.S. government finds it intolerable the way the Indian Ambassador used the American media to attack the Administration."[29]

On December 16, Pakistan capitulated. Nearly one hundred thousand troops surrendered and Yahya Khan was forced to resign. Bangladesh was recognized as an independent state.

The day before the war ended, Mrs. Gandhi wrote an open letter to Nixon:

This tragic war . . . could have been averted if, during the nine months prior to Pakistan's attack on us . . . the great leaders of the world had paid some attention to the fact of revolt, tried to see the reality of the situation and searched for a genuine basis for reconciliation. . . . The fact of the matter is that the rulers of West Pakistan got away with the impression that they could do what they liked because no one, not even the United States, would choose to take a public position [against them].[30]

In addition to the lifting of the arms embargo, the other major issue that arose in the spring of 1974 was India's entry into the nuclear community. India was not a signatory to the 1970 nuclear nonproliferation treaty because China, which already had nuclear capability, didn't sign the treaty, either. On May 18, India detonated a "peaceful" nuclear device underground at Pokhran in the Rajasthan desert, becoming the sixth nation in the world's nuclear club. Indians celebrated the achievement, but U.S. critics wondered aloud why India would pour millions into a nuclear program when so many of its citizens were in such dire need. While seen as "a serious setback to global nonproliferation efforts," it represented "relatively little strategic significance," in Kissinger's view.[31]

In May 1998, India again conducted nuclear tests near the border of Pakistan. Pakistan retaliated with nuclear testing of its own, heightening tensions between the two neighbors once again and engendering rebuke from the United States and other nations.

Because there was so much attention focused on India and its first nuclear tests, I made it a point prior to leaving Washington to meet with Dixy Lee Ray, former chairman of the Atomic Energy Commission. At the time, she was assistant secretary of state for oceans and international environmental and scientific affairs. I asked her about India's nuclear tests and whether such activity should be of concern to me as a representative of the United States.

"Don't worry about it, Bill," she said. "Everyone knows which nations have nuclear capabilities today. The technical know-how is widespread [this was late 1974, remember], so even Afghanistan could make an atomic bomb if it had the money and resources. Anyone can do it. I wouldn't worry about India."

Kissinger's next visit to India in October 1974 was somewhat less than a success. Mrs. Gandhi and others believed the CIA was meddling in India's affairs, even though Kissinger called a press conference to deny it. In a show of disdain Mrs. Gandhi left New Delhi in the middle of his visit, which annoyed Kissinger. He felt she was "hyper-sensitive to foreign criticism."[32]

Regardless, Mrs. Gandhi was convinced that the CIA was gunning for her. To those close to her she often "was to repeat . . . that 'they' wanted to do her in. She took care never specifically to identify who 'they' were. But, by innuendo and insinuation, she left little doubt that the accusing finger pointed to the CIA, if not to the government of the United States."[33]

Mrs. Gandhi and the Congress Party made it a point to blame the CIA for everything bad that happened in India. I'll never forget the first time I went up the main road there in New Delhi. The Congress Party had big anti-CIA banners across the road: "We're not going to be run by them," and so on and so forth.

That pot still was boiling in 1975 when I arrived, of course, and Mrs. Gandhi and I had some serious talks about that business. In May I returned to Washington for consultations and to Columbus for The Ohio State University commencement on June 13. Rocky received his law degree that day, and I was the commencement speaker and recipient of an honorary doctorate, but I spent most of my time in Washington. I met with William E. Colby, head of the CIA. I said, "Now look, Bill, I want to know what's going on in India because I'm going to tackle this thing, and if I find out that you're doing these things that I have no knowledge of, I'm going to announce it publicly and resign."

I was assured that we were responsible for none of the activity Mrs. Gandhi thought we were engaged in. When I returned to New Delhi, I went to Mrs. Gandhi on July 23 and told her of my talks in Washington.

I asked her if she knew who India's biggest customer of its exports was. "It's the United States," I said. "You don't sell anything to Russia. All you do is buy military equipment from Russia, and they don't buy anything from you." Unless India got off its anti-U.S. stance, "I'm going to go back to the states and say India is not our friend and you shouldn't do business with them." I don't believe I was quite that blunt with Mrs. Gandhi, but I was to the foreign secretary (Chavan) and his people. Well, that got their attention and things eased off for a while.

Mrs. Gandhi was one of the most admirable women I ever met, but I didn't agree with her political and economic views. She was too enamored of the London School of Economics philosophy, which she learned from her father and from her own studies and theories of socialism. She tried to keep such tight control on the economy that there was no room for human endeavor to expand and develop. It was called democracy, but it was the most socialistic type of democracy with its attempt to control everything.

One of the ways they maintained control was by not permitting anything to come into the country. That protectionist policy made it difficult for international companies to do business in India. For instance, India made it a rule that the executives who came in, like for Firestone and Good-year, both of which had plants there, could only stay a year in India. The government also demanded that Indians be given positions of responsibility in those plants. I think one of the reasons for the Bhopal chemical plant incident was that they required Indian engineers to run the machinery. Union Carbide was in overall charge, but its own engineers did not have their hands on the switch.[34]

India also made it virtually impossible for international corporations, American or otherwise, to take any profits out of India. Union Carbide had $200 million dollars in investments in the country, investments that went back to 1905. It established its first manufacturing plant in 1928. In the eyes of India's "democratic" government, none of that counted for much. Union Carbide tried everything to get its profits out of the country and to the stockholders. It resorted to dealing in gems, setting up a shrimp boat fleet, and other things. It was the dead hand of Indian government that was stifling the country.

The Indian government was irrational. It said, for instance, that Coca-Cola had to disclose its secret formula, so Coca-Cola closed down its operation in India. The government also said that all the maintenance and repair people for IBM in India had to be Indians. IBM refused and left the country. What the government said was, you can do business here, but you have to have Indians running your business.

In Mrs. Gandhi's defense she had a bureaucracy to deal with that was unbelievable by our standards. It was traditional in India, for example, for the men to do the shopping, so the government workers would all go out and do their shopping in the morning, when it was coolest, and not get to the office before 10:00 A.M. They'd take an hour off at noon—you'd see them out on the lawn playing cards. Around 1:00 P.M. they'd come back in and were gone by 4:00 P.M. That was more or less routine.

There seemed to be an indifference to work in the civil service. They claimed that if everyone in government came to work, there wouldn't be enough chairs for them. As a result, absenteeism was very high. They also had coolies—they called them coolies—who brought the office workers tea in their offices.

Corruption was rampant, even though the government denied it. As I told the Washington press during my May/June visit in 1975, the only way to get anything moving was to make an under-the-table payment. Slip the clerk a few rupees and your paperwork would miraculously move from the bottom of the pile to the top. The fact that government salaries had not been raised in twenty-five years or so contributed to the problem.

During the first few months of our time in New Delhi the Vietnam War was still going on. We had a demonstration outside the embassy at 5:00 P.M. every afternoon. The Vietnamese would hire a bunch of Indians, and they'd shoot firecrackers and demonstrate and then get in a bus and leave.

It became ludicrous, though. One time, the Indian demonstrators came to us and said they didn't get paid. They wanted *us* to pay them. Then the Indian government provided a platoon of soldiers to guard the embassy. The Indians set up tents just outside the perimeter in front of our place. Their laundry would be hanging out, and those guys loafing around out there, but there never was any need for them.

Having demonstrators outside the embassy upset Dolly. During our 1975 visit, she told the news media in Columbus that she did not enjoy everything about India. Of course, everything she said was reported in the Indian press, too. In New Delhi *The Mail* reported her unhappiness: "Not so pleasant," she said, "are the anti-American headlines in the newspapers every day and the student demonstrators who gather frequently outside the embassy. It's all very hard for us to understand," she said. "We always think we are the good guys, but as a government we are not very popular in India."[35]

I mentioned in the previous chapter the million dollars worth of generators the embassy purchased just for Kissinger's visit to India in 1974. Well, there's more to that story. Congressman Wayne L. Hays, D-Flushing, Ohio, had a hand in that. He was a power in the House and chairman of the House Administration Committee and chaired its subcommittee on international operations. Anyway, committee members decided they had to buy those two generators for $2 million. They supposedly shipped them to Bombay. When I got there they had been sitting in a Bombay warehouse for six months—never installed. I told the State Department, "We don't need the generators." We tried in vain to sell them to the Indians, but suddenly, without my knowledge, they were loaded on a tramp steamer and sent to Saudi Arabia. I knew that something was phony when the ship caught fire and sank, and when authorities examined the wreck, the generators weren't in it. Somebody had stolen them. Maybe there never were any generators. I just don't know.

There always was a lively social interplay between the various embassies. For instance, we had a very close relationship with our neighbors, the Russians. They entertained us and we entertained them. At the same time, we listened to them and they listened to us. That was one way to get information and to establish relationships, to know what their potential was, to know what their military situation was, to know what equipment they were selling to countries in the subcontinent. We were competing with Russia, of course, to supply American equipment.

The Russians put on good parties. They'd give you vodka and caviar, the best grade caviar available. But the Russian ambassador and his wife, Mr. and Mrs. Viktor F. Maltsev, did not speak English well. They tried hard and were very jovial, but it was difficult to carry on a conversation with either of them.

Private or personal, entertaining was inexpensive. Dolly determined one time that it had personally cost us forty dollars to entertain seventy-five guests for cocktails and a lot of snacks. We would hire the staff for our own parties as well as our household servants. I think we had ten or eleven of them in our quarters, which cost us something like three hundred dollars a month. We needed that many because each had a specific job, whether it was driving the limousine, cleaning the carpets, or serving dinner. No one doubled up on jobs; that way more jobs were available. But when you had to fire someone, that often would put an entire family out on the street.

Much of the "official" responsibility of the ambassador was to entertain and be entertained by representatives of other nations, each of which had its national and other special days. Almost every day there were luncheons and receptions and dinners with ambassadors of Denmark, Bhutan, Sweden, Australia, Morocco, and dozens of other countries. Then there were the special visitors, such as U.S. Secretary of the Treasury William E. Simon, who came in April 1975 with his wife and two teenage daughters. His itinerary, and mine, included visits to Bombay and the Taj Mahal in Agra, as well as talks with Mrs. Gandhi and other Indian officials.

On August 21, 1975, I accompanied visiting Sen. Thomas F. Eagleton, D-Missouri, to a tea hosted by Mrs. Gandhi at her residence. He and I settled on her settee, and Eagleton asked the first question of Mrs. Gandhi, who was attired in an ivory and pink sari. "I have seen the press reports concerning the political 'emergency' in India," Eagleton began. "Would you say these reports are accurate?" In reply, she launched into a fifty-minute monologue, and the scheduled thirty-minute tea ended an hour and a half later.

Three days later, Mrs. Gandhi came to Roosevelt House—her first visit there—for a small dinner party in honor of House Minority Leader Elford A. Cederberg, R-Michigan. Mrs. Gandhi was delightful, very relaxed and chatty.

Bart, Juli, and Rocky all spent some time with us during our first year in India. We enjoyed having them close. Juli became quite a social butterfly and was very popular on the diplomatic social circuit. Rocky and Suzy, who came with eight-month-old Sarah, won a private audience with Mrs. Gandhi, which was the highlight of their trip.

Among the many other visitors to New Delhi were General Quesada and his wife, Kate; William J. Keating, president of the *Cincinnati Enquirer,* who had been so instrumental in my being named U.S. attorney general; Dr. Harold L. Enarson, president of The Ohio State University; and my longtime political ally, J. D. Sawyer and his wife, Mickey.

Between the few duties I had, the visits, the golf, fishing, and hunting, I kept quite busy in India. The work was far from satisfying, though.

22

Huntin', Fishin', and Leavin'

Being an ambassador had become somewhat tiresome by early 1976. I notified the State Department that it was my intent to leave the post in the fall. Relations with India were deteriorating—it appeared that they were moving rapidly into total dictatorship—and we were gradually losing effective contact. I was determined that our country would not be pushed around, and that often meant confrontation.

Furthermore, the American business community in India was fast dwindling, and I concluded that those companies that invested in India were out of their minds. Americans, and me in particular, were often attacked by India's political leaders and by the press, the *Patriot* in New Delhi being among the most vocal.

There was plenty of blame to go around among those who pulled the strings. For instance, there is no question in my mind that the United States had the idea of reforming India, reforming its agriculture, reforming its industry, reforming its way of life. But when we employed finger-wagging, holier-than-thou policies, we shouldn't have expected India or any other country to welcome us with open arms nor be surprised or upset when they didn't appear to appreciate all that we did for them. We don't have all the answers, as anyone who has spent any time overseas can plainly see, so we shouldn't act as if we do.

Several times during my stay in India I stumped for better, more realistic, commercial and economic relations. "Each of us has a stake in the progress of the other," I said in a major address to the Indo-American Chamber of Commerce in Bombay. I feared, however, that India's 1976 Foreign Exchange Regulations Act would impose undue hardship on foreign investors. I told the chamber group: "The Indian government is perfectly within its right to enact any legislation or to frame any ground rules for foreign investments in India that it considers appropriate. While we do not question this right, we hope that its implementation of those rules will be in the spirit of business realism and administrative statesmanship."[1]

As I expected, my comments drew out the critics. An editorial in New Delhi's *National Herald,* noted in part:

> Mr. William Saxbe, the American Ambassador, is all sweet reasonableness in talking of Indo-U.S. relations and of Washington's desire to exploit the potentiality to the maximum mutual advantage. These noble sentiments, expressed volubly to an audience of big traders in Bombay, might sound original to Mr. Saxbe, but this is the kind of relationship India has been seeking with all countries, including Mr. Saxbe's, over the years. It is the U.S. that has not responded adequately but has tried to link economic cooperation and trade to political postures, a line unacceptable to India. . . . Mr. Saxbe's talk of business realism and administrative statesmanship seems to reflect the old line, which is unsuited to the new times.[2]

While in Washington for talks in the spring of 1975, when U.S.-Indian relations were in the pits, I told administration and congressional leaders that before any initiatives were proposed with India, they should consult India. If they don't want us to tell them how to improve their wheat crop, for example, don't force our knowledge on them. I don't think my thoughts had much impact on United States policy, though.

"Our relations with India are going from bad to ridiculous," I confided in a letter to Bill Monroe, host of "Meet the Press." We were operating in an atmosphere of hostility, fueled by Prime Minister Gandhi: "We have no basic differences but the prime minister is upset because western governments and the media are not rejoicing about her takeover. She attacks us almost daily, blaming us for a long list of real and imagined ills that beset the country. Dolly and I are enjoying our sojourn here, but it is rather depressing to preside over an immense embassy establishment doing little or nothing. Keeping my views bottled up never was my 'long suit,' as you know so well, but I am determined not to get into a shouting match with her [Mrs. Gandhi]."[3]

Actually, I felt I got along very well socially with the prime minister. I remember one time she had just Dolly and me for an informal family dinner at her residence. Both of her sons and a few other people were there all together. I understand that was the first time she had had a U.S. ambassador as a guest at a family dinner. We were honored. It was quite a lively—but nonpolitical—social evening.

India's prime minister, Indira Gandhi, joined in our bicentennial celebration at the United States embassy in New Delhi, February 1976.

Mrs. Gandhi joined us for our bicentennial celebration at the embassy on February 27, 1976. Among the twelve hundred other guests were Vice President B. D. Jatti and Minister for External Affairs Yashwantrao B. Chavan, a large contingent from the diplomatic corps, and an even larger group of Americans. It was a beautiful evening, with fireworks, of course.

Mrs. Gandhi, Jatti, other distinguished guests, and Dolly and I were seated on the front terrace of Roosevelt House. After the speeches, Mrs. Gandhi turned to Dolly and said, "Let's go down!" She wanted to circulate among the guests. Her security force, which was formidable, was quite perturbed, but she dismissed their concerns. "Oh, bother them," she said, and plunged into the crowd. They all loved it—and so did Mrs. Gandhi.

Many days there was little to do, other than attend some social function or other, so Dolly and I played a lot of golf at the Delhi Golf Club, which expanded to twenty-seven holes from eighteen shortly before we left India. It was best to play in the early morning, sometimes as early as 5:00 A.M., to beat the oppressive heat. It was a tough course—6,770 yards from the members' tees—with tight fairways and lots of sand. Four-hundred-year-old Moghul and Lodi tombs served as rain shelters on the course. The rough was as rough as it gets—damn near impenetrable. When the ball left the fairway, you forgot about it. There were all manner of monkeys, dogs, cobras, and other snakes in that jungle—and a few people you wouldn't want to meet, either.

I recorded my first and only hole-in-one at the club on August 17, 1975. It was on a 140-yard par 3. I was so happy that I was ready to sing "Ace in the Hole!"

American golf balls were hard to come by in India because of high tariffs. Most members played with the smaller British balls, but Ralph Waldo used to send me balls that he had swiped from members at Scioto Country Club in Columbus. Friends like H. K. "Bud" Crowl, Russ Schuler, John Arthur, and Cassie Sharp also would send a box or two of balls from time to time. Jack Nicklaus even sent me a box.

Like everything else I did in India, what I did on the golf course was noted in the Indian newspapers, and not always kindly, either. The *Indian Express* in Bombay reported: "The New York Times, the Bible for the India-watchers in and out of the Government, today pictured...Saxbe spending 'several hours a day at the Delhi Golf Club' and waiting for calls which never come from Indian officials and journalists. The paper said he has told his staff that if Indians wanted to improve relations with the United States, 'they know where I am.' Mr. Saxbe's decision to adopt a virtually passive role in New Delhi marks one of the lowest, perhaps oddest, points in relations between his country and India."[4]

In addition to the golf, the hunting and fishing was great, too, so I often was off doing one or the other, many times accompanied by Dolly. I remember a couple of memorable hunting trips in India. Bart was along—he was visiting his mother and me—as was Capt. Reggie Sawhney, my hunting and fishing companion. Reggie's mother was British, his father was an Indian professor. He had been a captain in the Indian navy, and he had run the cadet school. He had retired from the navy and was an agent for an American sugar company. When we went hunting, Reggie would bring a table and tablecloth and the silver service to set it up, so our lunch was ready when we came in.

On that particular trip we were going partridge hunting, which we did most of the time, traveling in a Land Rover. We got high centered between the ruts in the road, spinning the wheels with nothing but air under them.

A guy came along and told us the farmers in the area were having problems with a couple of nilgais, also known as blue buck. These are large, ugly, cow-size antelope that eat and trample the crops. Being Hindus, the farmers wouldn't kill anything, not even birds. In fact, the farmers would spend days and nights in the rice and wheat fields, banging pots and pans to keep the birds out. Would I shoot those nilgais, the man asked? I agreed, reaching for the rifle I always carried because you were frequently asked to do this sort of thing.

We took off and tracked the animals and finally came up on them, about three hundred yards ahead of us. But I didn't want to shoot because the land was flat and inhabited with people. Finally I got within about two hundred yards of a big male. I dropped down on one knee and prepared to shoot him right in the slats (his ribs) because there is less chance of missing and the bullet going into the populace. I hit him, and I saw the dust fly where I hit him, but he took off.

We tracked again, getting within about 150 yards that time. But by then, a crowd of villagers was following me. I was ready to shoot that buck again, and there came a guy on a bicycle, between the nilgai and me! So, I didn't get a chance when I had a good shot. As the nilgai disappeared over a dike, I hit him right in the ass, but he kept going.

By that time the crowd was thirty to forty people, all going with us. What a circus! The buck stopped in a grove of trees, which knocked out most of the danger. That time I got to within one hundred yards, and I hit him right in the ear. Down he went.

Now, there we were, in a grove without a damn thing but a pocketknife. A woman was cutting wood with a little hatchet, but she wouldn't lend us the hatchet. So Bart, my son the surgeon, gutted this animal with the pocketknife. It dressed out at about six hundred pounds.

Before we left there, a guy in a turban, an untouchable, arrived. We took the meat, of course, but the entire viscera were there on the ground. He unwrapped his turban into a wide, long piece of cloth. He took all the guts and squeezed the shit out of them, gathered them up in that cloth, put it over his back and disappeared. All that was left was a smear on the ground.

A scary hunt was a trip I made with my friend Avi Kohli, who ran hunting and fishing expeditions in the subcontinent. We were shooting partridge on the border of Rajasthan when I saw a gang of people coming over the hill. They were waving sticks and hollering. What we didn't know was that there was a Brahman village right over the hill. They don't believe in killing anything. The crowd gathered around Avi, waving those sticks and throwing clods of dirt at him. I thought they were going to kill him. I kept moving back towards the Land Rover, but the crowd spotted me and took off after me. "Get the hell out of here!" I yelled at our driver. I had a loaded gun in my hand, but I was not about to shoot anybody. We finally outran them and got to the little car we came in, an Ambassador.

The nearest police station was five miles away, so we drove there as fast as we could. At the station nobody spoke English. The head man, the lieutenant, was home taking a nap. We had to get him, so we loaded five or six Sikhs, all police officers, into that little Ambassador and headed down the road. With their long poles with steel tips sticking out every window, we looked like a motorized porcupine. With the lieutenant in tow, we raced back to the village at sixty miles an hour or more. Kohli had had lost some teeth and had big lumps on his head. He also had a lump on his face and was spitting blood. The villagers had taken his hat and coat and his birds. The lieutenant talked to the headman of the village, who stopped the beating. Then the officer turned to us and said, "Now you get in your car and get out of here, fast!" And we did. But it was a scary time for us all.

Hunting in Pakistan could be unusual, to say the least. I remember going boar hunting in a Mercedes. When we arrived at the hunting grounds, the servants first set up a tea table—white tablecloth and silver tea service. Nearby, off in a thicket, a boar was tied to a tree. The poor animal was the object of the "hunt." I didn't participate in the slaughter.

Another time we were supposedly duck hunting near Islamabad, the capital of Pakistan. That time the tea table was set up right in the boat. No self-respecting duck would come within a half mile of that thing! Out on the lake were flocks of mud hens that you could have killed with a fishing pole. That was the extent of that "duck" hunt.

Bird shooting and trout fishing were outstanding in Kashmir, India's northernmost state. We would bag snipe, partridge, duck, goose, and chukar, often stopping only when I was ashamed to shoot more. It was not unusual to come back from a bird hunt in India with several dozen birds. One time I had ninety, and all of them went into the embassy's freezer. In the clear-running streams at eight thousand feet or so we caught brown trout up to seven pounds. It was the best trout fishing I have ever enjoyed. It cost us $1.65 per day, plus $1 a day for the cabin.

Shopping for antiques, jewelry, clothes, and rugs was another pastime both Dolly and I enjoyed, and so did many of our visitors. When Secretary of the Treasury William E. Simon was there with his family, Dolly estimated they dropped fifty thousand dollars in Delhi and Bombay.

Dolly bought a couple of saris while in India. They were of beautiful material and vibrant colors, but I was not fond of them. The press once asked me if I had ever seen Dolly in a sari? "No . . . and I hope I don't," I said. "For a woman who hasn't been used to wearing a sari it [makes her look] like a mule in a horse harness."[5]

In March we returned to the States for a short visit, taking the long way around with our friends, W. F. "Al" Rockwell Jr., chairman of Rockwell International, and his wife, Connie. The Rockwells were touring the Far East in the company's twin-engine jet and invited us to travel with them and Frank Gard Jameson, a former vice president of Rockwell who was president of Ryan Aircraft. His wife, the actress Eva Gabor, also was along.

It was a grand trip, with stops in Singapore, Bali, New Zealand, Australia, Tahiti, and Hawaii before they dropped us off in Wyoming to see Juli and her new husband. Dolly stayed in Mechanicsburg while I went on to Washington and then on to Bremen, Germany, for a meeting of the pipe-puffing Tobacco Collegium (Das Bremer Tabak Kollegium). Rockwell and Jameson were there also, along with my friend John Galbreath of Columbus and senior executives from Gulf Oil, Westinghouse, Packard, Reynolds, Bethlehem Steel, Union Carbide, and other corporations.

By mid-April Dolly and I were back in New Delhi and looking forward to returning home permanently. In July I applied for membership to the District of Columbia Bar, having received several invitations to practice law in Washington upon my return. My main goal, however, was to return to Mechanicsburg before jumping into anything else.

My unhappiness with the job made it into the press by December 1975. The *Urbana Citizen* interviewed me by telephone, and I said that I intended to be home in Mechanicsburg by the following Christmas. In March, the Associated Press ran a story that I intended to resign, frustrated as I was with the assignment and deteriorating relations with India. The Indian press had a field day with that story. I guess they couldn't wait for me to leave town.

Dolly and I really loved the people of India and the country, but it is complex and difficult to understand. It has been overrun by wild tribes from the Hindukush, the Mongols, the Persians, and in more recent times, the British. Each has left their mark.

Few people realize that while India is mostly Hindu, it has nearly 100 million Muslims and remnants of dozens of other religions, such as Christian, Sikh, Buddhist, and Parsi. Hindi and English are the official languages, but there are fourteen national languages and dozens of regional tongues. There are still millions of tribal people and an outlawed caste system that includes the untouchables, despite the government's best intentions to rehabilitate them.

India is a sovereign democratic republic that seeks to be a world power, but that is difficult to imagine, given the factionalism of the states. Most important, though, is that the government must get the chip off its shoulder before it can be considered a world power.

By mid-September Dolly and I were all but packed and ready to leave. We had to get started early because most of our things had to be returned by ship. I didn't realize until they started to crate it how much we had accumulated in India.

Shortly before leaving New Delhi, I received a letter from my successor in the Senate, Howard M. Metzenbaum, D-Ohio, who said my "pithy comment" concerning Ford's selection of Bob Dole as national party chairman received "wide publicity." I was not a Dole fan, and when asked about his selection, I said I didn't think he could sell ass on a troop ship. Later, when others quoted what I had said, the commodity was changed to beer.

Metzenbaum also told me, "Word is going around here that you might run for Governor in 1978. I expect no comment on this subject from you." He wasn't about to get any, even if he wanted it. I had no intention of jumping back into the frying pan of Ohio politics.

We left India on November 22, returning home via London, where we spent two days in the home of Justin Dart, chairman of Dart Industries. We then boarded the QE 2, arriving in Boston on December 2, 1976. It was a glorious way to end my more than thirty years of public service, I admit, but I had expected fire boat salutes as we entered the harbor and a ticker tape parade.[6]

23

In Private Again

It was great to be back in Mechanicsburg and on the farm at Jubarock. Both Dolly and I were tired of living life in a fishbowl. We were content in Mechanicsburg, doing what we wanted to do. I ran the cattle operation, played golf, took trips, and so forth. I had never been in a position that allowed me to take off any time I wanted. I had never met a payroll. I never became involved in any major business enterprise of any kind. I just didn't want to get tied down. It's amazing I survived as well as I did. Sure, I opened a small law office in Mechanicsburg, as well as practicing later in Washington with the law firm of Pierson, Ball, and Dowd, but I was happiest putting down roots again and becoming reacquainted with a lifetime of friends in central Ohio.

Contrary to what I might have thought, not everyone was acquainted with me, though. I discovered my anonymity one night very shortly after my return. I tried to check into the Sheraton Hotel at Broad and Third Streets, in downtown Columbus. The report in the *Columbus Dispatch* was accurate:

> A punctilious desk clerk, filling out the registration card, asked where Saxbe worked. He replied he was unemployed. Well, the desk clerk sniffed, did he have any credit card identification? Saxbe produced an International Air Travel card. The desk clerk demanded a domestic card or two. Saxbe explained that he had been out of the country for two years, in India, and had no current domestic cards. "I have a suitcase and a wife," he said. "Will that do?" Apparently it would not. But, at that point, a Sheraton bellman who recognized the prominent and oft-photographed Saxbe, intervened and assured the desk clerk that if the prospective guest did not pay his bill, the bellman would. Saxbe got his room.[1]

That first summer home Dolly and I realized how much junk we had accumulated over the years. It was a lot—more than we really had room for at Jubarock. So we decided to have a garage sale for our friends and neighbors. Nearly three thousand items went on sale, from a bed of nails we brought from India to a walnut pie safe that had been in my family for more than one hundred years. A friend in Urbana bought the bed of nails, and also paid fifteen hundred dollars for a six-by-eight camel hair rug made in India. Books, clothing, rugs, dishes, furniture, and all manner of bric-a-brac were snapped up. I remember we had a rug from India or Pakistan priced at two hundred dollars, but we raised that when a rug expert and a friend said its value was fifteen times that.

In two days, more than one thousand folk—including reporters and photographers from the Associated Press, the *New York Times,* and other papers—attended, often backing up traffic something awful along Route 29 in front of the farm.

By the fall of 1977 I had had enough of Washington and returned to Ohio to join forces in Columbus with Jack Chester, Herbert Hoffman, and Roderick Willcox. The firm became Chester, Saxbe, Hoffman, and Willcox, and it stayed that way until I left. Subsequently Rocky became a partner and it became Chester, Willcox, and Saxbe.

I was invited to be on the Bank One board, which I was on for five years. I also was a director of Mohawk Rubber in Akron, Columbus Savings and Loan, Worthington Industries, and some other small interests.

From time to time my name would emerge for Ohio governor. Supporters and GOP party leaders would try to draw me into a race. At the time I decided to leave the Senate, a group of supporters urged that I make a run for governor. That, perhaps, was the most serious effort of all. Daytonian Harry K. "Bud" Crowl, a member of the GOP state executive committee and president of WAVI Broadcasting, led the campaign to draft me for the 1974 race against Rhodes in the primary and then against Gov. John J. Gilligan, the incumbent, in the general election. Chester and Sawyer were part of the group, too.

The arm-twisting began in the spring of 1973 and heated up that fall. Crowl wrote to those who were supporting my candidacy:

I think this information might be of interest to those who met at my home March 10th last to discuss Bill Saxbe and the Rhodes situation.

I am enclosing a copy of my today's letter to Jim Rhodes for what very little that may be worth [and] the results of the Montgomery County preference poll.... Then, we'll just have to see what happens.

I enjoy Herefords because they coexist with mice, don't shed like cats, and are nonviolent.

Hopefully these leaders [state and county GOP leaders] can be motivated to get a "grassroots" opinion, which might bring Jim Rhodes to his senses.

As for Bill, there is just no question he will run under the conditions he outlined over a year ago, i.e., a clear track and sufficient money to mount a strong campaign. I spoke with him as late as last Wednesday evening; there is no change.

No matter what he says or does publicly, he will head the 1974 ticket if the conditions are met. You must believe this.[2]

Crowl's letter to Rhodes, also dated October 26, came right to the point:

I believe you are aware, I am opposing your bid for a third term as governor. . . . I sincerely feel very strongly that you cannot win next November. Not only do I feel you cannot win, I further believe your candidacy in today's political climate is so impractical that its end result will be disastrous for the whole state ticket. Pragmatically, it could be disastrous enough to initiate the demise of the Ohio Republican Party.

... For everyone, there is a time to come on stage, a time to stay on stage, and then a time to leave it. The difficulty always ... is to discern when that latter time is.[3]

The mailing for the preference poll, conducted among some one thousand party workers and contributors in Montgomery County, was posted the day I announced that I would not seek a second term in the Senate. Then Crowl arranged to have the results leaked to Hugh McDiarmid, Columbus correspondent for the *Dayton Journal Herald*, and to the Associated Press. McDiarmid published the story, noting that I "trounced" Rhodes by a 3 to 1 margin in the head-to-head popularity survey. Among just party regulars, the margin was 2 to 1, and among contributors the margin jumped to 6 to 1.4.[4]

Rhodes had no intention of giving up his candidacy, and I just was not willing to fight him for the nomination, despite what the polls said. I know I disappointed a lot of people, but I was not ready for another Bender-like battle within the party.

When Rhodes wound up his fourth four-year term in 1983 and was barred from running for a third consecutive term, the press felt I might make a run for the nomination. I made the mistake of telling Gene Jordan, public affairs editor at the *Columbus Dispatch*, that my running for governor might happen if I got a case of "the simples or something, but I don't foresee that happening."[5]

I never was really that interested in the job. I'd seen enough of it and thought it was a housekeeping job. There is never enough money to do the things that you want to do, and you've got a patronage problem that is nothing but a nuisance. I talked to Dolly about it; we talked about everything. She didn't care. Dolly is not ambitious for me or for herself—never has been. Maybe it was a mistake, but I just didn't have the desire. You've got to have the fire in your gut if you want to go on in Ohio politics.

While I was with Chester's firm, I served as independent special counsel for Canadian Javelin Ltd. in Montreal and for its founder, John C. Doyle. It was one of the more interesting law assignments I had in an otherwise dull existence.

In an investigation that began in 1975, Doyle was accused of illegally selling unregistered stock. The Securities and Exchange Commission caught up with him and prosecuted him, charging that he manipulated Javelin's stock on the American Exchange. The government cut a deal with Doyle, telling him if he pleaded guilty, he'd get a fine but no time in prison. However, the judge gave him ninety days, so Doyle fled the country, eventually ending up in Panama, where the company had mining interests.

Doyle also got involved in a fiberboard company in Newfoundland, with government-backed bonds. It was a goofy deal that blew up, and Canada sought prosecution. Doyle again fled. The Mounties tried to kidnap Doyle and bring him back to Canada, but they never succeeded.

In 1978 Javelin dismissed its Washington counsel, which had been appointed by a federal court under terms of a 1974 consent decree involving Javelin and the SEC. That followed the SEC's fraud suit against Javelin. Although it was a Canadian company, it traded on the American Exchange and had a lot of U.S. stockholders. In any event, the company submitted my name to the court as "someone beyond reproach and acceptable to everyone—the SEC and the courts." In the fall of 1978, the SEC approved my appointment as special counsel to ensure company compliance with U.S. securities laws. I was paid fifty thousand dollars a year, which I badly needed at the time.

I discovered that the company was putting together their quarterly 10Qs and 10Ks with information that was not quite correct. I likened it to the Amazon Indians who gather raw rubber. They smoke the rubber and make a big ball with a rock in the middle to increase the weight. Then they take it down river and the buyer cuts it open and takes the rock out. The next time they do the same thing. I kept taking the rocks out at Javelin, every quarter. I stayed for four or five years, until the Canadian government finally moved in and threw the company into bankruptcy.

In March 1980, I got a call from the Horvitz family of Cleveland, whose members had been feuding for three years over control of the family businesses. They forwarded to the court my name for trustee of the family trust, and Cuyahoga County Probate Judge Joseph J. Nahra appointed two others and me. Our job was to direct the trust, which covered a $500 million communications, construction, and real estate conglomerate in Florida, Virginia, Ohio, and New York.

The three Horvitz brothers—Harry R., William D., and Leonard C.— couldn't get along, so I set up three separate trusts. Their father, Samuel A., had died in 1956. When I retired from the trust in 1998, I received a $225,000 pension, payable over five years.

That appointment came at a good time for me. As I said, I was tiring of routine law practice, and a substantial retainer gave me time to cast about for more interesting aspects of the law. It surfaced in Cleveland.

In June 1981 I left Chester, Saxbe, Hoffman, and Willcox and joined the much larger Cleveland law firm of Jones, Day, Reavis, and Pogue. They paid me sixty thousand dollars a year, and I had offices in Columbus and

Washington. I know Jack was very unhappy and disappointed, but I felt I needed a stronger, bigger firm where I could get more technical assistance. Three years later, I joined the Washington firm of Pierson, Ball, and Dowd, for reasons explained in the following chapter.

The George Steinbrenner case was an interesting one in which I became involved in the mid-1980s, after joining Pierson, Ball, and Dowd. Steinbrenner is probably best known as owner of the New York Yankees.

He was convicted in August 1974 for having made illegal corporate contributions of about $140,000 to Nixon's 1972 reelection campaign. He thought he was pleading guilty to a misdemeanor, but it turned out to be a felony. He avoided prison, but he was fined fifteen thousand dollars, and his American Ship Building Company, which had a large yard in Lorain, Ohio, was fined twenty thousand dollars for a separate campaign contribution to another candidate.

Edward Bennett Williams represented Steinbrenner at the time and tried to get him a pardon before President Jimmy Carter left office in 1980. Carter said he was going to grant it, but he didn't. As a result, Steinbrenner couldn't own a gun, he couldn't vote, he couldn't get a license to race horses, and many things that are applicable to a felony conviction. The only answer to it was a pardon.

Steinbrenner had exhausted his appeals before I became involved. One day I received a call from his attorney in Cleveland. I had met Steinbrenner casually because he was in Columbus when I was there, and when I was running for the Senate he supported me. After the attorney painted the picture for me, I called T. Timothy Ryan Jr., at our Washington office.

"Got a call from George Steinbrenner," I told him, "and he wants me to help him get a pardon." We talked about it and set a fee of fifty thousand dollars, which we thought would adequately cover us. The first time Tim and I met with Steinbrenner was in a New York steakhouse, a hangout for ball players. All he wanted to do was tell us about how he'd been mislead into that plea, which didn't help much with what we were trying to do.

We worked through the parole board in New York to get their recommendation, which was required before President Ronald Reagan would do anything. We emphasized to the board that Steinbrenner was a national force, not only in baseball but in industry. As a supplier of the military, he had done an outstanding job with his American Ship Building Company, building ships for the navy.

As we stated in his application for a pardon, his conviction was "a source of personal humiliation" and "a symbolic slap in the face for a man who has tried so hard to overcome his conviction and be a good citizen."[6]

We played up the fact that Steinbrenner had cooperated with several law enforcement operations. One instance involved some Russian at the United Nations in New York who the Central Intelligence Agency thought they could compromise. Above all else, the Russian loved baseball and the New York Yankees; he even wore a Yankees jacket. So the CIA used Steinbrenner to help compromise him. We put that in an affidavit to the Justice Department as a reason why they should endorse a pardon for Steinbrenner.

Over a long lunch at 21, one of New York's landmark restaurants, where our client was almost a fixture, surrounded by his kind of people, I told Steinbrenner, "Look, this is how we get a pardon. You've got to make these bastards feel guilty. They've been using you through this whole process. The CIA, the city, the FBI—all of them."

We talked to Steinbrenner over and over again. On two occasions we went to Yankee Stadium and sat in his box—blue ribbon treatment. The thing I best remember is that Steinbrenner's elaborate office adjacent to his box had a popcorn machine in it.

We also had to convince him to change his story. In order to get a pardon, contrition is a key component, and to be contrite you have to admit that you did something. After he pleaded guilty he told the whole world that the only reason he did it was because Williams told him he had to cut the deal. Probably to this day Steinbrenner would say he didn't do those things. But we had to convince him to sign an affidavit saying that he had, in fact, made campaign contributions that were illegal.

All that took a lot of time. It finally went to Reagan and sat there for a couple of years. We'd pretty much given up on the thing, but the day he left office, January 20, 1989, Reagan signed the pardon. That was a surprise. Tim and I called Steinbrenner to tell him the good news, and he started to cry tears of joy. It was a very emotional moment. Steinbrenner was very appreciative. He doubled our fee, paying us an additional fifty thousand dollars without us even asking for it.

All in all, life was good for Dolly and me. We were home in Mechanicsburg, and I was making more money that I ever had made before.

24

Teamster Times

George W. Lehr was a large man, broad shouldered and well over six feet tall, but what everyone noticed first about him was that he was on crutches. Lehr had been a big, tough, rough-and-tumble high school football player—a top prospect for college stardom. Then infantile paralysis crippled him.

I met Lehr for the first time in Cleveland in 1982, while I still was with the Jones, Day, Reavis, and Pogue law firm. He telephoned me there, identified himself as executive director of the Central States Pension Fund in Chicago, the largest such fund in the International Brotherhood of Teamsters, and said he wanted to come see me. A former state auditor of Missouri, Lehr was in charge of the fund under a consent decree that the Department of Justice and the Labor Department had brought against it. The fund was the racket-controlled pension fund that earlier had financed many of the early Las Vegas hotels. It was a clearinghouse for mob loans—a tough operation.

I had had a long association with the Teamsters in Ohio. I used to attend Teamsters affairs in Cleveland—they comprised a big voting bloc—and Bill Presser, Jackie's father, always supported me and invited me to important occasions. That's where I met Teamster boss James R. Hoffa for the first and only time. I never had any conversation with him.

Our paths crossed yet again in a rather oblique way. As U.S. attorney general and a cabinet officer, I was invited to lunch from time to time in the private dining rooms of other cabinet officers. It was a way to meet informally, talk about cases or problems, or just shoot the breeze and get to know one another better. The purpose of one particular luncheon surprised me, though. I did not know Labor Secretary Peter J. Brennan well. He served in both the Nixon and Ford cabinets, so I was delighted when he invited me to have lunch with him. When I arrived, Brennan introduced me to his other guest, Frank E. Fitzsimmons, the powerful president of the Teamsters.

Fitzsimmons assumed leadership of the union immediately after Hoffa was forced to give up the presidency, as a condition of the executive clemency President Nixon granted on December 23, 1971. Hoffa had been in jail since 1967 for pension fraud, jury tampering, and conspiracy. The Nixon pardon also was contingent on Hoffa's agreement to stay away from Teamster activity—but he didn't. He continued to battle to remove Fitzsimmons and regain control of the union. Some believe that led to Hoffa's disappearance July 30, 1975, the apparent victim of a mob hit. Hoffa was declared legally dead in 1983.

Personally, I thought Nixon erred by pardoning Hoffa. He should have served his entire thirteen-year sentence. As it was, he served half that time. In addition, the administration's cozy relationship with the union reeked of political expediency. Unusual favors were granted Teamster leaders by the Nixon administration, and the union's executive board returned the favors by voting, for the first time in its history, the membership's support of the GOP presidential candidate (Nixon) in the 1972 campaign.

At Brennan's luncheon, Fitzsimmons turned the conversation to Hoffa, his pardon, and Hoffa's efforts to regain the union's presidency in violation of the clemency agreement. Pulling a crumpled piece of paper from his pants pocket, Fitzsimmons laid out his "evidence" of Hoffa's deviousness. Written on the paper was a pledge "not to seek union office" if pardoned. It was signed James R. Hoffa.

Afterwards I could only assume that Fitzsimmons had asked Brennan to set up the meeting to get me—and the office of the attorney general—involved in the Hoffa affair. If that was his aim, he missed the target completely.

The 1982 Labor Department consent decree isolated the pension fund from the Teamsters union itself and its leadership. There were some unsavory characters, from Hoffa on down, who used the pension fund as a cash cow. They profited not so much from the interest or the loans, but from kickbacks for getting the loans and then on the skim from the Las Vegas gambling operations that resulted from the mob making the loans.

The first of two main provisions of the decree set up the fiduciary, selected by the trustees from among the twenty-five largest banks, the twenty-five largest insurance companies, and the twenty-five largest investment houses. Equitable Insurance was selected for the first two years. Then Morgan Stanley was chosen to determine where to allocate the fund's assets—in stocks, bonds, real estate, and other investments. The fiduciary also hired the investment managers and allocated monies to the different managers to manage. So one part of the consent decree, and an important part, was the management of the assets.

The second part was to set up the position of independent special counsel to see that the provisions of the decree were strictly applied. Lehr asked if would I be interested in that job. Unbeknownst to him, I had some familiarity with consent decrees. At the time I was getting fifty thousand dollars a year from the Canadian Javelin Corporation as an independent special counsel to see that it abided by a court-ordered consent decree. I said to myself, boy, this is for me. I can do this. I've had experience in this.

Lehr evidently got my name from former Democratic Sen. John Culver of Iowa, who was one of the pension fund attorneys. Other candidates for the spot were Wilson Wyatt, former secretary of labor and a lawyer, and Sen. Birch Bayh, D-Indiana. I received support from Fred Thompson, Sen. Howard Baker's attorney on the Sam Ervin Watergate Committee, a pension fund attorney and now Republican senator from Tennessee. Also, there was T. Timothy Ryan Jr., who played an important part as the head lawyer for the Department of Labor. We had never met.

So, I began to lobby for the job. I called Vice President George Bush; my influential friend, entrepreneur Marshall Coyne; my friends in the Senate; and others. I said it was a job I wanted. It came down to three candidates, I understand, but Lehr pulled some strings, assuring my selection. In announcing my appointment, Lehr said:

> We are extremely proud of the selection. Having interviewed dozens of qualified attorneys, we are convinced that there is no one in the country better qualified than [Saxbe] to assume the responsibility of independent special counsel.
>
> We believe that the appointment . . . demonstrates the fund's eagerness to comply with both the spirit and the letter of the Consent Decree. We welcome the assistance of a man of his stature and reputation for integrity and candor. . . . We are convinced we have found the best.[1]

At the time U.S. District Court Judge James B. Moran of Chicago made the appointment, the Teamsters pension fund totaled $4.4 billion. Today the number is more than $21.1 billion, providing benefits totaling about $130 million a month to nearly 200,000 retirees.

Eighteen months after my appointment, when the Central States Health and Welfare Fund also was in need of a trustee, U.S. District Court Judge

Hubert Wills had jurisdiction. "Well, you've got that one [pension fund]," he said, "why not this one, too?" By that time, I'd established a record and nobody opposed me, so I was appointed for both funds. Since Wills's death in 1994, Moran had presided over both funds.

In the official language of the decree, my job was to "assist in identifying and resolving problems that may arise in implementing the undertakings of the Consent Decree." In other words, I am like a parole officer. I give a written report to Moran every three months and a copy goes to the Department of Labor. Ryan was my attorney at the Teamsters; more recently it has been Virginia Lewey, who was a former attorney for the Labor Department. When I first went there I had an independent auditor, too, because I didn't know whether to trust the Teamsters' auditors.

I admit I had some concerns about getting involved with the Teamsters pension fund. I am sure everybody at Teamster headquarters in Chicago thought I was a crook, and I glanced furtively at them, too. It took me a while to realize that the crooks, virtually all of them, had been kicked out before I arrived. I worried about Lehr for a while, too, because Teamster President Roy Williams, also from Kansas City, and who later went to jail in connection with kickbacks from the mob, was one of his sponsors for the job of executive director.

The government also suspected that Lehr was part of the game, but an exhaustive investigation revealed he was totally straight. He told Ryan, "I'm basically here to work with you. My biggest problem is that I have a guy running the insurance company called [Allen M.] Dorfman, who is a total mobster. He spends all of his time putting on his putting green or flying around in a corporate jet, which we have, or he's up in our dining rooms or bedrooms playing around with some prostitute."[2] So one of Lehr's goals was to get rid of Dorfman and get the fund operating like it should.

Dorfman was still at the fund's Chicago headquarters when I got there. He was a key figure in the organized crime picture, a high-living insurance salesman who owed his riches and his power to former Teamster boss Hoffa. "'Dorfman probably was aware of more information on more [mob] people than maybe any other single individual around the country,' a federal prosecutor said. 'It wouldn't be beyond belief that he knew who killed Jimmy Hoffa.'"[3]

Within a few years of establishing the Union Insurance Agency and receiving from Hoffa the Teamsters' insurance business, Dorfman was said to be a millionaire.[4] The two men created a pair of giant pension and welfare funds under the name Central States by incorporating the funds of dozens of union locals. Dorfman collected the fees for processing health and welfare claims, "But the real scandal lay with the pension fund, which [Dorfman] served as a consultant. Under his guidance, the fund made hundreds of millions of dollars in questionable loans for speculative real estate ventures, to friends of Teamsters officials and to Nevada casinos."[5]

Ronald J. Kubalanza, who later succeeded Lehr as executive director of both Central States funds, told me:

Dorfman was a multi-faceted kind of guy, very smart in certain ways and very personable. He would personally lend money to his employees. He could walk up to you and maybe not see you for three or four years, but he would remember not only the facts about you, but what you may have discussed about your personal life, your marriage or your kids or problems with your life in some way. He would have celebrities come in—Dean Martin, Evil Knievel and other people from Las Vegas—and he would tour them around and introduce them to people. He was not shy about telling anybody how smart he was, either, able to outsmart "this whole fucking government. These guys [the government] think they're fucking smart, but they'll never get me."[6]

After frequent brushes with the law and the mob, including jail time and shotgun blasts ripping into the car in which he was riding, Dorfman was convicted in federal court on December 15, 1982, of conspiring to bribe Sen. Howard Cannon, D-Nevada. That was less than two weeks after my appointment.

The government's investigation of Dorfman that led to the indictments had the Chicago headquarters in turmoil. Kubalanza recalled those days in the early 1980s:

At one point I'd say we had maybe 40 to 50 full-time investigators in the building, copying documents and interviewing staff. They brought in one of those king-sized Xerox machines and copied pension fund documents by the bushel. There was a lot of confusion. Then shortly before the indictments were returned against Dorfman [and four others], 20 or 30 FBI agents appeared in the lobby. They had a court order to remove the listening devices they had planted in the building 13 months before, primarily on the second floor in and around Dorfman's offices. The devices were everywhere, in light bulbs, behind pictures, under tables—everywhere.[7]

Even though I had been independent special counsel for a very short time, I didn't need to be hit between the eyes with a pickaxe to realize that we needed to get Dorfman out—and quick. I told Lehr, "We've got to get an injunction against him," because this guy was not only running the health and welfare fund and robbing it, but he was exercising control over some of the fund's trustees. So, Lehr got an injunction against Dorfman, hired two policemen, and locked the doors to him and his people. He never did get back in.

As it turned out, someone else took Dorfman out of the Teamster picture entirely. On January 20, 1983, while on his way to lunch at Tessy's Restaurant in the Hyatt Lincolnwood Hotel, Chicago, he was shot eight times in the head with a .22-caliber pistol in the hotel's parking lot. What everyone agrees was a mob hit came three days after he had decided to become a cooperative witness for the federal government. Apparently they got quite a bit of information out of him for three days, but word leaked out that he was singing. As a headline in the *Chicago Tribune* accurately said, his was "A Death by Natural Causes."

I felt I had walked into an environment more deadly than I anticipated, but after the demise of Dorfman, there never was anything that looked even remotely sinister or improper. The pension fund began to operate smoothly, with Lehr being the dominant administrative figure, the trustees getting together two days a month, performing their functions well, and me watching over both funds to make sure they did everything the right way. Ryan gave me credit "for being a conscience and a steady force that [the trustees] appreciate. The trustees understand exactly what he [Saxbe] does for them. He is the best insurance policy they could ever have. He is not intrusive, yet when they ever shade to something that is headed in the wrong direction—we're not talking about anything illegal—his judgment's good enough so he can say, 'You really should look at that again.'"[8]

Not everything that was proposed sat well with me. I instigated a big lawsuit in Las Vegas that involved the sale of the Sands Hotel. There wouldn't have been a Las Vegas as we know it today without Central States and the mob. When Howard Hughes came in there with the big money and bought up the casinos, he bought them from the mob.

The pension fund and its fiduciary, Morgan Stanley, had some notes on a few casinos, including the Sands. The notes were sold to Las Vegas tycoon Steve Wynn with the understanding (or so everyone thought) that if he flipped the notes and sold them to somebody else at a profit, he'd share in the gain with the fund.

Well, unbeknownst to the fund, the lawyers never put that in writing, so the next day Wynn sells them at a 50 percent gain. Morgan Stanley looks bad, the fund looks bad, and Wynn looks awfully smart.

The fund's share of the Wynn sale totaled about $5 million, not an inconsiderable sum. Lehr and I and Gordon Gray of Morgan Stanley met in Washington, and I told Gray, "This is your problem. You're the fiduciary. You're going to have to prosecute this case. The choices are either you are going to be a plaintiff or you are going to be a defendant. If you don't prosecute, we're going to sue you because we've been robbed of $5 million." That's the last thing they wanted to hear. So they went to work and after several years we finally won. We got our money.

Hotels and casinos weren't the only pension fund investments in the old days. It had a stake in the jai-lai frontons in Bridgeport, Connecticut; a golf course on Long Island, New York; a trotting track in Aurora, Illinois; and many other investment properties. The Teamsters also owned a tract of land, seventy-some acres in the Bronx, just off the Hutchinson River Parkway. At the time I believe it was one of the largest tracts of undeveloped property in the five boroughs of New York. Lehr, Ryan, and I looked at it and realized it was a valuable piece of land. To let it go for taxes, which is what was being proposed, was ridiculous. We just felt there was something wrong.

We discovered that the taxes were unusually high for undeveloped land, so we successfully appealed for a reappraisal to get them reduced, to about $3 million, I believe. Then I began to get inquiries from U.S. Rep. Mario Biaggi, D-New York, the congressman from the Bronx.[9] He evidently was trying to steal the property. He'd call me and say, "You know, this property isn't worth anything. It's full of trash and fill from the Gowanus Canal," and so forth.

I stopped the plan to let it go for taxes. We put up "For Sale" signs and sold it for $9 million. I am sure Biaggi or somebody would have wanted it for $3 million, or less even.

The pension and health and welfare funds ran up tremendous legal bills of some $30 million a year. When I came to the funds, I brought Jones, Day in as my attorney. They were paid substantial sums—about $350,000 in 1983, for instance, according to Lehr.[10] Jones, Day assigned an attorney to me from the Cleveland office. Then I discovered that he was also representing another company against the Teamsters' pension fund in a Toledo case. He was using the file we created for his own case against us. I fired him and took on a lawyer from the firm's Columbus office. He was a very nice guy, but he didn't know everything and he wasn't about to.

I didn't particularly like the way Jones, Day operated, anyway. They hounded me continually to solicit new clients. I was supposed to be out recruiting. Well, hell, I wasn't about to do that. I didn't think it was a lawyer's business to go out and pressure people to be clients. I guess it is now— who do you know, who'd you meet this month—that sort of thing.

Those legal fees were an enormous problem for the two Teamster funds. I was determined to cut back on all the parasitic lawyers sucking up the money. One of the firms that didn't get the message was Jones, Day, even after I complained to them about their fees.

I called my friend, Dean Burch, former GOP party chairman, and related to him my unhappiness with the Jones, Day firm. Burch invited me to join his Washington law firm, Pierson, Ball, and Dowd, which is where Tim Ryan was. I became acquainted with Ryan because I had to go meet with him at the Labor Department. After more than two years as solicitor of labor, he left the department in April 1983 to join Pierson, Ball, and Dowd. Later the firm merged into an even larger firm, Reed, Smith, Shaw, and McClay.[11]

Both Ryan and I realized that probably there would be some criticism of my joining the firm, inasmuch as he had a hand in picking me as independent special counsel, as well as in laying out the entire consent decree. The *Chicago Tribune* reported that "it looks a wee bit fishy."[12] However, Judge Moran approved my serving the firm as "of counsel" and my use of Ryan as counsel on matters that clearly were not in conflict with what the court perceived as appropriate.

Tragically, Lehr died in office in March 1988. He had a brain tumor and had been dying for a year. He was a very outgoing, public kind of a guy, just the man they needed to get those funds in order.

Today the Central States Pension Fund is operating as it should, and it has honest, good people. It has been restored to health and trust.

EPILOGUE: FINAL THOUGHTS

As this book came together I gave a lot of thought to the trips, adventures, and jobs I've had over the last seventy years that have little or nothing to do with the book. On the other hand, they have been an important part of my life, important because they reflect the way I am now and the way I was.

Those incidents and my attitudes ranged from the sometimes irresponsible and frivolous to the important and sometimes dangerous: being curious in my adolescence; running away from home at age eleven; owning a high-powered motorcycle at age fifteen; acting rebellious and indifferent in high school; taking a job driving long-distance trucks before I finished high school; dropping out of college several times to go hunting in Florida; working as an ordinary seaman on a freighter to South America.

Those incidents alternated with periods of relative sanity or even brilliance that got me through high school and college and married to a wonderful life partner. Other less important and questionable intervals included joining a horse cavalry regiment while in college and jumping around in the army, serving in more branches of it than anybody I know: the cavalry, infantry, armored force, air corps, then the general staff and selective service, all over a period of thirty years.

All that with thirty years in politics, fifty years of active law practice, sixty years of marriage and, with Dolly, raising a fine family despite having moved twenty-seven times and never living in a house with a mortgage.

There is no doubt that my most serious problem was being unable to say no to any seemingly reasonable suggestion or invitation. I didn't plan to be a "been there, done that" person, but it turned out that way. It was once my intention to write a book and call it, *Hell, I've Been There.* Another suggested title was, *He Did What?!* after I left four big-time law firms and seven or eight corporate boards.

The most important "he did what?!" came up after the successful 100th Ohio General Assembly when Ray Bliss wanted me to run for governor. Dolly and I took off the day after adjournment. Another was when I

My mother, who
died in June 1972,
always watched
over me.

announced I would not run for a second term in the Senate. A third arose
when I returned from India and announced I was quitting politics.

Some incidents were not so smart, such as when Pat Williams and I
ended up in Cuba for three days. Dolly had a conference with the kids, and
they said, "Beat him up but don't leave." She didn't, but I was very contrite.

Other times Dolly and I went on adventures just as frivolous. One day I
got a call from our friends, the Byerlys, inviting us to go with them to New
Orleans. "When?" I asked. "Right now. Let's go!" Dolly was teaching school,
so she got a substitute teacher and a baby sitter, put on her hat, and walked
out the door with me. That night the four of us drove from Mechanicsburg
to New Orleans.

I never missed an opportunity to go fishing or shooting or to a golf
outing, sometimes as a guest, but more often at personal expense. Shooting or fishing took me to Holland for ducks; Ireland, Scotland, and England for driven birds; Canada, Iceland, Norway, and Russia for salmon;
and South and Central America, Mexico, India, Africa, Australia, New
Zealand, and most states for a wide variety of game.

Dolly went on many of those excursions. She cast a fly with the best and
was my loader in the British Isles. We spent some wet and uncomfortable
nights in tents and others in the finest lodgings in the world. We traveled
on EuroRail without making reservations and got on or off anyplace we
chose. In 1953 we left Rotterdam on an excursion train for five days in Paris
and discovered we were the only Americans. We spoke no Dutch, but some
of the Dutch spoke English and took us under their wing. We had a ball.
Total cost: twenty-six dollars apiece.

In retrospect I don't know how we did it. We lived hand-to-mouth, drove used cars (and still do), lived in only one new house, one I built myself using truck crates for walls and a salvaged bowling alley for floors. But we lived it up and didn't miss a thing. I collected a five thousand dollar fee and spent it on a mink jacket for Dolly and a used Cadillac convertible. I told her we had to spend the money before we pissed it away on necessities.

When we returned from India and left politics behind, we had a net worth of less than one hundred thousand dollars, and that included my inheritance from my father and mother. So I went to work. In almost sixty years of marriage we have never considered ourselves hard up. I thought we lived well. The children went to prep schools and colleges of their choice. The most money I made in a government job was the forty-four thousand dollars I received as ambassador to India. We were never in serious debt, and I saved money from every job I ever had, in or out of politics. I have never had an unpaid bill except for twelve dollars that I owed Bonds in Columbus for a suit—two pair of pants—that I missed a payment on when I was in college.

I have a loving family, including nine grandchildren. Dolly holds Trevor, our great-grandson. This photo was taken on Thanksgiving 1995.

There is no question that I have been fortunate and, yes, lucky, in my life. First I had a family, both before and after marriage, that loved and supported me even when I was wrong or foolish. Then I had good friends—in college, in the practice of law, and in politics. Finally, I arrived in politics when voters were looking for new faces and new ideas. And I was lucky that I survived the old cars, the motorcycle, and the B-26, which was called the "widow maker." It was said you didn't make the same mistake once. Also, I survived the hundreds of thousands of miles I drove and flew in Ohio, in good weather and bad. I had good advisers, like Bland Stradley, who talked me into law school when I was headed for the cattle business or the Episcopal ministry.

I never envisioned writing a book about my life, especially one that anyone would want to publish and read. I am both pleased and amazed: pleased that it is done and amazed that I was able to sit still long enough to work on it. Somehow the whole shebang seems to fit together.

I deeply appreciate Dolly's love and support throughout and the work of my collaborator, Pete Franklin. He kept me at the job, organized the story, researched the references, and removed the bad spelling and most of the profanity.

And so here I am at age eighty-four, still working, still enjoying good health and my favorite sports, and still surrounded by good friends and a loving and successful family, all of whom shaped my destiny. Would I change anything, were that possible? I doubt it. There are things I regret, but those are too late to change. Should I have stayed in Ohio? In Washington? Stuck to the cattle business or a big-time law practice? I think not.

I look at the political scene today and rejoice that I got out when I did. I always had an aversion to political fund-raising and still do. Raising enough money to mount a campaign is such an important factor today that it has to affect your thinking and actions. The problem can be solved, but I see little inclination to do so.

Also, the media is so dominant today. They would beat me to death for my indiscretions and loose lips. They did a pretty good job of it even in my day.

I thank God for the interesting and exciting life Dolly and I have shared together, and I pray that we can hang on and enjoy life for a few more years.

Yes, I have seen the elephant.

NOTES

2. BECOMING WORLDLY

1. A rick is a stack of wood of varying lengths that stands four feet high and eight feet long.

2. While I was envoy to India, bar owner Larry Paoletti informed me that Apartment 203 at 2034 North High Street had been designated the William B. Saxbe Suite, and a plaque noting that had been placed outside the two-room apartment.

5. THE LAUDABLE 100TH

1. Hal Conefry, "Saxbe Named Speaker of Ohio House," *Columbus Citizen,* December 9, 1952.

2. Editorial, "The Lobby and the Republican Dilemma," *Ohio State Journal,* March 31, 1953.

3. Sine die: without setting a day to reconvene.

4. Editorial, "Record of the 100th," *Akron Beacon Journal,* July 18, 1953.

5. Editorial, "The 100th General Assembly," *Toledo Blade,* July 16, 1953.

6. Editorial, "An Impressive Record," *Cleveland Plain Dealer,* July 16, 1953.

6. LOSING A GOOD FIGHT

1. Reed Smith, Associated Press, "Pressure Mounting for GOP to Form 1954 State Ticket; Bender-Rhodes Slate Hinted," *Springfield (Ohio) Sun,* December 13, 1953.

2. "Saxbe May Be Governor Candidate," *Urbana Daily Citizen,* December 11, 1953.

3. Katherine Sullivan, "Dolly's 'Needlework' Put Husband in Race," *Columbus Citizen,* March 29, 1954.

4. Bender later said that Senator Taft told him to be "a cheerleader" on the convention floor, even naming the songs to be sung.

5. Alvin Silverman, "Saxbe Fights Bender for Senate Race," *Cleveland Plain Dealer,* January 14, 1954.

6. Smith, Associated Press, "Bid by Saxbe for Seat in U.S. Senate Called Week's Top Political Surprise," *Springfield Sun,* January 16, 1954.

7. "Ohio G.O.P. Faces a Bitter Primary," *New York Times,* April 25, 1954.

8. "Young Taft Slapped Down by GOP, But Very Lightly," *Columbus Citizen,* April 18, 1954.

9. Carl Ebright, "Bender Ahead: Saxbe Claims He Is Gaining," *Columbus Dispatch,* April 18, 1954.

7. TACKLING OHIO LAW

1. Krenzler served as cochair of the Saxbe for Senator Committee in Cleveland in 1968.

2. John J. Chester, interview by Peter D. Franklin, tape recording, Columbus, Ohio, May 6, 1996.

3. Before returning to the attorney general's office, Donahue was Ohio's tax commissioner.

4. James T. Keenan, "Saxbe Answers Sheppard Lawyers on Trial Evidence," *Cleveland Press,* February 14, 1966.

9. HERE I COME, READY OR NOT!

1. J. D. Sawyer, confidential "Senate Study," November 1968.

2. Sawyer, interview, Peter D. Franklin, tape recording, Naples, Florida, March 15, 1996.

3. William B. Saxbe, speech, National Oil Jobbers Council, San Francisco, October 21, 1973.

4. Robert J. Havel, "Unionists Vote Saxbe a Hit," *Cleveland Plain Dealer,* May 2, 1969.

5. Jesse Shaffer, "Saxbe Voting Scored as 'Too Liberal,'" *Cincinnati Enquirer* (undated).

6. Allen L. Otten, "Senator Saxbe's Surprising Behavior," *Wall Street Journal,* July 30, 1969.

7. Saxbe, letter to Art Flemming, February 6, 1970.

8. Gov. Nelson A. Rockefeller appointed Goodell to the Senate seat held by Robert F. Kennedy.

9. William Safire, *Before the Fall* (Garden City, N.Y.: Doubleday, 1975), 318–19.

10. Joe Rice, "Saxbe Stumps for Goodell, Blasts GOP 'Kamikazes,'" *Akron Beacon Journal,* October 10, 1970.

11. "Saxbe Says That Many Could Replace Agnew," *Cleveland Plain Dealer,* December 9, 1970.

12. James R. Dickenson, "Senator Dole, GOP's Petrel, Comes on Hard," *National Observer,* December 28, 1970.

13. Richard M. Nixon, *RN: The Memoirs of Richard Nixon* (New York: Grosset and Dunlap, 1978), 416.

14. Joan Hoff, *Nixon Reconsidered* (New York: Basic Books, 1994), 189.

15. Nixon, press conference, April 18, 1969; *Congressional Quarterly,* April 25, 1969, 607.

16. The debt, which was half that amount, was paid.

17. Stephen E. Ambrose, *Nixon—The Triumph of a Politician—1962–72* (New York: Simon and Schuster, 1989), 289–90.

18. Nixon, letter to Saxbe, December 11, 1969.

19. "Saxbe Shuns Nixon-Bliss Fete for Trip with Ted," *Cleveland Plain Dealer,* April 6, 1969.

10. VIETNAM ALL OVER AGAIN

1. Allen L. Otten, "Senator Saxbe's Surprising Behavior," *Wall Street Journal,* July 30, 1969.

2. H. R. Haldeman, *The Haldeman Diaries: Inside the Nixon White House* (New York: G. P. Putnam's, 1994), 110–11.

3. Nixon was born in Whittier, California, because his father, Francis Anthony "Frank" Nixon, sought warmer climes in 1907 after his feet became frostbitten while working in the open cab of a streetcar in Columbus.

4. Nixon, *In the Arena* (New York: Simon and Schuster, 1990), 333.

5. Ibid.

6. Herbert S. Parmet, *Richard Nixon and His America* (Boston: Little, Brown, 1990), 566.

7. Henry Kissinger, *Years of Upheaval* (Boston: Little, Brown, 1982), 87.

8. Ibid., 87–88.

9. Walter Isaacson, *Kissinger: A Biography* (New York: Simon and Schuster, 1992), 246.

10. Nixon, *In the Arena*, 33.

11. Killed were Sandy Scheuer, Youngstown, Ohio; William Schroeder, Lorain, Ohio; Jeffrey Miller, Plainview, New York; and Allison Krause, Pittsburgh, Pennsylvania.

12. Safire, *Before the Fall*, 191.

13. Nixon first referred to the "great silent majority" in a major Vietnam policy address to the nation on November 3, 1969. It also established the administration's battle line between his "silent majority" and what Nixon speech writer William Safire referred to as the "noisy minority."

14. Saxbe, "Recapturing Our Values: The Path to Destiny," commencement address, Ohio Wesleyan University, June 14, 1970.

15. In May 1971, a letter from Saxbe's eldest son, Bart, also was read into the *Congressional Record*. As a doctor at the Peter Bent Brigham Hospital in Boston, Bart wrote to his father concerning the "growing discontent and impatience with the [health] system" and the deteriorating services to the poor in hospitals.

16. *Congressional Record*, June 23, 1970, 209–10.

17. The so-called Christmas bombing of North Vietnam by United States B-52s began on December 18 and ended December 30, 1972. Nixon authorized up to 120 strikes a day against military targets.

18. Havel, "Saxbe Splits With, Denounces Nixon on Bombing," *Cleveland Plain Dealer*, December 29, 1972.

19. During the ten years of the Vietnam War, more than forty-seven thousand United States service men and women lost their lives and another one hundred fifty thousand were wounded.

11. A COUPLE OF VOTES FOR JUSTICE

1. Nominated by President Lyndon B. Johnson to be chief justice, Fortas resigned in the face of Senate opposition regarding his relationship to Louis E. Wolfson, a financier indicted three years earlier for securities violations. Fortas denied any impropriety.

2. Jonathan Aitkin, *Nixon: A Life* (Washington D.C.: Regency Press, 1996), 392.

3. Jack A. Gleason, memorandum to Kevin Phillips, October 15, 1969.

4. Gordon S. Brownell, memorandum to Harry S. Dent, October 16, 1969.

5. Gleason, memorandum to Phillips, October 17, 1969.

6. Preston Wolfe was the politically powerful president of the Dispatch Printing Company, publisher of the *Columbus Dispatch*. Gleason, memorandum to Phillips, October 22, 1969.

7. Dent, memorandum to the attorney general and Bryce Harlow, October 31, 1969.

8. Gleason, memorandum to Dent, November 4, 1969.

9. James B. Pearson, R-Kansas; John Sherman Cooper, R-Kentucky; Robert Packwood, R-Oregon; Thomas J. Dodd, D-Connecticut; Winston L. Prouty, R-Vermont; Henry M. Jackson, D-Washington; and William B. Spong Jr., D-Virginia. Dent, memorandum to attorney general and Harlow, November 11, 1969.

10. William Vance, "Saxbe Pressured on Justice Vote," *Akron Beacon Journal*, November 19, 1969.

11. The Van Darby Club is the hunt/social club I founded in Mechanicsburg.

12. John Ehrlichman, *Witness to Power* (New York: Simon and Schuster, 1982), 122.

13. Len B. Jordan, R-Idaho, and Richard A. Schweiker, R-Pennsylvania.

14. Bruce Oudes, ed., *From: The President—Richard Nixon's Secret Files* (New York: Harper and Row, 1989), 70.

15. *Congressional Record*, Senate, March 16, 1970, p. 7487.

16. Frank Kane, "Saxbe Backs Carswell for Supreme Court Post," *Toledo Blade,* March 13, 1970.

17. Saxbe, letter to Nixon, March 30, 1970.

18. Nixon, letter to Saxbe, March 31, 1970.

19. Editorial, "Judge Carswell: The President's 'Right of Choice,'" *Washington Post,* April 2, 1970.

20. Robert Webb, "Saxbe Would OK Firing of Mitchell," *Cincinnati Enquirer,* April 11, 1970.

21. Dan Rather and Gary Paul Gates, *The Palace Guard* (New York: Harper and Row, 1974), 109.

12. THE FINISHING TOUCHES

1. Robert H. Snyder, "Saxbe to Run Again, Ohio Republicans Say," *Cleveland Plain Dealer,* July 21, 1973.

2. Robert B. Reich, "Party Favors," *New Yorker* (October 13, 1997): 11–12.

3. Michael A. Genovese, *The Nixon Presidency: Power and Politics in Turbulent Times* (New York: Greenwood Press, 1990), 38.

4. Jack Anderson, "Haldeman Blacklisted GOP Senators," *Washington Post,* July 9, 1973.

5. Nixon, letter to Saxbe, November 24, 1972.

6. The committee's formal title was the Senate Select Committee on Presidential Campaign Activities.

7. David Hess, "Saxbe Had Eyes on White House," *Akron Beacon Journal,* October 14, 1973.

8. Hess, "Saxbe Can't Resist Political Zingers," *Akron Beacon Journal,* February 25, 1973.

9. Glenn Waggoner, "Sen. Saxbe: He Didn't Like the Job or the Town," *The (Lorain) Journal,* October 10, 1973.

10. Associated Press, "Saxbe Denies Tie to Draft Effort," *Cleveland Plain Dealer,* October 12, 1973.

11. Oudes, *From—The President,* 592.

12. Geoffrey Carroll Shepard, memorandum to Ken Cole, September 14, 1973.

13. Alexander M. Haig Jr., *Inner Circles* (New York: Warner Books, 1992), 396.

14. Nixon, *Memoirs,* 1004.

13. DESPERATE TIMES

1. Frank Mankiewicz, *U.S. v. Richard M. Nixon: The Final Crisis* (New York: Quadrangle, 1975), 53.

2. In the fall of 1973, Keating was named president of the *Cincinnati Enquirer.*

3. Haig Jr., interview with Franklin, tape recording, Washington, D.C., October 3, 1996.

4. Loye Miller Jr. and Robert S. Boyd, "Even GOP Doubtful Nixon Can Survive," *Detroit Free Press,* October 28, 1973.

5. In a memorandum dated October 26, 1973, to Haig, Timmons urged that the president nominate for attorney general Sen. Marlow Cook, R-Kentucky, or Sen. Howard Baker, R-Tennessee.

6. Wauhillau LaHay, "Sense, Humor Needed, Dolly Says," *Columbus Citizen-Journal,* November 2, 1973.

7. Betty Beale, "The Book Arrived with the Dearest Love," *Washington Star-News,* November 11, 1973.

8. David Hess, "Cabinet Topic as Saxbe Visits White House?" *Akron Beacon Journal*, October 31, 1973.

9. "Saxbe Could Rise to Top, Hughes Says," *Cleveland Plain Dealer*, October 31, 1973.

10. James Grohl, "GOP Questions Saxbe 'Sacrifice,'" *Columbus Citizen-Journal*, October 31, 1973.

11. "Right Wing Fears Vacancy for Left," *Cleveland Plain Dealer*, October 31, 1973.

12. Nixon, *Memoirs*, 944.

13. The plumbers were a secret "dirty tricks" team created by Nixon to cause political disorder and to stop information leaks within the administration.

14. Monica Crowley, *Nixon off the Record* (New York: Random House, 1996), 17.

15. The *New York Times* noted that "rarely, if ever, has a prospective presidential appointee spoken so freely before his nomination has been announced." Douglas E. Kneeland, "Nixon Due to Name Saxbe, with Texan as Prosecutor," *New York Times*, November 1, 1973.

16. Herbert Brownell Jr., a prominent New York attorney, served as United States attorney general in President Dwight D. Eisenhower's administration. He also chaired the GOP National Committee.

17. Haig, interview.

14. A CONSTITUTIONAL QUESTION

1. Walter Rugaber, "1969 Rise in Cabinet Pay Could Prove Bar to Saxbe," *New York Times*, November 2, 1973.

2. Hong Kong was the final stop for Dolly and me after an official visit to Dacca, Bangladesh, August 10–13. On the trip we also visited Istanbul, New Delhi, Kashmir, and Bangkok.

3. "Senator Backs Nixon on Tapes," *Hong Kong Standard*, August 24, 1973.

4. Stanley I. Kutler, *Abuse of Power: The New Nixon Tapes* (New York: Free Press, 1997), 635.

5. Susanna McBee, "Saxbe Won't 'Flounce Out' if the Going Gets Tough," *Lorain Journal*, November 2, 1973.

6. Geoffrey Carroll Shepard, "Justice Without Leadership," memorandum to Ken Cole, November 8, 1973.

7. Shephard, memorandum to Cole.

8. William E. Timmons, memorandum to Haig, November 9, 1973.

9. Mary McGrory, "Saxbe, Converted, Zips Through the Senate," *Washington Star-News*, December 18, 1973.

10. Richard G. Thomas, "Ervin: Saxbe Barred," *Dayton Daily News*, November 15, 1973.

15. A VERY MODEL OF A MODERN ATTORNEY GENERAL

1. A swamper is a handyman who cleans an establishment.

2. I was the sixth Ohioan to be United States attorney general. My predecessors were Edwin M. Stanton (1860); Henry Stanbery (1866–68); Alphonso Taft (1876–77); Judson Harmon (1895–97); and Harry M. Daugherty (1921–24).

3. Columbus artist Roswell Keller painted my portrait (fifty-five by forty-two inches) in acrylics. The artist scrapped an earlier portrait because he was unhappy with it. The second painting was unveiled in Washington on February 3, 1975. There were so many attorneys general in the Nixon administration that a group portrait was considered.

4. Ymelda Dixon, "For Republicans, It Was Like an Inaugural Party," *Washington Star-News*, January 7, 1974.

5. Vic Gold, "Enter Saxbe—Fasten Your Seatbelts," *Washington Star-News,* January 17, 1974.

6. Nixon, *Memoirs,* 970–71.

7. Gerald S. Strober and Deborah Hart Strober, *Nixon: An Oral History of His Presidency* (New York: HarperCollins, 1994), 423.

8. Richard G. Zimmerman, "Saxbe Confidant's Role in Watergate Defense Raises Questions," *Cleveland Plain Dealer,* January 26, 1974.

9. In an interview on January 3, 1974, the day before I was sworn in as attorney general, I described the Senate's subpoena of four hundred Watergate tapes as "a fishing expedition. ... To keep in business, the committee has to have grist for its mill. If they can, they will keep dredging stuff up. They'll go on forever."

10. In 1973 a group of Senate aides listed me as one of the Senate's ten best-dressed.

11. Elliot L. Richardson, memorandum, "Reorganization of the Department of Justice," October 17, 1973.

12. Sawyer, memorandum, "Reorganization of the Department of Justice," April 1, 1974.

13. Sawyer, memorandum.

16. WALKING ON EGGS

1. Helen Thomas, United Press International, *Jackson Citizen Patriot,* May 12, 1974.

2. United Press International, "Saxbe Says Execution Answer to Kidnappers," *Columbus Dispatch,* February 22, 1974.

3. A warrant was issued for Patty Hearst's arrest as a material witness in the robbery. The other participants were charged with bank robbery.

4. "Saxbe: Dad's Hearst Statement Bad," *Akron Beacon Journal,* April 29, 1974.

5. Two years later, Patty Hearst was sentenced to seven years in prison for aiding the bank robbers. In February 1979, President Jimmy Carter commuted her sentence.

6. Phil Kerby, *With Honor and Purpose* (New York: St. Martin's Press, 1998), 201.

7. "If Nixon Is Impeached?" *U.S. News and World Report* (February 4, 1974): 22–26.

8. McBee, "Impeachment Is Doubted by Saxbe," *Washington Post,* February 28, 1974.

9. According to *The Breaking of a President* (City of Industry, Calif.: Therapy Productions, 1975), 215, Nixon reported income of $328,162 in 1969 when in fact it totaled $464,235. As a result, he paid only $72,682 in tax, or $171,055 less than he should have.

10. Saxbe, letter to Leon Jaworski, April 4, 1974.

11. Nixon, *Memoirs,* 676.

12. Genovese, *The Nixon Presidency,* 182.

13. Marvin Kalb, *The Nixon Memo* (Chicago: University of Chicago Press, 1994), 210.

14. Actually, Jaworski took himself out of the Connally probe because as a Texas attorney he had oblique links to those under investigation. Jaworski's senior deputy, Henry Ruth, took charge of the case.

15. Isaacson, *Kissinger: A Biography,* 226–27.

16. Safire, *Before the Fall,* 166–67.

17. Kissinger, *Years of Upheaval,* 1123.

18. Isaacson, *Kissinger: A Biography,* 225.

17. NIXON BOWS OUT

1. It was Haldeman who in 1970 convinced Nixon to install the sophisticated taping system so that the Nixon presidency would be recorded for posterity.

2. Nixon, *Memoirs,* 1052.

3. Haldeman, *The Ends of Power* (New York: Times Books, 1978), 217.

4. Ibid., 318.

5. Kutler, *Abuse of Power*, 69.

6. Nixon, *Memoirs*, 1064.

7. Aitkin, *Nixon: A Life*, 518.

8. Haig, interview.

9. Gerald R. Ford, *A Time to Heal* (New York: Harper and Row, 1979), 18–19.

10. Nixon, *Memoirs*, 1065.

11. David N. Parker, memorandum to Ford, "Talking Points—Cabinet Meeting, August 6, 1974."

12. Bob Woodward and Carl Bernstein, *The Final Days* (New York: Simon and Schuster, 1976), 387.

13. Ford, *A Time to Heal*, 21.

14. One day before he resigned, Nixon vetoed the bill. It was the final piece of legislation that bore his signature.

15. Haig, interview.

16. Kissinger, *Years of Upheaval*, 1204.

17. Ibid.

18. THE TRANSITION

1. James Cannon, *Time and Chance* (New York: HarperCollins, 1994), 324.

2. Philip W. Buchen, "Memorandum for the Vice President," August 8, 1974.

3. Ford, *A Time to Heal*, 126.

4. In a letter to Ford, Senator Robert Taft recommended me among fifteen others to fill the vacancy of vice president.

5. Ford, *A Time to Heal*, 131.

6. Ford and the head of his transition team, Donald Rumsfeld, already had decided cabinet changes would be made by the end of January 1975. Rumsfeld, who became chief of staff and later secretary of defense, felt Ford should act as quickly as possible to "move from an illegitimate government in the minds of the American people to a legitimate government."

7. Jerald F. terHorst, "Ford's Door Slammed by Nixon Holdovers," *Chicago Tribune*, November 1, 1974.

8. Ford, *A Time to Heal*, 132.

9. Gary Trudeau, *Doonesbury*, Universal Press Syndicate, September 9, 1974.

10. Kenneth R. Cole Jr., memorandum, "Meeting with Attorney General Saxbe," August 12, 1974.

11. Ford, interview with Franklin, tape recording, Palm Springs, California, November 27, 1996.

12. Ford, interview.

13. Stephen E. Ambrose, *Nixon: Ruin and Recovery 1973–1990* (New York: Simon and Schuster, 1990), 449.

14. Ford, *A Time to Heal*, 164.

15. Two days earlier Haig informed Watergate Special Prosecutor Leon Jaworski that Nixon would take all his documents with him when he left the White House, according to Seymour M. Hersh, *Atlantic* 252 (August 1983), 69.

16. Benton L. Becker, interview, Franklin, telephone conversation, March 23, 1998.

17. Cannon, *Time and Chance*, 365.

18. Saxbe, letter to Ford, September 6, 1974.

19. Cannon, *Time and Chance,* 383.

20. Orr Kelly, "Saxbe Goes on the Stump for the Old Morality," *Washington Star-News,* June 26, 1974.

21. Nixon, memorandum for the Attorney General, July 16, 1974.

22. Saxbe, memorandum for Nixon, undated.

23. Saxbe, letter to Haig, July 31, 1974.

24. Ford, *A Time to Heal,* 269.

19. TELEPHONES AND COINTELPRO

1. In 1949, while Harry S Truman was president, the Justice Department filed a divestiture suit against American Telephone and Telegraph (AT&T), but it was settled without divestiture during the Eisenhower administration.

2. Columnist Jack Anderson reported in the *Washington Post,* on November 15, 1974, that a suit against AT&T "is all but ready" to be filed by the Justice Department.

3. Phillip Areeda, memorandum to Ford, November 20, 1974.

4. Robert T. Hartmann, *Palace Politics: An Inside Account of the Ford Years* (New York: McGraw-Hill, 1980), 300.

5. Steve Coll, *The Deal of the Century: The Break-up of AT&T* (New York: Atheneum, 1986), 70–71.

6. William E. Simon, memorandum for the president, November 22, 1974.

7. Simon, memorandum.

8. Subsequently, after my departure, the FBI revealed five additional counterintelligence programs.

9. The Citizens Commission to Investigate the FBI.

10. James Kirkpatrick Davis, *Spying on America: The FBI's Domestic Counter-Intelligence Program* (New York: Praeger, 1992), 173.

11. Jaworski, letter to Saxbe, October 12, 1974.

20. IN KIPLING'S FOOTSTEPS

1. Anderson, "Goodell for Attorney General?" *Cincinnati Post,* October 16, 1974.

2. "Washington Wire: Saxbe Successor?" *Wall Street Journal,* November 29, 1974.

3. Editorial, "Saxbe Should Be Retained," *Toledo Blade,* October 20, 1974.

4. Charles R. Saxbe won the 75th District Ohio House seat on November 5 by beating Democrat Courtney A. Metzger by some forty-six hundred votes.

5. "A Grave Mistake," *Akron Beacon Journal,* November 24, 1974.

6. Terence A. Todman, a career diplomat and former ambassador to Guinea, was named United States envoy to Costa Rica.

7. Leonard Garment, memorandum "for the President," July 12, 1974.

8. Daniel P. Moynihan, *A Dangerous Place* (Boston: Little, Brown, 1978), 44.

9. November 30, 1974.

10. Waldo made a record of the concert, and a Boston radio station ran a contest to determine if anyone could identify the vocalist. Nobody could.

11. National Association of Manufacturers dinner, New York, December 6, 1974.

12. I had been invited by Ed Wolfe to return with him to Columbus on that ill-fated plane so I could attend a dinner in my honor at the Scioto Country Club.

13. Ford, *A Time to Heal,* 235.

14. Ibid., 235–36.

15. Ibid., 236.

16. On the same day it was revealed that my predecessor at the Justice Department, Elliot L. Richardson, would be nominated envoy to the Court of St. James.

17. Ford, personal letter to Saxbe, December 13, 1974.

18. Associated Press, "Saxbe to be Named U.S. Envoy to India," *Cincinnati Enquirer,* December 12, 1974.

19. James F. DeLeone, letter to Ford, December 12, 1974.

20. Buchen, letter to DeLeone, January 3, 1975.

21. Chester, letters to Ford and Buchen, January 8, 1975.

22. Buchen, memorandum to Areeda, undated.

23. Editorial, "Saxbe as Ambassador," *Cincinnati Enquirer,* December 26, 1974.

24. Editorial, "Saxbe to India? Oh, No!" *Cincinnati Post,* December 14, 1974.

25. Kutler, *Abuse of Power,* 451.

26. Saxbe, letter to Ambassador Viron P. Vaky, March 6, 1973.

27. At the time the Costa Rican legislature was debating the repeal of the "Vesco Law," so named because it served to protect the financier from extradition.

28. Warren S. Rustand, memorandum for the attorney general, December 18, 1974.

29. Donnie Radcliffe, "The Washington Exit: Saxbe's Farewells," *Washington Post,* February 6, 1975.

30. Ibid.

31. Ibid.

21. TIPTOEING INTO INDIA

1. Jack Anderson with George Clifford, *The Anderson Papers* (New York: Random House, 1973), 217.

2. Kissinger, *Years of Renewal* (New York: Simon and Schuster, 1999), 82.

3. Anderson, *The Anderson Papers,* 4.

4. Kissinger, memorandum to Ford, August 21, 1974.

5. Anderson, *The Anderson Papers,* 4.

6. The classmate, Jon Rohde, was assigned to the Dacca Cholera Project.

7. Warren Unna, "Saxbe Interested in Agriculture," *The Statesman,* December 21, 1974.

8. *Private View,* cartoon, *Indian Express,* January 18, 1975.

9. Galbreath wrote a personal congratulatory note to me on December 18, 1974, saying that India's complex political scene would be no match "to anyone who has mastered Ohio politics."

10. Beale, "Washington Letter . . . Saxbe Says," *Columbus Dispatch,* January 26, 1975.

11. In the summer of 1975, the Congress Party held more than three-fifths of the seats in India's Parliament and controlled nineteen of India's twenty state governments.

12. "Saxbe Admits Failure on Arms Ban Issue," *Deccan Herald (Banglalore),* February 25, 1975.

13. "Postponement of Saxbe's Arrival Causes Anger," *The Motherland,* February 23, 1975.

14. "Non-arrival of Saxbe Surprising," *Patriot (New Delhi),* February 23, 1975.

15. H. W. Brands, *India and the United States: The Cold Peace* (Boston: Twayne, 1990), 144.

16. When Kenneth Keating succeeded Galbreath as ambassador, he had a plaque installed to also honor the other Roosevelt who was president, Theodore Roosevelt.

17. Lewis M. Simons, "Saxbe Sees U.S., India at Arm's Length," *Washington Post,* March 19, 1975.

18. Ibid.

19. Editorial, "Petty," *Patriot,* March 22, 1975.

20. "5 MPs Decry Remarks by US Ambassador," *Times of India,* March 24, 1975.

21. Dolly Saxbe, "Dolly's Delhi Diary," 51.

22. Three weeks later, in a meeting in the Oval office with India's External Affairs Minister Chavan, Ford backtracked, expressing an interest in meeting Mrs. Gandhi one day. Both Kissinger and I attended the October 6, 1975, meeting.

23. Ford, interview.

24. Pranay Gupte, *Mother India: A Political Biography of Indira Mrs. Gandhi* (New York: Scribner's, 1992), 409.

25. Isaacson, *Kissinger: A Biography,* 374.

26. Gupte, *Mother India,* 407.

27. This was the same day that Nixon welcomed to the White House with considerable fanfare Pakistan's new ambassador to the United States, Nawabzada Agha Mohammad Raza.

28. Anderson, *The Anderson Papers,* 228.

29. Pupul Jayakar, *Indira Mrs. Gandhi: An Intimate Biography* (New York: Pantheon Books, 1992), 178.

30. Gupte, *Mother India,* 410–11.

31. Kissinger, memorandum to Ford, October 6, 1975.

32. Kissinger, memorandum to Ford.

33. Inder Malhotra, *Indira Mrs. Gandhi: A Personal and Political Biography* (Boston: Northeastern University Press, 1989), 291.

34. In December 1984, a leak of methyl isocyanate gas at the Bhopal plant left thirty-three hundred dead and twenty thousand injured.

35. "Hatred Towards US Irks Envoy's Wife," *The Mail,* May 17, 1975.

22. HUNTIN', FISHIN', AND LEAVIN'

1. Saxbe, keynote address, Indo-American Chamber of Commerce, Bombay, March 4, 1976.

2. Editorial, "India and U.S.," *National Herald,* New Delhi, March 6, 1976.

3. Saxbe, letter to Bill Monroe, February 17, 1976.

4. "Golfing Saxbe and His Low-Key Approach," *Indian Express,* May 28, 1975.

5. Beale, "Washington Letter... Saxbe Says."

6. Three days after she suffered defeat in the national election, March 19, 1977, Mrs. Gandhi resigned as prime minister. She was reelected in January 1980 and served her second term as prime minister. On the morning of October 31, 1984, Mrs. Gandhi walked from her residence at 1 Safdarjung Road to her adjacent office at 1 Akbar Road, where British actor and humorist Peter Ustinov waited to televise an interview with her in the garden. Before she had completed her short walk, two of her Sikh bodyguards mortally wounded her in a hail of gunfire.

23. IN PRIVATE AGAIN

1. "Former India Ambassador Passes Hotel Credit Check," *Columbus Dispatch,* January 23, 1977.

2. Harry K. Crowl, form letter, October 26, 1973.

3. Crowl, letter to James A. Rhodes, October 26, 1973.

4. Hugh McDiarmid, "Saxbe Beats Rhodes," *Dayton Journal Herald,* October 29, 1973.

5. Gene Jordan, "Saxbe Hints at Campaign for Governor," *Columbus Dispatch*, April 23, 1981.

6. Jill Abramson, "Up for a Pardon, George Steinbrenner Defeated the Odds," *Wall Street Journal*, February 3, 1989.

24. TEAMSTER TIMES

1. Central States Pension Fund, news release, December 3, 1982.

2. T. Timothy Ryan Jr., interview with Franklin, tape recording, New York, September 6, 1996.

3. Douglas Frantz, "Double Life of Allen Dorfman," *Chicago Tribune*, January 21, 1983.

4. The agency grew into Amalgamated Insurance Agency Services Incorporated in Chicago, the linchpin of his fourteen-company empire.

5. Frantz, "Double Life of Allan Dorfman."

6. Ronald J. Kubalanza, interview with Franklin, tape recording, Chicago, May 8, 1998.

7. Ibid.

8. Ryan, interview.

9. Biaggi, who represented New York's 19th District, was convicted in 1988 of racketeering.

10. Pete Earley, "Teamsters Fund Overseer Seeks to Join Ex-Solicitor's Law Firm," *Washington Post*, August 29, 1984.

11. Ryan left Reed, Smith, Shaw, and McClay in January of 1993 to join J. P. Morgan as a managing director in charge of Financial Institutions, Bank Insurance, Government Institutions, Central Banks and Real Estate (FIGRE).

12. "Office Search in Washington," *Chicago Tribune*, August 21, 1984.

INDEX

Hodgson, James D., 213
Hoffa, James R., 243–44, 246
Hoffman, Herbert, 237
Hoiles, William, 77, 120, 143; as administrative assistant, 84, 85, 145–46
Hollings, Ernest "Fritz," 88, 123, 208
Homes, Saxbe: Bill built, 30, 34; in Costa Rica, 130, 206; first married, 20; at Fort Riley, Kansas, 23, 25; in Houston, 27–28; living in Dolly's parents', 33; in Louisiana, 28; Roosevelt House in India, 215; in Washington, 87–88, 130. See also Jubarock
Hong Kong, Dolly and Bill visiting, 120
Hoover, J. Edgar, 172–73, 191–93
Horvitz family, Bill as trustee for, 240
Hughes, Oscar F., 37
Hughes, Robert E., 135
Hummel, Edward J., 36–37
Humphrey, George, 53
Humphrey, Hubert H., 82, 84, 86, 88
Hunter, Bill "Chomp," 78
Hunting, 137, 207; in Cuba, 68, 252; on Election Day, 81–82; by father, 4–5, 7, 9; with father, 10, 16; to feed family, 26; in India, 227, 231–33; travel for, 68, 121–22, 125, 252
Hushen, John W., 162

Immigration, illegal, 183, 198
Immigration and Naturalization Service, 154, 183, 198
Impeachment proceedings, against Nixon, 133; and House Judiciary Committee, 130, 170, 175; responses to, 164, 165
In the Arena (Nixon), 99
Independent special counsel, Bill as, 239–40, 245–50
India, 11, 234; Bill and Dolly preparing to leave, 234–35; Bill as ambassador to, 207, 209–34; Bill's interest in ambassadorship to, 197–98, 201–2; Dolly and Bill visiting, 119–20; nuclear weapons of, 210, 222; politics of, 211, 220, 223–24, 234; relations with Pakistan, 213–14, 220–22; relations with U.S., 213–14, 218, 220–23, 228–29; State Department moving people through, 216–17
Ingersoll, Robert S., 203

Inouye, Daniel K., 135
Intelligence school, Bill sent to, 24
Internal Revenue Service, and Nixon, 168
International Business Machines (IBM), antitrust suit against, 187–88
Ireland, hunting trip to, 125
Ireland, R. L., 55
Isaacson, Walter, 172–73

Jameson, Frank Gard, 234
Jatti, B. D., at bicentennial celebration, 230
Javelin Ltd., Bill as special counsel for, 239–40, 245
Javits, Jacob K., 90, 161
Jaworski, Leon, 138–40, 148, 153; Bill pledging independence of, 148, 168–69; Bill's relationship with, 168–69, 174–75; probe of Connally, 170; resignation, 194–95
Jha, Lakshmi K., 214, 221
Johnson, Cynthia, 66
Johnson, Fred H., 35
Johnson, Lyndon B., 96, 99, 137–38
Johnston, J. Bennett, 152
Jones, Day, 249–50
Jones, Day, Reavis, and Pogue, 240–42
Jones, Fred E., 201; and Bill's campaigns, 64, 81; insurance businesses of, 64–65; and Saxbe's Haynsworth vote, 113–14
Jordan, Gene, 239
Jordan, Len B., 114
Jubarock (Saxbe farm), 59, 236–37
Judiciary Committee: House, 130, 169, 175; Ohio House, 36–37, 41, 46; Senate, 148, 174–75, 192
Justice, Department of, 152, 200; disarray of, 157–58, 182; duties of, 135, 163, 181; illegal business practice suits by, 169, 187–91; and impeachment, 155–56, 166; and ownership of Nixon papers, 183–85; portraits of attorneys general in, 154; problems of, 143, 169; reorganizations of, 144–45, 157–59. See also Attorneys general, U.S.

Kalb, Marvin, 168
Kaul, Triloki Nath, 207–8, 209–10
Kauper, Thomas E., 189
Keating, Kenneth, 120, 217

Mitchell, John N., 111, 138, 143, 206; proposing names for Supreme Court, 110, 115, 117; and wiretapping requests, 171–72

Mitchell, Martha, 117, 153

Mondale, Walter, 131

Monroe, Bill, 229

Moore, Jonathan, 144

Moran, James B., 245–46, 250

Morrison, Hugh P., 189

Morton, Rogers C. B., 181

Moscow, Bill's travel to, 95

Motorcycle, Bill's, 13

Moynihan, Daniel Patrick, 197–98, 207–8, 211–13, 217

Mundt, Carl E., 93

Murphy, George, 85, 94, 123–24

Muskie, Edmund S., 82, 148

Myers, Davis J., 65

Nahra, Joseph J., 240

Name voting, 50

National Association of Manufacturers, Bill addressing, 199–201

National conventions, 1972 Republican, 123

National Guard, Bill in, 22–27, 86

Neer, Joseph C., 34–35

Nelson, Gaylord, 88, 92, 208

Nepal, Dolly and Bill visiting, 115, 120

New York, Bill delivering trucks to, 14

Nicklaus, Jack, 231

Ninth Armor Division, cavalry becoming, 27

Nixon, Richard M., 73, 82, 120, 123–24, 244; and Agnew, 166–67; and antitrust suit against AT&T, 187–88; and Bill as attorney general, 153–54, 163, 167–69; and Bill's attorney general nomination, 130–39, 148–49; Bill's disillusionment with, 130–31, 174, 179; Bill's opinion of administration of, 126–27, 127; Bill's relationship with, 97, 97–100, 136–37; Bill's Senate votes in support of and against, 95–97, 126; campaigning, 76, 79–80, 80, 99, 123, 124, 241; concern about crime rates, 185–86; and Connally, 166, 170; "Dear Bill" letters from, 93, 124; denying involvement in Watergate, 137–38, 166; enmity with Congress, 117, 122; and Ford, 180–86,

194, 196; House Judiciary Committee and impeachment of, 170, 175; and India, 210, 221–22; library of, 178–79; meetings with Bill as senator, 88, 123; and opposition to Sentinel ABM, 91–93; papers of, 183–85; personality of, 155, 172; and Republicans, 91–92, 110–14, 136; resignation of, 175, 176–78; and "Saturday Night Massacre," 127–29; seeing senators to reward or punish, 88–89, 97; strong-arm tactics to keep Republicans in line, 90–91, 110–14; Supreme Court nominees of, 96, 110–17; tax return of, 168; and truckers' strike, 164, 165; and Vietnam War, 103–4, 108–9; vindictiveness of, 122, 168, 178; and Watergate, 125, 155–56, 164–66, 168; and Watergate tapes, 143, 156–57, 165–66

Nixon Off the Record (Crowley), 137–38

Nolan, James, 72

Nuclear weapons: Bill's opposition to Sentinel ABM, 91–93; India's, 210, 222; Pakistan's, 222

Ohio: neglect of state responsibilities, 45–46; pressure from constituents on Haynsworth vote, 113–14; response to Bill's voting record in, 96–97

Ohio Division of Conservation, Bill lecturing for, 18–19, 23

Ohio legislature, 39; Bill's first term in, 34–38, 40; Bill's second term in, 41, 45–49, 51; makeup of, 39–40, 50–51; reapportionment of House, 72–73; 100th session of, 45–51; Un-American Activities Commission of, 63

Ohio National Guard, 30–31, 42, 103–4

Ohio State University, The, 98, 223; Bill at, 15–19, 22

O'Neil, Anna F., 51

O'Neill, C. William "Billy," 45, 54, 65; antagonism toward Bill, 40–41, 60, 61–63; Bill's campaign following, 61–62; campaigning, 52, 61–62

O'Neill, Thomas P. "Tip," 184

Orkin, Louis H., 65

Pakistan: Bill visiting, 120, 233; relations with India, 119–20, 220–22; U.S. policy toward, 119–20, 209–10; U.S. selling arms to, 213–14

Palace Guard, The (Rather and Gates), 117

Park, Tongsun, 207

Parties, 154; and Bill and Dolly, 89, 157; at embassies in India, 225–26; farewells for Saxbes, 207–8

Pay raise controversy, 141–42, 147–49, 153–54

Percy, Charles H., 90

Peterson, Henry E., 153, 170, 192–93

Phillips, Kevin, 111

Photo interpretation, for G2, 24–26

Pierce, Henry, 55

Pierson, Ball, and Dowd, 236, 241, 250

Pierson, James B., 90

Pilot, Bill as, 27–30

Plea bargains: Agnew's, 167, 194; for Watergate, 169

Political organizations, Ohio, 53; and Bender, 54, 74; of Rhodes, 73–74

Politics: Bill quitting, 66, 252; of fund-raising, 119; over reapportionment of Ohio House, 72–73; over Supreme Court nominees, 116–17

Pommerening, Glen, 144

Portman, Frank A. "Duke," II, 79, 146

Pottinger, Stanley, 193

Preble, Jack, 64

Presidency, 169, 220; Bill considering run for, 126, 135–36, 203; Nixon campaigning for, 79–80; Nixon trying to protect, 155–56, 176; relation to Senate, 116–17; and Rhodes, 73

Press, 254; on AT&T antitrust suit, 190; on Bill as ambassador to India, 203–6, 204–5, 211, 213–14, 218–19, 229, 231, 234; on Bill as attorney general, 135, 138–39, 160, 196–97; on Bill as senator, 54–55, 93–94, 118; on Bill's Watergate tape comment, 142–43; on Hearst kidnapping, 160–62; Nixon's paranoia about leaks to, 172; praise for 100th session of Ohio legislature, 48–49; Sheppard case in, 71–72; on state attorney general campaign, 60–61

Presser, Bill, 243

Price, Ray, 175

Price-fixing: in food industry, 198; and Justice Department, 169, 200–201

Primary campaigns: for Senate, 77; for

state attorney general, 60–62, 68–69

Prine, Malcolm M. "Mack," 59

Quesada, Elwood R. "Pete," 88, 134, 153, 227

Rakestraw, Vincent W., 77, 213; as assistant attorney general, 146; duties of, 85; in India, 217; as legislative assistant, 82; office for, 84, 153; and pay raise controversy, 141–42

Ramen, Sheikh Mujibur Abdul, 120

Randolph, Edmund, 142

Rather, Dan, 79, 117

Ray, Dixy Lee, 210

Reagan, Ronald, 154, 220, 241–42

Reed, Smith, Shaw, and McClay, 250

Regan, Sheila J., 163, 200

Reich, Robert B., 119

Religion, Saxbes', 32–33

Renner, Gordon, 38, 41–43, 45

Republicans, 91; on Bill being sent to India, 203–4; effects of Watergate on, 177–78; election losses, 65–66, 124; and Nixon, 91–92, 110–14, 136; response to Bill's voting record, 90, 96–97

Republicans, Ohio, 65, 73, 76, 136, 237–38; Bill's involvement with, 11–12, 35; filling Taft's Senate seat, 52–53, 53–58

Rhodes, James A., *63, 74;* Bill's relationship with, 41, 73–74, 153; as governor, 41, *76,* 150; and Nixon, 79–80, *80,* 88; in Ohio politics, 72, 118; running for governor, 52–53, 53, 237–39

Richardson, Elliot L., 166, 168; and Bill as attorney general, 136, 151; reorganization of Justice Department by, 144–45, 157–58; resignation of, 127–29, 143; staff loyalty to, 144–45

Right-to-work legislation, 64–65

Roberts, J. Eugene, 60

Roberts, Kline L., 44

Robinson, Kenneth A., 46

Robson, John, 197

Rockefeller, Nelson A., 73

Rockwell, W. F. "Al," Jr., 122, 234

Rogers, William P., 120–21, 131

Roosevelt House, in India, 215–16, 226

Ross, Charles D., 135

Ruckelshaus, William D., 129, 143–45, 157

I've Seen the Elephant

was designed & composed by Will Underwood

in 10½/14 Minion on a Power Macintosh G3 using PageMaker

at The Kent State University Press;

printed by offset lithography on Turin Book Natural Vellum

(an acid-free, totally chlorine-free paper),

Smyth sewn, bound over binder's boards in Arrestox B cloth &

Multicolor endpapers, & wrapped with dust jackets

printed in two colors finished with

polyester gloss film lamination

by Thomson-Shore, Inc.;

and published by

The Kent State University Press

KENT, OHIO 44242